VIETNAMESE
FOOD & COOKING

VIETNAMESE
FOOD & COOKING

Discover the exotic culture, traditions and ingredients of Vietnamese and Cambodian
cuisine with over 150 authentic step-by-step recipes and over 750 photographs

GHILLIE BAŞAN

WITH PHOTOGRAPHY BY MARTIN BRIGDALE

HERMES
HOUSE

For Antonia, who is about to embark on her own culinary journey

This edition is published by Hermes House

Hermes House is an imprint of Anness Publishing Ltd
Hermes House, 88–89 Blackfriars Road, London SE1 8HA
tel. 020 7401 2077; fax 020 7633 9499; info@anness.com

A CIP catalogue record for this book is available from the British Library.

Publisher: Joanna Lorenz
Editorial Director: Judith Simons
Senior Editor: Doreen Gillon
Editor: Molly Perham
Photographer: Martin Brigdale
Home economist: Lucy McKelvie and Bridget Sargeson
Stylist: Helen Trent
Designer: Nigel Partridge
Jacket Design: Chloe Steers
Production Controller: Wendy Lawson

1 3 5 7 9 10 8 6 4 2

Many of the recipes in this book have previously appeared in *Vietnamese*.
Front cover shows Beef Noodle Soup – for recipe, see page 78.

Notes

Bracketed terms are intended for American readers.

For all recipes, quantities are given in both metric and imperial measures and, where appropriate, in standard cups and spoons.
Follow one set, but not a mixture; they are not interchangeable.

Standard spoon and cup measures are level.
1 tsp = 5ml, 1 tbsp = 15ml, 1 cup = 250ml/8fl oz.

Australian standard tablespoons are 20ml. Australian readers should
use 3 tsp in place of 1 tbsp for measuring small quantities of
gelatine, flour, salt, etc.

American pints are 16fl oz/2 cups. American readers should use 20fl oz/2.5 cups in place of 1 pint when measuring liquids.

The nutritional analysis given for each recipe is calculated per portion (i.e. serving or item), unless otherwise stated. If the recipe gives a range,
such as Serves 4–6, then the nutritional analysis will be for the smaller portion size, i.e. 6 servings.
Measurements for sodium do not include salt added to taste.

Medium (US large) eggs are used unless otherwise stated.

Names of ingredients are given in Vietnamese only.

CONTENTS

INTRODUCTION

Vietnam and Cambodia are known for their warm, friendly people, their lively culture and superb cuisine. With such a long history of colonial rule and frequent, brutal wars, it is a wonder that the cultural life of the former Indo-china has survived in any shape or form. However, despite suffering more inhumanity to man than it is possible to imagine, the people have survived. Their strong belief in preserving ancient cultural traditions while at the same time absorbing the new is particularly evident in their fascinating culinary culture.

CULINARY INFLUENCES

Nearly all South-east Asian countries share the influence of China in their cuisines. In the case of Vietnam and Cambodia, the effects of Indian and Western colonial occupation have also added a bit of spice and variation to the gastronomy, making the culinary cultures of both countries quite distinctive in their own right.

Vietnamese cooking is most heavily influenced by China, apart from the southern cuisine, notably that of Ho Chi

Below: Hmong women overlooking the terraced fields in the Muong Hoa Valley, Vietnam.

Minh City, where Indian and French influences are vivid. More than any of its neighbours, it is an example of fusion cooking, balancing ancient with modern, and Chinese with Indian.

Indian customs and spices are more evident in the culinary heritage of Cambodia, combined with Khmer traditions, Contemporary Cambodian cuisine is both distinct and similar to its neighbours Laos and Thailand. As a cuisine it is not as sophisticated and

Above: A typical rural scene of thatched houses and paddy fields, near Siem Reap, Cambodia.

diverse as Vietnamese, which is partly due to the decades of severe destruction of the land and the people at the hands of the debilitating regimes of Pol Pot and the Khmer Rouge. There are a number of Cambodian noodle dishes, enriched with coconut milk, which are similar to the old favourites of Thailand and Malaysia, but richer than many of the Vietnamese noodle recipes. The popular hot and sour soups, often flavoured with chillies, coconut milk and fresh pineapple, resemble many dishes that are found in Thailand and the southern regions of Vietnam.

YIN AND YANG THEORY

A basic principle of South-east Asian cuisine is yin and yang, which evolved in China in the 4th century BC, This theory balances the Taoist connection with nature with the Buddhist search for enlightenment. An effective way of achieving this harmony is by balancing the yin and yang properties of food. As yin signifies female, darkness and cold, and yang signifies male, brightness and warmth, these principles could be applied to food by devising a "hot-cold" food system, in which certain foods have a cooling effect on the body, and

Above: Two boys making rice flour pancakes on griddles.

others are warming. In the yin category, are ingredients such as green vegetables, some fruits and some animal proteins; the yang category includes some animal proteins and seafood, herbs and spices. Each meal is formed with these principles in mind so that it is balanced and beneficial to the body. Wherever the influence of China has spread, the yin and yang theory has been incorporated into the food culture.

FIVE FLAVOUR NOTES

An extension of the yin and yang theory is the concept of five flavour notes: salty, bitter, sour, spicy and sweet. Each of these notes corresponds to the five elements – water, fire, wood, metal and earth – which are believed to be present around us and within us. When it comes to food, water is represented by salty and black, fire by bitter and red, wood by sour and green, metal by spicy and white, and earth by sweet and the colours yellow, orange and brown. This way of combining the properties and elements of food gives every meal balance.

THE JOY OF COOKING

In Vietnam and Cambodia, as well as other parts of South-east Asia, the idea of food "speaking" and pots "singing" is a common concept. Sizzling and bubbling are the favourite tunes – the noises of food cooking. In Vietnam, the joy of the food's singing is reflected in some of the names of dishes, such as the "happy crêpes" of the central region and the "sizzling crêpes" of Ho Chi Minh City. The moment the ingredients sizzle in the wok, or rice bubbles in the pan, the cook knows the food is on its way to being cooked. The pleasure of cooking and eating begins in the markets, where a great deal of squeezing and smelling of vegetables and fruit takes place, ensuring the freshest, the ripest or even the most tart item is selected for the meals that day. Back in the kitchen, the cook will taste each dish before serving to check the seasoning and the balance of flavours.

KEY INGREDIENTS

Both Vietnam and Cambodia share a rainy subtropical climate that enables them to employ the same key ingredients – rice, coconuts, ginger, garlic and chillies. Fish plays an enormous role in the diet of most Vietnamese and Cambodians. Generally, the fish is grilled (broiled) or stir-fried, wrapped in lettuce or spinach leaves, and dipped into their national local fish sauces, to which Cambodians often add finely ground chopped peanuts. Lemon grass and fresh, leafy herbs, such as mint and coriander (cilantro), find their way into almost every hot or cold dish, giving them a refreshing flavour – culminating in two striking cuisines that bewitch the senses with their vibrant colours and warm, tangy tastes.

Below: Women gutting fish for sale in the market at Hoi An, Vietnam.

VIETNAM TODAY

Today Vietnam is a thrilling place to be. Resplendent with colour, exotic smells, and delicious tastes, it has risen from the ruins with its spirit intact. From the border with China in the north to the rice mills of the Mekong Delta in the south, this land of rivers and lush, emerald-green paddy fields hums with activity. There are unspoiled beaches, peaceful lagoons, dense jungles and rugged mountains with roaring waterfalls. Visitors are graciously accepted and the Vietnamese people, in spite of their history of hardship and suffering, are always smiling and friendly.

Since the opening of Vietnam to tourism, there has been a new wave of excitement in all aspects of its culture, with a growing emphasis on the cuisine. And, with the spread of Vietnamese refugees to different corners of the world, authentic restaurants have mushroomed in Sydney, Paris and California, all presenting an intriguing fusion of flavours and history.

Below: The floating market at the village of Phung Help, in the Mekong Delta.

The Vietnamese are keen snackers. Life is generally lived in the streets so wherever you go there are markets, small restaurants, cafés and makeshift stalls made out of bamboo, selling or cooking every type of snack. The southern city of Ho Chi Minh City is abuzz with the sounds and sights of culinary activity. The streets are so enticingly thick with the smell of cooking you could almost bite the air. From the minute the city awakens just before dawn, the tables and stools are ready for early workers who come to slurp their bowls of the classic noodles soup *pho*. Other people sit waiting for the slow drip of coffee filtering into cups. Pungent spices like cinnamon, ginger and star anise tickle your nose as you walk about among the chaos of sputtering motorbikes, pedestrians dodging traffic, tinkling bicycles with ducks and hens spilling out of baskets and fruit sellers weaving their way through the crowds, pushing carts of pineapple, mango or papaya, freshly peeled and kept cool on a bed of ice. You don't have to look for food in Vietnam; it finds you!

Above: Preparing food at a market stall in Hoi An.

MARKETS

Along the Mekong Delta, some markets are on boats. The best known is the floating market Cai Ran, where the boats converge at dawn. It is a colourful sight as boats laden with bright green bitter melons, long, white radishes, scarlet tomatoes, yellow fruits and freshly cut herbs, bob peacefully in the water.

The countryside village markets are more reminiscent of a busy barnyard. The squawking and cackling of hens and ducks, and other forms of livestock, remind you that one striking fact about the Vietnamese is that there is little they don't eat. Roasted dog's head, stir-fried ducks' tongues, grilled field rats, monkey roasted on a spit or the heart of a venomous snake are all part of the daily fare. In these live markets, you will also find fish bladders, cockerels' testicles, crunchy insects, bats, toads, sparrows and turtle doves, crocodiles, armadillos, bears and sea horses.

GEOGRAPHICAL INFLUENCES

Vietnam has often been described as a "pearl necklace" perched on the edge of Indochina. The Mekong branches out into the South China Sea below Ho Chi Minh City and serves as a highway for boat traffic and trade. Its source is a stream in the Tibetan Himalayas, from where it tumbles down through steep gorges in south-western China, through the jungles of Laos and Cambodia until it flows at a leisurely pace through the lush pastures of southern Vietnam.

As the Vietnamese will point out, their country is shaped like a *don ganh*, the traditional bamboo pole that is slung over the shoulder with a basket of rice hanging from each end. These baskets represent the rice bowls of Vietnam, the Red River Delta in the north and the Mekong Delta in the south, joined by a mountainous spine. A long coastline and the numerous flowing rivers and streams that carve up the land, provide Vietnam with such a volume of water that it has a steady supply of its two most important ingredients: rice and *nuoc mam*, the fermented fish sauce.

The north

In the mountainous region of northern Vietnam there is still a large Chinese population, and the emphasis of the cuisine is on contrasting flavours and textures within the meal. The food is milder than the spicy dishes of the south, relying on mild black pepper and the indigenous herbs, which include basil, mint and coriander (cilantro).

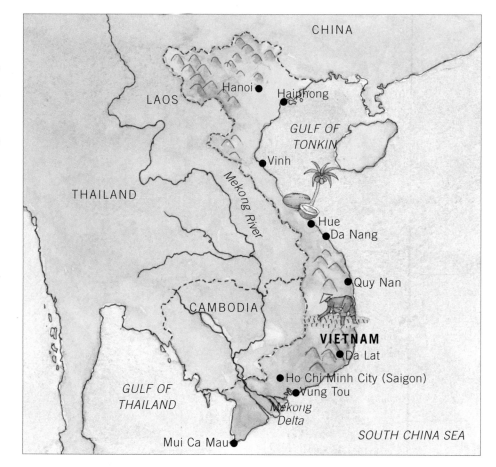

Hanoi, the principal city in the north, is reputed for its rice rolls, sweet snacks made with mung beans, and its snail dishes. The communal dish *lau*, which is often translated as "hotpot" but is in fact more akin to the French meat fondue, is attributed to the north, as is the favourite noodle soup, *pho*.

Hue

Of all the cities in Vietnam, there is none so representative of culture and learning as the historic, garden city of Hue. Once the imperial city, Hue was considered the centre of *haute cuisine*. The emperor Tu Duc, who reigned from 1848 to 1883, demanded ingenuity from his kitchens to create a refined cuisine. To achieve this, he expected 50 dishes to be prepared by 50 cooks and served by 50 servants at each meal. In Hue today, service remains formal and food is still presented in many small bowls as if feeding the emperor. Here you might find crab claws stuffed with pork, beef wrapped in wild betel leaves, and minced prawns wrapped around sugar cane (*chao tom*). A variety of crops are grown in this part of Vietnam, such as aubergines (eggplants), bitter melons, pumpkins, mangoes, pineapples and artichokes. Game birds, river fish and seafood are in abundant supply.

Ho Chi Minh City

The southern region of Vietnam is characterized by Ho Chi Minh City, formerly Saigon. At one time the languid Paris of the Orient, it is the centre of commerce and trade. The food relies heavily on the rice bowl and growing pastures of the Mekong Delta, and most produce comes from around Dalat. Just about anything grows here, including avocados, white strawberries, peaches, cauliflowers, tomatoes, tropical fruits and salad vegetables, all of which are incorporated in the region's dishes, which are served with French bread almost as often as with rice or noodles. Coconuts and sugar cane provide the base ingredients for many dishes.

VIETNAMESE CUSTOMS AND FESTIVALS

As eating plays such an important role in Vietnamese society, there are certain requirements of dining etiquette, although this can vary from region to region. For example, in northern and central Vietnam, it is custom for the oldest family member to sit nearest the door and everyone else to be arranged in descending age. The eldest will also be the first to help himself to food and a host will often serve the guest. In the south where the traditions of etiquette are more relaxed, everyone can dive in and help themselves. If you are the guest, one tradition that is important to remember is the bearing of a small gift. Whether you are invited to eat in a home or restaurant, throughout Asia, from Turkey to China, it is polite to bring your hosts a little box of something sweet or a bunch of fresh flowers – although in Vietnam the flowers should never be white as this signifies death.

COMMUNAL DINING

As with most Asian countries, dining is a communal affair. A selection of dishes may be put on a table and each diner will be given their own individual bowl into which the food is spooned. When passing the food around, two hands are used to hold the dish and the exchange is acknowledged with a nod. Food is usually eaten with fingers, chopsticks or

Below: Delicate lotus flowers are used to decorate tables and plates of food.

spoons, although the Vietnamese have a knack of sipping their food from the spoons without ever putting the spoon into their mouths.

The proper way to eat is to take some rice from the communal dish and put it in your bowl, then use the ceramic spoon to transfer the meat, fish or vegetables onto your rice. Hold the bowl up near to your mouth and use the chopsticks to shovel in the tasty morsels. It is polite for the host to offer more food than the guests can eat but, equally, it is polite for the guests not to eat everything in sight.

Depending on the complexity of the meal, there will be a number of individual dipping bowls, containing sweet or spicy condiments, and there may also be bowls of chillies or pickled vegetables to crunch and chew on between mouthfuls. When the Vietnamese eat, there is a great deal of gutsy enjoyment and noisy slurping. Eating is almost a game – there are crabs to crack, prawns to suck, food to be wrapped and rolled, and a lot of mess as they love lingering over food.

Above: A vendor selling the pungent fruit durian and other local fruits in Ho Chi Minh City.

FAMILY CELEBRATIONS

For the Vietnamese, to show a "big face" is a sign of prestige. Weddings and family celebrations are often elaborate and ruinously expensive for some families, but the cost is less important than "losing" face. A great deal of preparation goes into these events so that the food is overflowing. Each celebration calls for traditional, time-consuming specialities, and opulent dishes will appear, such as the Vietnamese roast duck, sliced into juicy slabs, drizzled with the piquant fish sauce (*nuoc cham*), and wrapped in lettuce leaves; sticky rice cakes steamed in lotus leaves and decorated with lotus flowers; and highly prized whole fish, grilled (broiled) or steamed with the head presented to the guest who is destined for good fortune. On these occasions, the habitual fragrant tea may be cast aside for a little merriment with beer and wine.

RELIGIOUS FESTIVALS

Vietnam's calendar is full of festivals, all of which call for elaborate feasting and celebration. The national celebrations include Liberation Day, which marks the date that Saigon surrendered; National Day on 2 September, to mark the Declaration of Independence of the Democratic Republic of Vietnam by Ho Chi Minh in 1945; and Ho Chi Minh's Birthday.

The religious festivals take place according to the lunar calendar, so the dates change from year to year. Important religious festivals include Buddha's Birthday, *Phat Dan*; Christmas; the Holiday of the Dead, *Thanh Minh*, when people visit the graves of dead relatives to light incense and make offerings of food and flowers; Wandering Souls Day, when offerings of food and gifts are made for the forgotten dead; and the mid-Autumn Festival, which lands on the fifteenth day of the eighth moon. To celebrate the harvest, children take part in an evening procession, holding colourful lanterns in the form of dragons, fish, boats and unicorns, while the drums and cymbals play and festive snacks and sweets, such as sticky rice cakes filled with lotus seeds, peanuts, and candied watermelon seeds, are sold in the streets.

Tet – Vietnamese New Year

Tet Nguyen Dan, meaning "New Dawn", is the most important festival of the Vietnamese lunar year. It falls some time between mid-January and mid-February and lasts for three days. It is a time of renewing and reaffirming beliefs in life, love, family and community. Families reunite in the hope of success and prosperity in the coming year. Cemeteries are visited and the spirits of dead relatives are invited home for the *Tet* celebrations. Homes and graves are cleaned and decorations are put up. The rites for *Tet* begin a week in advance.

The first rite is the ascension of the Spirits of the Hearth to the heavens. These kitchen gods dwell in every kitchen and must ride on the backs of fish to report on the year's events to the Jade Emperor in the hope of bringing

back good luck for the family. To aid them on their journey, families all over Vietnam put live carp into the rivers and lakes and leave offerings of food and fresh water at the altars. At the stroke of midnight on New Year's Eve, the noise of drums and cymbals mark the beginning of the celebrations as the gods are welcomed back.

The first meal of *Tet* is one for the ancestors as they are believed to have returned to the world of the living. The head of the family will offer a grace, light three incense sticks, then invite five generations of the deceased, whispering their names, to join in the family feast. This ceremony of "ancestor calling" takes place at the morning and evening meals for the three days of *Tet*. The second day of *Tet* involves visiting the wife's family and close friends and the third day is for embracing the community. Families visit the school teachers, patients visit their doctors, and many people visit astrologers to hear the year's fortunes. On the evening of the third day, the ancestors depart.

The principal *Tet* speciality is *banh chung*, sticky rice cakes filled with bean paste and, traditionally, wrapped in a green *dong* (similar to a banana leaf) parcel and tied with bamboo twine. Throughout the festivities, stacks of *banh chung* are piled high in the stalls next to watermelons and dragon fruit,

Above: Street vendors selling sweet snacks and fruit.

sweets, lotus seeds dyed a festive red to represent joy, truth and sincerity, and the popular *mut*, a candied concoction of vegetables and dried fruits, which are on display among the woven, painted masks. Lucky money is placed on trees as offerings to the ancestors and homes are decorated with trees, such as pretty, fruit-laden kumquats, or peach and apricot trees, resplendent in perfumed blossom, to ward off evil spirits.

Below: Traditional dancers performing in Hue, Vietnam.

CAMBODIA TODAY

For most of its recent history, Cambodia has been shut off from the rest of the world, but that has all changed. Today, it is open to tourists, foreign investors and international trade. It is one of the poorest countries in South-east Asia, but there is a will to rebuild and get on with living. The capital, Phnom Penh, has emerged from economic ruin and military occupation to become a captivating place to visit with a lively, international atmosphere. And no visitor should miss the stunning temples of Angkor, which are a mesmerizing blend of symmetry and spirituality. Not only do they display man's devotion to his gods, but they are the heart and soul of Cambodia as they represent a time when the Khmer empire was the greatest in South-east Asia. Many Cambodians make pilgrimages to the temples of Angkor, and tourists can explore them on foot, by bicycle, on the back of an elephant or view them from a helicopter.

To the Cambodians, their homeland is called Kampuchea, which is derived from the word *kambu-ja*, meaning "those born of Kambu", who was the mythical founder of the country. After years of conflict, many displaced Cambodians and refugees have now

Below: Rice sellers on the Tonlé Sap Lake, Cambodia.

returned to their homeland to start life anew in this moment of peace. With them they have brought fresh ideas and wealth accumulated in countries of the Western world which, combined with the UN influence and foreign aid, makes Cambodia an interesting place to be. In the countryside, the peasants still struggle to survive from fishing and rice growing, whereas cities like Phnom Penh and Siem Reap seem to be thriving. There are Western bars and restaurants, selling beers and pizzas, adjacent to Chinese and Cambodian restaurants selling deep-fried frogs' legs and noodles. Young urban Cambodians are into MTV and Western fashion, while the older generations cling to their traditions. But, most of all, in spite of the suffering that simmers beneath the surface of every family, the Cambodian people are unfailingly enthusiastic and friendly.

CAMBODIAN CUISINE

The cuisine of Cambodia is experiencing a revival. Restaurants serving traditional Khmer dishes are popular in the cities, as well as in Cambodian communities in Australia, France and America. There are also many restaurants and stalls selling Chinese, Thai or Vietnamese food, all of which play a part in the overall cuisine of the country. Although rice and fish are the staple foods,

Above: A Kreung woman in a krama scarf selling custard apples and bananas in Ban Lung, Rattankiri province.

Cambodia's culinary culture has been influenced by India, Thailand, China, France and Vietnam. As a result, there are many dishes that resemble each other in Cambodia and Vietnam, with a strong emphasis on the coconut milk, and spices and herbs, particularly garlic, ginger, lemon grass, chillies and coriander (cilantro). Both cultures also enjoy the French colonial legacy of fresh baguettes, ice cream, and coffee.

On the whole, Cambodian cuisine is not as sophisticated as Vietnamese, which is partly due to the decades of severe destruction of the land and the people at hands of brutal regimes. But it should not be forgotten that the once mighty Khmer empire spread over large sections of Thailand, Laos and Vietnam as well as Cambodia and would have played a big role in influencing the court cuisine at Hue, thus some of the imperial dishes of Vietnam could originally have been Cambodian.

MARKETS

The markets of Cambodia resemble those of Vietnam. Lively, colourful and atmospheric, they display the country's fish, livestock and agricultural produce, while the aroma of freshly cooked snacks wafts from the makeshift stalls and noodle shops. The countryside markets also offer a similar selection of livestock and wildlife, including endangered animals, such as bears, tigers and rhinos, which are sold for

their meat, paws, hides, hooves and penises. There is one market in the small town of Skuon, near Phnom Penh, that differs from all others as it features large, black, furry spiders. Bred in holes to the north of the town, the spiders are deep-fried for breakfast, lunch and supper. Cracked open like crab, the spiders are devoured by pulling the legs off and sucking out the flesh.

GEOGRAPHICAL INFLUENCES

Cambodia lies at the heart of Indochina, bordered by Laos and Thailand to the north, and Vietnam to the east. It is linked to Vietnam by the Mekong River, which unifies their culinary ingredients. The north-east of Cambodia is wild and mountainous, home to Cambodia's ethnic minorities and much of its wildlife, which includes Asian elephants, Asiatic wild dog, black gibbons, leopards, tigers and dugongs. Wild animals are also found in the dense jungles in the east, and in the Cardamom and Elephant Mountains in the south-west. A variety of bamboos and palms grow in these mountainous regions. The symbol of Cambodia is the sugar palm tree, which is used in construction, and in the production of medicine, wine and vinegar.

The country's rice bowl is in the Battambang region to the west, and extensive rice paddies are found in the central lowlands, where dry crops such as maize and tobacco are also grown. Vegetables, fruit and nuts grow in the central and southern lowlands, and salt is extracted from the sea near Kampot, on the Gulf of Thailand.

Water sources

The two most important geographical features in Cambodia are the Mekong River, which is almost 5km/3 miles wide in places, and the Tonlé Sap Lake. The largest lake in South-east Asia, the Tonlé Sap provides fish and irrigation water for almost half of Cambodia's population, who live on the low-lying

Right: Women washing clothes on a floating village on the Tonlé Sap Lake in Cambodia.

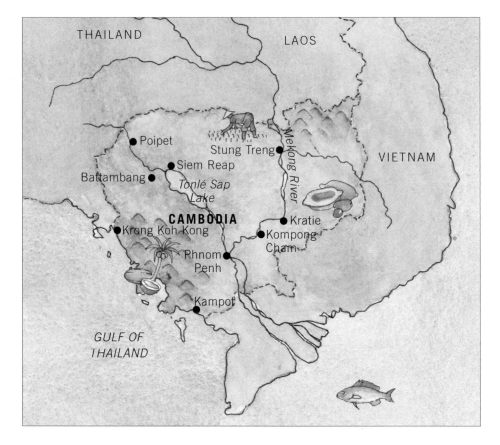

plain around lake and the upper Mekong Delta. The Tonlé Sap is linked to the Mekong by a 100km/60 mile channel, which is also called the Tonlé Sap. In the rainy season, when the level of the Mekong rises, the water backs up the channel causing it to flow into the lake, which swells up. When the water levels fall, it is drained back into the Mekong from the lake. This unusual process makes the lake one of the richest sources of freshwater fish in South-east Asia, and the flooded land is ideal for spawning.

CAMBODIAN CUSTOMS AND FESTIVALS

On the whole, Cambodia is a very traditional society with an emphasis on strong family values and religion. The traditional greeting, the *sompiah*, involves pressing hands together in prayer and bowing. Generally, the higher the hand and the lower the bow, the more respect is shown. Compared to Vietnam, the culinary customs of Cambodia are fairly relaxed. When eating at home, the women and the men sit on floor mats with their feet to the side rather than the lotus position. Traditionally, they followed the Hindu custom of using a hand to eat, but nowadays forks and chopsticks as well as hands are used.

CAMBODIAN MEALS

Most Cambodian dishes are cooked in a wok, known locally as a *chnang khteak*. For breakfast most Cambodians eat rice porridge, *bobor*, often with the addition of a little fish or pork. A traditional Cambodian meal almost always includes a soup, *samla*, which is eaten at the same time as the other courses. While rice is the country's staple, fish is the most important source of protein. Most of the fish eaten in Cambodia is freshwater, caught in the Tonlé Sap lake or Mekong River. Traditionally, fish is eaten wrapped in herbs and lettuce leaves and dipped in the national fish sauce *tuk trey*, which is similar to the Vietnamese *nuoc mam*.

FAMILY CELEBRATIONS

At weddings and festive banquets, there are a number of sweet snacks made in the home, or sold in the markets, such as sticky rice balls stuffed with banana, sticky rice cakes in banana leaves. and pumpkin pudding in banana leaves or *nom l'poh*.

Right: Frogs and fish for sale at a stall on a street in Phnom Penh.

Below: Women making a communal meal around cooking pots and open fires in a typical village near Siem Riep.

FESTIVALS AND HOLIDAYS

The majority of Cambodians are followers of Theravada Buddhism, There are a number of religious festivals and national holidays, such as the Day for Remembering the Victory over the Genocidal Regime (7 January); the Chinese New Year, which usually falls around the same time as the Vietnamese *Tet*; the King's birthday; the Royal Ploughing Ceremony, *Chat Preah Nengkal*, held in early May in Phnom Penh to bless the farmers with successful crops in the coming year; and Independence Day on 9 November; the Khmer New Year; Buddha's birth, enlightenment and death; *Bon Om Tuk*; and Independence Day.

The Khmer New Year

Chaul Chnam, the Khmer New Year, lasts for three days in mid-April. Pilgrimages are made to the temples of Angkor and offerings are made at the temples and wats. Homes are cleaned out, gifts of new clothes are exchanged and food is shared. Water plays an important role in the celebrations as it

Below: A Khmer bride unwrapping the sacred coconut at a Buddhist wedding in Cambodia.

symbolizes cleansing and renewal. Religious statues are bathed in water and so is just about everyone else, as children and adults throw water missiles and fire water guns at anyone who goes by. Talcum powder missiles are also popular, spraying powder over people, cars and bicycles.

Above: Men rowing a long boat in the Retreat of the Waters during the Bon Om Tuk *festival in Phnom Penh.*

Bon Om Tuk

This is one of the most important festivals in Cambodia. Held in early November, it is a celebration of the reversal of the current of the Tonlé Sap. Just as the dry season begins, the water that is backed up in the lake begins to empty into the Tonlé Sap (the channel that links the lake to the Mekong) and on into the Mekong – a cause for much celebration. Boat races are held on the Tonlé Sap and on the moat around Angkor Wat.

Buddha's Birth, Enlightenment, and Death

Both Vietnam and Cambodia celebrate this event, which falls on the 15th day of the sixth lunar month. The festivities take place at pagodas and temples, which are decorated with lanterns and offerings of food. In the evening, a variety of processions take place – one of the most impressive is the candlelit procession of Buddhist monks at the ruins of Angkor Wat.

HISTORY OF VIETNAM AND CAMBODIA

Mountainous terrain and wide, rolling rivers made northern South-east Asia relatively inaccessible, so indigenous tribes thrived there for much longer than in other places. Early records show that a form of primitive agriculture took place in the region of northern Vietnam and that Cambodians lived in houses on stilts and survived on fish. The most comprehensive records start with the Indianized kingdom of Funan, which took hold from the 1st to the 6th century AD along the coastline of southern Vietnam, which at that time was inhabited by Cambodians. Funan acted as an important seaport on the spice route between China and India and evidence shows that rice was cultivated in the area and that canals were constructed to irrigate the land and provide a route for transporting the wet rice.

In the late 2nd century, another Indianized kingdom, Champa, arose around Danang in central Vietnam. A semi-piratic society, the Chams were continuously at war with the Vietnamese to the north and the Khmers to the west, as they raided the whole coast of

Below: Poklongarai Cham tower, a 13th-century brick-built monument.

Above: A Vietnamese woman ploughing a field using a metal plough and ox.

Indochina. Through their trade with India, both of these early kingdoms adopted Buddhism and Hinduism, employed Sanskrit as a sacred language, were influenced by Indian art, and incorporated Indian spices in their cuisines, which is still evident in the culinary cultures of southern Vietnam and Cambodia today.

CHINESE RULE

Over the centuries, ancient empires rose and fell in the region that later became known as Indochina. The Chinese, who ruled Vietnam for a thousand years from before 100 BC to AD 939, probably made the first dramatic impact on the culinary history of northern Vietnam and Cambodia. When they conquered the Red River Delta in the north of Vietnam, the Chinese encountered the Viet, a nomadic, clan-based society, similar to the hill tribes today, who were reliant on hunting and fishing. The Chinese rulers had a huge influence on the culture and government of Nam Viet, as well as on the development of its cuisine. They introduced the use of the metal plough and oxen, dykes and irrigation, the artistry of chopsticks, stir-frying in oil, the use of noodles, ginger, soy sauce and beancurd, and the cultivation of rice. Chinese scholars and travellers taught ancestor worship, Confucianism, and Mahayana Buddhism, while the Indians sailing eastwards on the India–China trade route introduced

Theravada Buddhism. The travelling Buddhist monks from both civilizations were highly regarded for their knowledge of science and medicine, which they passed on to the Vietnamese monks, who didn't take long to produce their own doctors, botanists, scholars, and vegetarian cooks.

Below: Monks threshing rice in Nha Trang, Vietnam.

Above: The imperial city of Hue, Vietnam, with its Chinese-style gate.

THE KHMER EMPIRE

While the northern region of Vietnam and the north-eastern reaches of Cambodia were affected by Chinese rule, farther south the competing kingdoms were beginning to unite to form the Khmer empire (AD 802–1432). Regarded as the greatest in South-east Asia, this flourishing empire spread over the bulk of Thailand, Cambodia, Laos and central Vietnam, and included the famous imperial city of Hue. The influence of Khmer traditions combined with ancient Chinese techniques and the indigenous cooking of the region produced a unique, lavish court cuisine. The imperial city meals consisted of a selection of tasty bite-size morsels, such as crab claws stuffed with minced (ground) pork, beef wrapped in wild betel leaves, and the exquisitely sweet and juicy *chao tom*, grilled shrimp paste on bamboo skewers.

The construction of the temple city of Angkor Wat has often been considered to be the cause of the Khmer empire's demise, as it drained the empire of all resources, paving the way for centuries of Thai control.

FRENCH INFLUENCE

Like its neighbour Vietnam, Cambodia was also colonized by the French in the 19th and 20th centuries. Under French rule, the ports and drainage systems improved, and coffee, tea and rubber plantations emerged, but the colonial policies made the people of Indochina very poor.

Typically, the positive impact made by the French was a gastronomic one, as they introduced baguettes, coffee, ice cream, pâté, avocados and asparagus, which is used in the Vietnamese French-inspired Crab and Asparagus Soup.

THE VIETNAM WAR

In both Vietnam and Cambodia, a period of Japanese occupation and social unrest followed World War II and the Franco–Viet Minh War, until the first US troops landed at Danang in March 1965. This marked the start of the long, bloody Vietnam War, which destroyed vast tracks of land and suppressed any cultural life for years. Thousands of Vietnamese and American lives were claimed by war, and the Vietnamese fled the country by any means they could. Many refugees died in their desperate flight, but those who survived settled in Australia, the USA, France and Great Britain. As the Vietnamese communities began to grow and thrive around the world, the cultural traditions and culinary heritage of Vietnam was preserved while the country itself continued to be wrecked by war.

The Vietnam War came to an official end in 1975 when Saigon fell to the North Vietnamese troops, who renamed it Ho Chi Minh City, but the fighting did not end for the Vietnamese. There were repeated attacks on the Vietnamese border by the Khmer Rouge. Chinese forces also invaded Vietnam in 1979, and the Khmer Rouge, supported by the Chinese and the Thais, continued their war against the Vietnamese for the next ten years.

Below: Baguettes were introduced to Vietnam and Cambodia by the French.

THE KHMER ROUGE

While Vietnam was locked in its deadly internal conflict, Cambodia was also targeted by the US carpet-bombing missions desperate to flush out any communists, but thousands of civilians lost their lives instead. The loss of lives and suffering didn't end there, though, as Phnom Penh surrendered to the Khmer Rouge in 1975, which marked the beginning of one of the most brutal regimes known to man and the death of any form of cultural life for decades. Proclaimed the Year Zero, Cambodia was cut off from the rest of the world, as the Khmer Rouge forced the entire population of Phnom Penh and the provincial towns, including the sick and the elderly, to live and work as slaves in countryside camps. Hard, physical labour lasted for 12 to 15 hours a day, rations consisted of a meagre bowl of watery rice-porridge, and families were separated. It is not known how many Cambodians died at the brutal hands of the Khmer Rouge – researchers put it at millions.

Below: Angkor Wat temple in the soft evening light at Siem Reap, Cambodia.

VIETNAMESE INVASION OF CAMBODIA

The Vietnamese intervened and invaded Cambodia in 1978. They succeeded in overthrowing the Khmer Rouge, but they in turn caused the destruction of rice stocks and unharvested rice fields, resulting in widespread famine and the flight of hundreds of thousands of Cambodians to Thailand. Civil war ensued for a further decade as the

Above: A Buddhist shrine within the 12th-century ruins of Banteay Kdei Ta Prohm, Angkor, Cambodia.

Vietnamese sought to control Cambodia, while the Khmer Rouge retaliated in guerrilla warfare by planting mines along roads and in rice fields, attacking buses and lorries, blowing up bridges, and killing administrators and teachers.

As a counter-attack, the Vietnamese laid the longest minefield in the world, the K-5, which stretched from the Gulf of Thailand to Laos, and stripped the forests along the roads to prevent ambushes. In September 1989, Vietnam withdrew from Cambodia to deal with its own economic problems, but fighting between the Khmer Rouge and the government forces continued, causing more deaths and refugees for several years. The conflict came to an official end in 1992, and the people of Vietnam were able to get on with their lives, rebuild their towns and villages, and to plant their crops and enjoy a life of peace for the first time in many years.

CAMBODIAN TOURIST ECONOMY

Not surprisingly, the effects of this long period of suffering and civil war took its toll on the Cambodians and their once vibrant culture, and these have not yet been fully shaken off. Many memories and traditions have been lost along with those who died, and most of the surviving population are too young to remember how things were. Until recently, Cambodia has been shut to the outside world and those tourists that have ventured there have done so at considerable risk.

Today, Cambodia is one of the poorest countries in Asia and welcomes tourists to boost its struggling economy.

To date, unlike its neighbours Vietnam and Thailand, foreign visitors are still rather thin on the ground and tend to concentrate on Phnom Penh with its cosmopolitan atmosphere and influx of restaurants offering Khmer specialities as well as Vietnamese, Chinese, Indian and French cuisines, or they take a tour around the magnificent, ancient temples of Angkor. For this reason, much of Cambodia is unfamiliar and

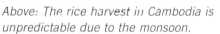

Above: The rice harvest in Cambodia is unpredictable due to the monsoon.

little is known about the traditional cuisine and the cultural customs of the countryside.

Unlike densely populated Vietnam, 85 per cent of Cambodia's population live in the countryside and are dependent on the unpredictable harvests, which are reliant on the South-western monsoon. Even today, rural livelihoods are subject to the hardships of disease and the landmines left over from the years of civil war and Vietnamese occupation. Between the Cambodians and Vietnamese there is a degree of mistrust, some of which dates back to historic battles over territory, but it does not make it easy for the Vietnamese communities in Cambodia, nor for the Khmer Krom, the ethnic Khmers living in southern Vietnam. However, one area in which these two countries are clearly harmoniously united is in their cuisines, which share many ingredients and culinary techniques, even if they differ in their cultural traditions.

Left: The French colonial-style Royal Palace compound, Phnom Penh.

THE VIETNAMESE AND CAMBODIAN KITCHEN

The culinary cultures of Vietnam and Cambodia have both been influenced by the cuisines of India, Thailand, China and France so there are inevitably many similarities. Fish and rice are the staples of both countries and there is a strong emphasis on coconut milk combined with spices and herbs, such as ginger, lemon grass, garlic, chillies and coriander.

RICE

In Vietnam and Cambodia, there are three main groups of rice: long grain, short grain, and sticky "glutinous" rice. The most widely grown and the most frequently consumed is the long grain; in the cooler northern regions of Vietnam and Cambodia, the plumper short grain sometimes takes preference. Sticky rice is often used in porridge-style dishes and wrapped in banana leaves to make savoury and sweet "cakes".

Rich in carbohydrate and containing vitamins A and B, rice is one of the healthiest staple foods. It is used to make vinegar and wine, and it is indispensable when ground into flour to make French-style baguettes and crêpes, the ubiquitous, paper-thin wrappers used for spring rolls, and dried and fresh noodles. Traditionally rice is boiled or steamed, then may be stir-fried; sticky rice is steamed until it resembles porridge.

In Vietnam, rice is regarded as the "staff of life". It plays an important role as a staple food as well as in the economy and the culture. There are even rigorous rice-cooking competitions based on the tradition of preparing rice for soldiers going into battle. With lush carpeted valleys and hillside terraces of fertile, well-irrigated rice crops, this long, narrow country manages to rank third in the rice-export game, behind

Below: A woman ploughing rice fields in the traditional way with a buffalo.

the United States and Thailand, producing a number of varieties that differ in aroma, flavor, and gluten content. Vietnam's principal rice bowls can be found in the land around the Red River in the north and the Mekong Delta in the south.

In Cambodia, rice is equally important. Grown primarily in the emerald-green rice paddies of the Battambang region in the west, it is the principal ingredient in everyday meals as well as in snacks and festive foods. A typical Cambodian breakfast consists of a bowl of *bobor*, rice porridge, which is sometimes accompanied by a little fish or pork. Both the regular and glutinous varieties are popular with a stronger emphasis on the red and brown grains, which still retain their bran husks. Although the texture and nutritional qualities of the red and brown grains are much greater, most Vietnamese dishes call for the polished varieties to form the basis of a meal that will then be balanced by vegetables, herbs and spices for their texture, colour and flavour.

Within their groups, there are many types of rice, all of which the Vietnamese and Cambodians can differentiate by the aroma or taste of the raw grain. When buying, the quality and texture of the grain will be discussed at length as each cook requires a particular rice for the meal that day. Several long grain and glutinous varieties are available in Asian stores and supermarkets.

Above: Jasmine or Thai fragrant rice has tender, aromatic grains. It is widely available in supermarkets in the West.

LONG GRAIN RICE

Gao, or long grain, rice is the daily staple of all South-east Asian cooking. Often delicately scented, such as fragrant jasmine rice, the grains should be dry, thin, firm and translucent when raw. Once steamed the tender grains should still retain some bite and turn white and fluff up easily with a fork. Whether polished or unpolished, aromatic or nutty, long grain rice is used throughout Vietnam and Cambodia as the absorbent bed for many fish and meat curries and stews. The Vietnamese prefer the long grain jasmine variety (*gao thom*), cooked using the absorption method.

WHITE STICKY GLUTINOUS RICE

Often referred to as sticky or sweet rice (*gao nep*), these grains are soaked for several hours, sometimes overnight, before cooking. Glutinous rice comes in both long and short grain varieties. The long grain is used for both savoury and sweet dishes, such as the popular porridge-style dishes of South-east Asia, whereas the plumper short grain is favoured for dumplings, puddings and festive sweets. In contrast to long grain rice, the highly polished, glutinous rice grain is an opaque white colour due to the starch content when raw and turns translucent when cooked. Although the grains retain a degree of firmness, they do tend to stick to one another, thus lending themselves ideally to being handled in clumps and moulded into

Above: Patna rice is one of the many types of long-grain rice.

balls to dip into a sauce, or to be flavoured with a dollop of sweet bean paste, to be used as fillings for cakes wrapped in banana leaves. In the streets of Vietnam and Cambodia, glutinous rice is often eaten as a filling snack, sweetened with a little coconut milk and sugar sprinkled over the top.

BLACK STICKY GLUTINOUS RICE

This unpolished, wholegrain glutinous rice is reserved for sweet dishes throughout South-east Asia. When soaked in water and cooked, the grains turn a deep reddish-purple colour. Sometimes called forbidden rice, it has a distinct nutty flavour. More filling than white rice, it is often eaten as a snack, sweetened with coconut milk and sugar. It is especially popular in the mango and durian season. Black sticky rice is available in some Asian markets.

Kralan

From the jungles of Cambodia comes this glutinous rice speciality. Requiring no cooking utensils, the raw grains are mixed with coconut cream and shredded coconut to form a stiff mixture, which is then stuffed into the hollow of a bamboo tube. The bamboo is then placed over a fire for about an hour, until the rice is cooked and the charred bamboo can be peeled off like a banana skin.

RICE PRODUCTS

The primary staple of both Vietnamese and Cambodian cooking, rice is used in many forms.

Rice flour

Bot gao, or rice flour, is made by grinding the raw grain until it is a very fine powder. All types of grain can be used and the packets are usually labelled accordingly. Long grain and medium grain rice flour is used to make the dough for fresh and dried rice noodles, as well as for dumplings, crêpes, buns, and the Vietnamese rice papers.

Glutinous rice flour, sometimes called sweet rice flour, is reserved for sweet pastries, pancakes and cakes. Rice flour, also called rice powder, is available in Asian stores and should be kept in an airtight container in a dry place.

Toasted rice flour

Thinh, or toasted rice flour, imparts a coarser texture and smoky flavour to particular dishes, such as the Vietnamese speciality of shrimp paste grilled on sticks of sugar cane. It is usually made with short grain rice by shaking a few handfuls of the raw grains in a dry, heavy-based pan over a

Below: Black and white glutinous rice.

Above: Rice flour is finely ground and thoroughly pulverized. As a result, it has a very light texture and is used in desserts such as pancakes.

medium heat, until they turn golden brown. The toasted grains are then ground by hand, using a mortar and pestle, or in a conventional coffee grinder, to a powder. Home-made toasted rice flour tends to be grittier than the commercial fine powders. Store toasted rice flour in an airtight container in a dry place.

Rice papers

Unique to Vietnamese cuisine, these delicate triangular or circular rice papers or wrappers (*banh trang*), made from rice flour, water and salt, are brittle to hold. They are dried in the open air in the sun on bamboo mats that leave their criss-cross pattern on the wrappers. In Cambodia, these wrappers are used when preparing Vietnamese specialities, otherwise the Chinese spring roll wrappers made from wheat flour are more common, just as they are in Thailand.

Once they have been reconstituted in water, these wrappers are used for making the fried Vietnamese spring rolls, *cha gio*, and the light summer rolls, *goi cuon*. They are also put on the table to be used as wrappings for salads, meatballs, grilled meats and stir-fried dishes. Wrapping tasty morsels and dipping them in sauce is a typical Vietnamese way of enjoying a meal.

Above: Rice papers are dried on bamboo mats, which give them their familiar cross-hatch pattern.

Not all rice papers are plain, some are flavoured with coconut, ginger or pandanus (similar to vanilla). The papers that are made with glutinous rice flour are toasted so that they puff up and have a chewy texture.

Packets of dried rice papers are available in Asian stores and some supermarkets. Before using, the dried rice papers must be separated and soaked in water, two to four at a time, until soft and pliable. Keep any remaining papers in an airtight container or they will dry out and curl up.

Fresh rice papers

In addition to dried papers, the Vietnamese make fresh rice papers (*banh uot*), which are used exclusively for wrapping minced (ground) meats.

Rice wine and vinegar

Rice is often distilled to make wine and vinegar. The clear, clean-tasting vinegar is used for pickling vegetables and in cooking. Both the wine and vinegar are made from fermented rice grains which lend a distinct, sharp taste. Bottles are available in Asian and Chinese stores.

Above and right: Amber and white rice vinegar have a distinctive sharpness.

PREPARING AND COOKING RICE

Most rice grains are cooked using the absorption method, except glutinous rice, which is soaked and steamed.

Long grain rice

In Vietnam and Cambodia, long grain rice is the most frequently eaten grain. If the main dish doesn't include noodles, then a bowl of steamed rice or rice wrappers will provide the starch in the meal. The volume of rice grains doubles when cooked. As a guide for four people, you will need about 200g/7oz/ 1 cup of rice in 600ml/1 pint/2½ cups water, but the proportion of water and cooking time will vary slightly with different grains.

Rinsing rice

Long grain rice should always be rinsed to remove the excess starch, so that the cooked grains are light and fluffy and separate easily.

1 Put the measured quantity of grains into a bowl and cover with cold water. Swirl the grains in the water until it becomes cloudy, then leave to settle.

2 Strain the rice through a sieve, then return it to the bowl and repeat the process several times.

Cooking rice

The traditional way to cook rice in South-east Asia is by absorption. The measured grains are put into a heavy pan or clay pot, with a proportionally measured amount of water, and the rice is cooked until all the water has been absorbed.

1 Put the rinsed grains into a heavy pan and pour in the measured water. Bring the water to the boil, stir once, then reduce the heat to low.

2 Cover the pan with the lid and leave to cook gently for about 20–25 minutes, until all the liquid has been absorbed.

3 Remove the pan from the heat and leave to stand for 5–10 minutes to allow the rice to steam a little longer. Fluff up the tender grains with a fork and serve.

Sticky glutinous rice

This type of rice needs to be soaked in water for a long time before cooking – at least 6 hours, preferably longer. For the best results, glutinous rice should be steamed, preferably in a traditional bamboo steamer. There is no need to partially cook the rice first. The volume of rice grains doubles when cooked. For four people you will need about 200g/7oz/1 cup sticky rice, and the cooking time may vary slightly from grain to grain.

Soaking and rinsing the rice

1 Put the rice grains into a bowl, cover with cold water and leave to soak for at least 6 hours.

2 Drain the rice through a sieve. Rinse it thoroughly under running cold water, then drain again.

Additional flavourings

Very often a little extra flavour is imparted by adding a bouquet garni of fresh herbs, or spices such as star anise, fresh ginger or lemongrass, to the cooking liquid. Rice is also delicious cooked in coconut milk or a well-flavoured stock, instead of water.

For a quick, filling snack
While still hot, spoon sticky rice into bowls, pour over a little coconut milk and sprinkle with sugar. In Vietnam, sticky rice is often topped with stewed, sweetened red beans; in Cambodia, the sticky rice is cooked in coconut milk with boiled, sweetened black-eyed peas stirred in.

Steaming the rice

1 Fill a wok one-third full with water. Place a bamboo steamer, with the lid on, over the wok and bring the water underneath to the boil. Alternatively, use a conventional steamer.

2 Lift the lid off the steamer and place a dampened piece of muslin (cheesecloth) over the rack. Put the rice in the middle and spread it out a little. Fold the edges of the muslin over the rice, put the lid back on the steamer and steam for about 25 minutes, until the rice is tender but still firm.

Food safety
Never keep cooked rice warm for more than a short time, or you may risk food poisoning. Rice is susceptible to a bacterium, *Bacillus cereus*, which is killed by cooking, but can leave behind spores that germinate if cooked rice is insufficiently reheated or kept warm for long periods of time. When buying fresh rice products store carefully and use within 12 hours.

NOODLES

South-east Asian cooking uses noodles in great quantities. If the main dish doesn't contain rice to provide the starch content of the meal, then it will consist of noodles. They are eaten at all hours of the day, in a soup for breakfast, simply stir-fried for a quick and filling snack, or more elaborately incorporated into a main dish with meat, fish and vegetables. It is no wonder that the most common type of food stall in Vietnam and Cambodia is the "rice and noodle" shop, as these two ingredients form the basis of every dish.

In Vietnam and Cambodia, there are a variety of noodles, many of them made from rice. The everyday noodles in Vietnam fall into three main types: *bun*, which are long and thin, similar to Italian vermicelli and called rice sticks – they are used in soups, side dishes, and as a wrapping for meat and seafood; *banh pho*, also called rice sticks, but they are flatter, thicker and sturdier, ideal for substantial soups such as *pho*, and stir-fries; and the fine *banh hoi* which resemble angel hair pasta and are primarily used in thin broths.

In addition to the common rice noodles, the Vietnamese and Cambodians both cook with wheat noodles, egg noodles, which are often referred to as Cambodian-style noodles in Vietnam, and the translucent Chinese cellophane noodles which are made from mung beans.

DRIED RICE "VERMICELLI" NOODLES

Often referred to as vermicelli, these dried rice noodles (*bun*), made from rice flour, salt and water, are thin and wiry and sold in bundles. Before using, they must be soaked in water until pliable and then the noodles only need to be cooked in boiling water for a few seconds, until tender and *al dente* like Italian pasta. In Vietnam and Cambodia, these noodles are used in soups and salads – they are often used to wrap around raw vegetables and herbs in Vietnamese table salad, as well as to wrap around grilled meats and shellfish.

DRIED RICE STICKS

These flat, thin dried rice noodles (*banh pho*) resemble linguine and are available in several widths, which start at around 2mm/1⁄16in. Also made from rice flour, salt and water, they are used in salads and stir-fries, after being softened in water.

FRESH RICE NOODLES

Known as *banh pho tuoi,* fresh rice noodles are thicker than dried ones. They are often served as a side dish with curries and vegetable dishes. Like the dried variety, they require minimal cooking. In some recipes they are just dipped in warm water to heat them up, or they are added at the last moment to stir-fried and steamed dishes. Use them on the day of purchase.

PREPARING DRIED RICE NOODLES

Dried noodles can be bought in various packaged forms from most Asian stores and supermarkets. The basic principle is that thinner varieties require less cooking time and are served with light ingredients and thin broths, whereas the thicker noodles take a little longer to cook and are balanced with heavier ingredients and stronger flavours.

Before cooking, dried rice noodles must be soaked in warm water for about 10 minutes, until pliable. The dry weight usually doubles on soaking. The rule is to soak well to soften, but to cook briefly. If the noodles are cooked for too long they will become soggy. Once softened, both the rice vermicelli and rice sticks need to be cooked in boiling water for seconds, rather than minutes, until tender and firm, just like *al dente* Italian pasta. Divide the noodles among individual bowls and ladle stock or a meat broth over them or put them in a wok to stir-fry.

Below: Soaking dried vermicelli noodles.

MAKING FRESH RICE NOODLES

A variety of dried noodles are available in Asian stores and supermarkets, but fresh ones are quite different and not that difficult to make. For a snack, the freshly made noodle sheets can be drenched in sugar or honey, or dipped into a sweet or savoury sauce of your choice. Similarly, you can cut them into wide strips and gently stir-fry them with garlic, ginger, chillies and *nuoc mam* or soy sauce – a popular snack enjoyed in both Vietnam and Cambodia.

Left: Different widths of dried rice vermicelli noodles.

As a guide to serve four, you will need about 225g/8oz/2 cups rice flour to 600ml/1pint/2½ cups water. You will also need a wide pot with a domed lid, or wok lid, a piece of thin, smooth cotton cloth (like a clean dish towel), and a lightly oiled baking tray.

Preparing the batter

Place the flour in a bowl and stir in a little water to form a smooth paste. Gradually, pour in the rest of the water, whisking all the time to make sure there are no lumps. Beat in a pinch of salt and 15ml/1 tbsp vegetable oil. Set aside for 15 minutes.

Preparing the steamer

Meanwhile, fill a wide pot with water. Cut a piece of cloth a little larger than the top of the pot. Stretch it over the top of the pot (you may need someone to help you), pulling the edges down over the sides so that the cloth is as taut as a drum, then wind a piece of string around the edge, securing the cloth with a knot or bow. Using a sharp knife, make 3 small slits, about 2.5cm/1in from the edge of the cloth, at regular intervals. If you need to top up the water during cooking, pour it through these slits.

Cooking the noodle sheets

1 Bring the water in the pot to the boil. Stir the batter and ladle a portion (roughly 30–45ml/2–3 tbsp) on to the cloth, swirling it to form a 10–15cm/4–6in wide circle.

2 Cover with the domed lid and steam for a minute, until the noodle sheet is translucent. Carefully, insert a spatula or knife under the noodle sheet and gently prize it off the cloth – if it doesn't peel off easily, you may need to steam it for a little longer.

3 Transfer the noodle sheet to the oiled tray and repeat with the rest of the batter. As they accumulate, stack the sheets on top of each other, brushing the tops with oil so they don't stick together. Cover the stack with a clean dish towel to keep them moist.

COOK'S TIP
During the cooking, you may have to top up the water through one of the slits. The cloth might occasionally need to be pulled tight again if it begins to sag, otherwise the batter will form a pool and be too thick.

Right: Egg noodles are available dried and fresh in the West.

MUNG BEAN NOODLES

Also called cellophane or glass noodles (*mien*), these dried mung bean threads are as thin as rice vermicelli and white in colour. When cooked they turn transparent, resembling strips of cellophane or glass. On their own, they do not have much flavour but, when cooked with other ingredients, they absorb the flavours, so they are often used to add texture and starch to mixtures for filling spring rolls.

Soak the delicate noodles in warm water for about 15 minutes, until pliable, and then drain, cut into shorter strands and cook as required.

EGG NOODLES

Made with wheat flour and eggs, the Vietnamese often refer to these as Shanghai-style or Cambodian noodles or *mi*. Firmer and denser than rice noodles, they are used in stir-fries and soups. They are sold fresh in Asian stores.

BREAD

The people of Vietnam and Cambodia eat a lot more bread (*banh mi*) than those in the rest of South-east Asia. Having both been influenced by French colonization and wartime occupation, bread has become a daily feature. Somewhere between a long, crispy French baguette and the wider Middle Eastern loaf, the bread of Vietnam and Cambodia is usually made from a combination of wheat and rice flours and is shorter than a baguette with a slit down the middle. Whether used for grilled meat and salad sandwiches, flavoured with fresh herbs and chillies, or smeared with a local pork pâté and a splash of chilli sauce, freshly baked loaves are available in the streets of southern Vietnam just as easily as noodles. Torn into chunks to dip into stews and curries, bread is also served as an alternative to noodles or rice.

And then there is the ice cream sandwich. A popular sweet snack with children in both Vietnam and Cambodia – thick chunks of baguette are halved lengthways and a wedge of ice cream is tucked in between them – a South-east Asian version of an ice cream cone.

Buns and dumplings fall into the bread category, as they start with a dough made from wheat flour and

yeast. However, following ancient Chinese tradtions, buns and dumplings are often stuffed and usually steamed, although some buns are baked after steaming. Flatbreads and wrappers, used for folding around morsels of food and for spring rolls, can also be included in the bread culture. Made from rice or wheat flour, they are baked on griddles, or left in the sunshine to dry.

In the main shopping areas of cities such as Phnom Penh and Ho Chi Minh City, bakeries and patisseries, stuffed

Left: A woman baking traditional rice flatbread in Hoi An, Vietnam.

Above: In the markets of Ho Chi Minh City, stalls are laden with freshly baked baguettes, which are eaten almost as much as rice and noodles.

full of enticing, freshly baked cakes, pastries and a variety of sweet and savoury loaves, reflect the French influence, as well as the travels of many refugee Khmer and Vietnamese who have returned to their homelands to set up business. International favourites such as jam tarts, chocolate éclairs, gingerbread men and sponge cakes, all baked on the premises, are enjoyed by passers-by with a good cup of tea or coffee.

MAKING TRADITIONAL BREAD

Some loaves are made from wheat flour alone but, in order to achieve the unique lightness and subtle flavour of traditional Vietnamese and Cambodian bread, it is essential to mix the wheat with rice flour. Once the dough has risen for the second time, use a sharp knife to make a slit lengthways along the top before baking it in the oven. As the freshly made bread is so delicious, one loaf won't go very far, so it is worth making at least two.

TO MAKE 2 LOAVES:

15g/½oz fresh yeast
450ml/15fl oz/scant 2 cups cold water
350g/12oz/1½oz cups unbleached strong white bread flour
350g/12oz/2 cups rice flour
15g/½oz sea salt
15ml/1 tbsp vegetable oil

COOK'S TIP

If using dried yeast, sprinkle 10g/½oz over 60ml/4 tbsp of water and 2.5ml/ ½tsp sugar in a small bowl. Stir the yeast, sugar and water until the yeast is well blended. Set aside for about 15 minutes, until the mixture is foamy. Follow the recipe from step 2.

Above: Baguettes are a common sight alongside the noodles and vegetables in southern Vietnamese markets and are frequently eaten smeared with pâté.

1 Crumble the yeast into a bowl with your fingers. Add 60ml/4 tbsp of the water and cream the yeast to a smooth liquid. Sift the flours and salt into a large bowl. Make a well in the centre and pour in the yeast mixture. Pour the rest of the water into the well in the centre.

2 Using your hand, draw a little flour into the centre and mix well. Draw in a little more flour and mix until you have formed a thick, smooth batter in the centre. Sprinkle a little of the flour over the top of the batter to prevent a skin forming and leave it to froth for about 20 minutes.

3 Using your hand, draw in the rest of the flour and work the mixture into a springy dough. Lift it on to a floured surface and continue to knead for about 10 minutes. Shape it into a ball.

4 Clean the bowl and lightly oil it. Put the dough into the bowl and cover it with a damp dish towel. Leave to rise and double in size – at least 2 hours. Knock back the risen dough by punching it with your knuckles. Lift it on to a floured surface and knead it.

5 Divide the dough into 2 pieces and knead them into sausages, about 30cm/ 12in long. Place both lengths of dough on a baking tray and, with a knife, slit the surface of each piece lengthways. Cover with a damp dish towel and leave again to double in size. Preheat the oven to 220°C/425°F/Gas 7.

6 Sprinkle the loaves with flour, or brush with egg yolk and bake for 15 minutes. Reduce the heat to 190°C/375°F/Gas 5 and bake for 20–25 minutes, until the loaves sound hollow when tapped.

VEGETABLES

Raw, stir-fried, braised, pickled or salted, vegetables are worked into every meal in some manner in Vietnam and Cambodia. Almost every dish includes a few vegetables but, in addition, there may be a vegetable side dish, salad, pickled vegetables, or leaves to wrap around the food. The main thing to remember is that a meal must be balanced with vegetables, protein and starch. Texture is also important, so "salads" might include such ingredients as fruit, meat, shellfish and rice noodles.

In the warm southern regions of Vietnam and the central lowlands of Cambodia, the growing season is long and abundant, providing the regional cuisines with a vast choice of indigenous, and adopted, roots and leaves for exciting vegetable dishes and refreshing, crunchy salads. In the cool north of Vietnam, vegetables are more often steamed, stir-fried and preserved, borrowing traditional Chinese methods. And following ancient Taoist philosophy,

Above: Tiny pea aubergines are bright green and grow in clusters.

some vegetables are believed to possess cooling "yin" qualities, others the warming "yang". It is thought that If these yin and yang forces are not balanced, illness will ensue. This ancient belief is most prominent in the culinary culture of Chinese-influenced northern Vietnam, where a number of Chinese communities still live.

AUBERGINES/EGGPLANT

Technically fruits, but eaten as vegetables, aubergines (*ca tim*) originally came to Vietnam and Cambodia from India and Thailand. Regarded as cooling, they are widely used in both countries. The most common aubergine is long and thin, in shades of pale green and purple. This is the most popular variety as the flavour is sweet with very little bitterness. Incredibly versatile, it is added to stews, curries and stir-fries so that the flesh absorbs all the delicious spices and flavours of the dish. It is often called an "Asian" aubergine and is available in Asian stores and some supermarkets. When choosing, look for smooth, unblemished skin and firm flesh. Thai aubergines are also used in Vietnam and Cambodia. Round and firm, the size of a ping-pong ball, these

Left: Thai aubergines are mostly small and round.

streaky pale green and cream-coloured aubergines are usually halved and added to stews and curries. The tiny, green pea aubergines are also popular throughout South-east Asia. Literally the size of garden peas, these aubergines grow in clusters and have a slightly bitter taste with a pleasantly firm texture. In Cambodia, pea aubergines are added to spicy dipping sauces and curries.

BAMBOO SHOOTS

Dense bamboo groves are a common feature on the South-east Asian landscape. Technically a giant grass, bamboo has many important uses. The long, thin stems or "trunks" are used for making baskets, furniture and conical hats, as well as many kitchen utensils, such as

Above: Bamboo shoots are available fresh, but sliced, canned shoots are easier to find.

steamers, strainers and chopsticks. The leaves are fermented and distilled to make a popular pale-green liqueur, and the shoots are harvested for their tender, delicious flesh. The small, pine cone-sized shoots (*mang*) that are dug up just before they emerge from the ground are very tasty.

In Vietnam and Cambodia, the bamboo "trunks" are also used as cooking vessels. The hollow is stuffed with marinated pork, fish or chicken and placed over an open fire to cook. The long, narrow, pointed leaves have their culinary use too. Dried and sold in

Above: Long beans are similar in flavour to Western green beans.

bundles in the markets, they are soaked in water until pliable and then used to wrap food that is to be steamed, imparting their own unique flavour to the dish.

Fresh, pickled or dried, bamboo shoots are popular throughout Vietnam and Cambodia. To prepare the shoots, the sheaths are stripped off and the tough base removed. Once peeled, the inner core is sliced and blanched in boiling water for a few minutes, then drained and rinsed under cold water. The creamy-white, fresh shoots have a wonderful texture and flavour and are delicious added to stir-fries and soups. Dried shoots require soaking before use. When cooked, they should retain a crunch and taste slightly sweet. Fresh shoots are available in Asian stores, but cans of ready-cooked shoots, preserved in brine, can be bought in most stores.

LONG BEANS

Sometimes referred to as "snake beans" or "chopstick beans", these long, green beans (*dau dau*) are the immature pods of black-eyed beans (peas) and can measure up to 60cm/2ft in length. Generally they are stir-fried just with a few basic flavourings such as garlic and ginger and eaten as a side dish. Pencil-thin and dark or light green in colour, they are available fresh in Asian markets.

PULSES

Dried beans are used extensively in Vietnam and Cambodia, in both sweet and savoury dishes.

Red beans

Dried red beans, also called azuki beans, are some of the smallest available. In Vietnam, they are generally reserved for sweet dishes of Chinese origin. Boiled until soft, they are mashed to form a sweet bean paste, which is eaten with sweet rice, or used to fill steamed buns and dumplings. They are also served as a sweet soup or drink. In Cambodia, black-eyed beans are more common, and are used in a similar way.

Above: Red or azuki beans.

Mung beans

These small beans (*dau xanh*) are prized in Vietnam and Cambodia. Whole dried mung beans, with husks on, are green in colour, whereas the peeled ones are yellow and sold whole and split. Both require soaking in water before cooking. Popular and versatile, mung beans are used in savoury dishes and fillings, as well as in puddings, sweet snacks, and iced drinks. Whole or split mung beans are available in Asian stores, health stores and most supermarkets.

Right: Both mung and soya beansprouts are widely used in Vietnamese cooking.

Beansprouts

Popular throughout Vietnam and Cambodia, as well as the rest of South-east Asia, beansprouts (*gia*) can be eaten raw or added to stir-fries and soups for their crunchy bite. The most common sprouts come from mung beans and soya beans. They are similar in appearance, except soya beansprouts are almost twice the size at about 8cm/3in long. The stems of both are white, but soya bean heads are green, while those of mung beans are yellow. Soya beans are sturdier and stronger in flavour, whereas mung beans are delicate and watery. Both types are nutritious, rich in vitamins and minerals.

Fresh sprouts can be stored in the refrigerator for up to 2–3 days. Packets of mung beansprouts are available in most supermarkets. Soya beansprouts can be found in Asian stores and some health stores.

Growing beansprouts

First soak the dried beans in water overnight. Drain and rinse thoroughly, then put them in a large plastic lidded container. Punch holes in the lid for air. Alternatively, use a jar covered with muslin (cheesecloth). Put in a warm, dark place for 4–5 days, rinsing in lukewarm water three times a day, until they sprout. Take the sprouts out of the container and rinse them, picking out the husks and beans that have not sprouted.

GOURDS AND SQUASHES

Frequently used in Vietnamese and Cambodian cooking, gourds and squashes are often stuffed or added to stir-fries.

Bitter melon

This gourd, *kho qua,* looks like a fat, knobbly cucumber and is, in fact, a bitter relative. It is considered nutritious and medicinal, as it contains high levels of quinine. It has a rather sweet and fragrant smell. Before cooking, the gourd needs to be slit lengthways to remove the seeds and inner membrane. The outer shell is then sliced into half-moons and stir-fried, blanched or pickled to retain the crunchy texture. In some parts of Vietnam and Cambodia, the gourd is kept whole, hollowed out from one end and stuffed with a minced (ground) pork and mushroom filling.

Bitter melons are sold fresh in most Asian stores. A firm, green bitter melon should be allowed to ripen a little before use and will keep for 3–4 days, but a soft yellowish one should be used within a day or two.

Luffa squash

Dark green with ridges running lengthways, luffa squash (*muop*) has sweet and spongy flesh and is usually harvested when it's about 30cm/1ft long. Generally, it is sliced and used in stir-fries and soups, much the same way as you would cook a courgette (zucchini). Luffa squash is available in Asian markets.

Above: A luffa squash has a sweet, delicate flavour when young.

If the luffa is young, all you need to do is wash and slice it. Luffas seldom need peeling, but sometimes the ridges toughen as the vegetable ripens, in which case remove the ridges but leave the skin between, so that the luffa is striped green and white. If the skin is very tough, it is best to peel it completely. Unlike cucumber or young, tender courgettes, luffa is never eaten raw. Keep fresh luffa in the refrigerator, but do not store it for too long as within 2–3 days of purchase it will start to go limp.

Kabocha squash

This is a stout, pumpkin-shaped vegetable with a beautiful dark-green skin patterned with yellow spots and green lines. The flesh is pale orange, fragrant, sweet and creamy, lending itself to a variety of dishes, including curries and desserts. An average kabocha (*bi ro*) weighs about 1–1.5kg/2–3lb and has edible skin. They are available in Asian markets and supermarkets.

Winter melon

Large, mild-flavoured gourds, winter melons (*bi dao*) can weigh 5.4kg/12lb or more and grow up to 25cm/10in in diameter. Egg- or pear-shaped and dark green, they are harvested in the summer (but traditionally stored for winter) and sold whole or cut into wedges. The white flesh tastes like marrow or courgette (zucchini) and is believed to cool fevers. Prepared and cooked in the same way as a pumpkin, winter melon is added to soups, stews and stir-fries, as the flesh absorbs the flavours of the dish. The rind must be cut off and the seeds and coarse fibres at the centre scooped out before the flesh is cut into strips or wedges. Winter melons and fuzzy melons can be used interchangeably, as they are similar in flavour. Both come in various shapes and sizes and are available in Asian markets and supermarkets.

Below: A large winter melon.

Right: Bitter melon is highly regarded in Vietnamese and Cambodian cooking.

MUSHROOMS

Fresh and dried mushrooms are used in many dishes in Vietnam and Cambodia. Dried mushrooms, however, are favoured for stir-fried and savoury fillings because of their texture and delicate taste.

Chinese black

Sometimes known as Chinese shiitake, these pungent mushrooms (*nam huong*) are usually sold dried. Usually light brown in colour with white markings on the surface, they have thick-fleshed caps which can grow to about 5cm/2in in diameter and have a meaty flavour and a distinct texture. Once softened in warm water for about 30 minutes, the stems are removed and the caps are added to stews, stir-fries and fillings.

Straw mushrooms

Also called bulb mushrooms in Vietnam and Cambodia, straw mushrooms (*nam rom*) look like tiny brown eggs. The whole mushrooms are often used in braised dishes for appeal and texture. Once peeled, however, they reveal small dark-brown caps and stocky, cream-coloured stems which look lovely in clear broths. Very delicate in flavour and texture, straw mushrooms are available in cans. They must be drained and thoroughly rinsed before use.

Below: Sliced straw mushrooms, showing their "umbrella" pattern.

Above: Fresh and dried shiitake mushrooms have a meaty flavour.

Above right: Pale and delicate oyster mushrooms are now widely available.

Cloud ears/wood ears

Reminiscent of a human ear in shape, these wonderful looking mushrooms (*nam meo*) are also called tree ears. Harvested from tree trunks, where they grow as natural fungi, they are valued for their nutritional qualities and are believed to cleanse the blood. Usually sold dried, they are thin and brittle and they need to be soaked in water, where they swell up and resemble frilly clumps of rubbery seaweed. The larger tree ears are two-toned, black and tan-coloured, and can be tough; the smaller black ones are more tender.

The dried fungus expands to six or eight times its volume after soaking, so use plenty of water. Leave to soak for about 30 minutes, then drain and rinse well, and drain again. On cooking, the mushrooms become quite translucent and gelatinous, but still retain a bite. Prized for their chewy texture, rather than taste, they are chopped up and added to stuffings and stir-fries. In Vietnam and Cambodia, these mushrooms are particularly popular in vegetarian dishes.

Oyster mushrooms

In the wild, oyster mushrooms grow in clumps on rotting wood. The caps, gills and stems are all the same colour, which can be pearl grey, pink or yellow. Once thought of as wild mushrooms, they are now grown commercially and are widely available in Western supermarkets.

The flavour is mild, with a hint of seafood. Oyster mushrooms are popular in soups and stir-fries, and they are also used in noodle and rice dishes. They seldom need trimming. Large ones should be torn, rather than cut into pieces. The soft texture becomes rubbery if they are overcooked, so always add them to cooked dishes at the last moment. Buy oyster mushrooms that smell and look fresh, avoiding any with damp, slimy patches and those that have discoloured. Store in a paper bag in the vegetable compartment of the refrigerator, and use as soon as possible after purchase. They do not keep for more than 2–3 days.

Below: Tree ears are also known as cloud or wood ears.

ORIENTAL GREENS

Cabbages and greens are grown all over Vietnam and Cambodia.

Pak choi/bok choy

This perennial, green, leafy cabbage is popular throughout South-east Asia. The ribbed, white stems are juicy and crunchy; the dark-green leaves are succulent and tasty. The tender stems of small cabbages are often eaten raw with a dipping sauce, or cut into strips and added to the Vietnamese table salad. The leaves, which are mostly composed of water, require little cooking and lose a lot of volume in the process. It is a good idea to cook the leaves and stems separately, as the stems take slightly longer. Generally, they are stir-fried quickly to retain their texture and flavour. These fresh cabbages are available in Asian stores and supermarkets.

Flowering cabbage

With its yellow flowers, long, slender stalks, and crisp leaves, the flowering cabbage (*cai xanh*) is much prized by Vietnamese cooks. It is picked to be eaten when in flower, so it is beautiful to

behold as well as to taste. One of many Chinese cabbages, it is mild and tender, mainly reserved for stir-fried dishes of Chinese origin. Sold tied in neat bundles, like spinach, flowering cabbages are available in most Asian markets. Choose crisp leaves and keep stored in the refrigerator for a day or two.

Mustard greens

Also known as Chinese cabbage, mustard greens (*cai tau*) look a bit like a head of lettuce such as cos or romaine, except that the leaves wrapping the heart are thick stalks. The leaves are sharp and robust in flavour but, once blanched, they mellow in taste and lose some of their bitterness. Traditionally regarded as peasant fare, mustard greens are added to stir-fries and vegetable dishes in rural areas,

Left: Dark green pak choi tastes similar to spinach. The white stems can be cooked and eaten separately.

Above: The stalks, leaves, and flowers of the flowering cabbage are all edible.

otherwise they are mainly used to wrap food that is to be steamed. Fresh mustard greens are available loose, or in plastic bags, in Asian markets and will keep for a few days in the salad compartment of a refrigerator.

Preserved cabbage

In Vietnam, the tender hearts of mustard greens (*cai man*) are preserved in brine. Quite salty to taste, preserved cabbage is used sparingly and is usually reserved as a garnish for soups and noodle dishes of Chinese origin.

Chinese leaves

There are almost as many names for this member of the brassica family as there are ways of cooking it. In the West, it is generally called Chinese leaves, but it is also known as Chinese cabbage, Napa cabbage (mainly in the USA) or celery cabbage. It is a cool season vegetable, most abundant from November through to April, but available all year round. There are three common varieties which all look similar, but differ in length, width and tightness of leaf. Chinese leaves have a delicate sweet aroma with a mild cabbage flavour that disappears completely when the vegetable is cooked. The white stalk has a crunchy texture, and it remains succulent even after long cooking. It is a very versatile vegetable and it can be used in stir-fries, stews, soups or raw in salads. It will absorb the flavours of any other ingredients with which it is cooked – be they fish or shellfish, poultry, meat or vegetables – and yet retain its own characteristic taste and texture. Restaurant chefs blanch the vegetable in boiling stock, which enhances the flavour, before frying.

Chinese leaves can be stored for a long time without losing their resilience. Keep in the salad compartment of the refrigerator and they will stay fresh for up to 10–12 days. Don't worry if there are tiny black specks on the leaves as this is quite normal and will not affect the flavour.

Below: Chinese leaves have a crunchy texture and a delicate aroma.

Above: Water spinach, which has a flavour that is reminiscent of spinach, is widely eaten throughout South-east Asia.

Water spinach

Also called swamp cabbage or morning glory, this attractive leafy green vegetable (*rau muong*) is traditionally grown in swamps or ponds, near rivers and canals, although it does grow on dry land too. In Vietnam it is so popular it could be considered the national vegetable. Unrelated to regular spinach, it does have a spinach-like taste with crunchy stems and tender, light-green, arrow-shaped leaves.

Sold in big bunches, water spinach is often added to stir-fries and soups, or it is simply stir-fried by itself with garlic. In Vietnam, the hollow stem is often eaten raw, trimmed or curled and added to salads. When cooked, the stem tips stay firm, but the leaves rapidly become limp.

Quite difficult to find outside South-east Asia, water spinach is available in some Asian markets and supermarkets. It is highly perishable and must be used promptly. High in flavour, water spinach provides a good measure of vitamins and minerals. Several variations are cultivated in Vietnam and Cambodia. Look for fresh bundles, which may be sold under the name *kang kong* in Asian and Chinese markets.

Preparing Chinese leaves

1 Discard any damaged outer leaves and trim off the root.

2 It is not usually necessary to wash the leaves. Simply cut the head of Chinese leaves crossways into thin shreds.

3 You may prefer to wash the Chinese leaves, before using them raw in a salad, for instance. Separate the leaves, then wash under plenty of cold running water. Shake off any excess water before shredding and pat dry. This type of cabbage can be stored, before prepration, in the salad compartment of the refrigerator for over a week.

TUBERS AND AQUATIC ROOTS

The crunchy texture of tubers and aquatic roots is enjoyed in fillings and salads and stir-fries.

Cassava

Also known as manioc, cassava (*khoai mi*), is a large tuber similar in shape and size to a sweet potato, with skin like a firm brown bark. It originated in Brazil, and is also popular in Africa and the Caribbean as well as the rest of South America. The creamy-coloured flesh of the root is starchy and often reserved for sweet, sticky puddings. Fresh cassava tubers are available in Asian markets. An extremely versatile vegetable, sweet cassava can be cooked in a number of different ways.

Above: Sweet cassava is a versatile tuber and can be cooked in many ways.

Above: Tapioca pearls prepared for drying on trays.

Preparing cassava

1 Scrub the root, peel, then cut into fairly large pieces, removing the fibrous core.

2 Drop the pieces into a bowl of acidulated water to prevent discoloration. Drain, then boil, steam, bake or fry the cassava pieces until tender.

Tapioca flour

This silky flour (*bot nang*) is made from the starch of the cassava root. Primarily, it is used to thicken sauces and custards for ice cream, but it is also used to make fresh rice papers to give them a translucent sheen. Tapioca flour is available in Asian stores and markets.

Tapioca pearls

These small noodles (*bot bang*) are made from tapioca flour. The pearls range in size from tiny teardrops to green peas, the smallest being the most delicate. They are used primarily in sweet puddings, combined with coconut milk, and in some thick soups. Tapioca pearls are sold dried. They are white in colour, but become transparent when cooked. In Vietnam and Cambodia, tapioca pearls are used primarily for sweet, thick puddings, but in some areas they are cooked in place of rice to accompany fish or a stew. Available in Asian stores, packets of tapioca pearls can also be found in some health stores and supermarkets.

Daikon

White in colour, this root vegetable (*cu cai trang*) looks very similar to a large carrot. Also known as Oriental white radish or mooli, it is crisp, juicy and slightly hot and nips the tongue. It can be eaten raw or cooked and it is a popular vegetable throughout Vietnam and Cambodia for salads and pickles, as well as soups, stir-fries and stews. Daikon can be found in Asian markets and supermarkets.

Above: Raw daikon has a delicious, crisp and crunchy texture.

used in festive sweets and cakes; the large leaves are used for wrapping sticky rice and steamed snacks, in a similar fashion to banana and bamboo leaves; the stems are peeled, sliced and added to salads and soups; and the bulbous roots are cooked in braised dishes and soups. Lotus roots are tan-coloured with a pinkish hue. Juicy and mildly fragrant, they taste similar to water chestnuts. When sliced, the root reveals small holes which hold the seeds. Following ancient Chinese traditions, the nourishing lotus root is believed to aid the blood circulation and to increase virility. In Vietnam and Cambodia, the lotus root is used in braised dishes and clear broths. The roots, stems and seeds of the lotus plant are available, fresh, dried and preserved, in most Asian stores. If dried, all of them need to be soaked overnight and then cooked until tender.

Above: The flesh of a jicama is a cross between an apple and a potato.

Jicama

Resembling a large turnip, this root vegetable (*cu san*) has a delicate taste with a crunchy texture, similar to water chestnuts and lotus roots. Simply peel before use and cut into chunks or slices for soups, salads and stir-fries. Jicamas can be found in most Asian stores.

Lotus flower and root

The beautiful aquatic lotus plant, or water lily (*sen*), with its delicate pink and white flowers, is quite unique. Not only does it symbolize beauty and purity throughout South-east Asia, it is also edible in its entirety. The stamens are infused to make a fragrant tea; the seeds are dried and then boiled to be

Below: Fresh lotus roots have pinky beige skin and look like linked sausages.

Taro

This root vegetable, known as taro (*khoai mon*), requires warm, damp growing conditions and is usually harvested in the winter. Generally, it comes in two varieties. One is small and egg-shaped; the other is about 25cm/10in long and shaped like a barrel. Both are covered in short hairs with white purple-flecked flesh.

Above: Taro is a rough-skinned tuber.

Along with sweet potatoes and yams, taro is used like a potato – mashed and baked, or added to soups, stews and curries. The larger variety is firm with a nutty flavour; the smaller one is creamier and sweeter, lending itself to sweet cakes and puddings. Taro roots are available in Asian stores as well as in some supermarkets.

In Vietnam, the stem of a particular variety of taro is also used. Long and thick, it is peeled and cut into diagonal slices which are added to soups and stews, as their spongy texture absorbs the flavour and sauce of the dish.

Water chestnut

Technically a corm, water chestnuts are grown on rice paddies but harvested when the soil is dry. Sold fresh in the markets, they are often covered with earth. Once the brown skins have been peeled off, the water chestnut is white and crunchy, about the size of a large chestnut off the tree. Juicy and slightly starchy, the texture is similar to that of an Asian pear. Regarded as cooling and beneficial to the digestive system, water chestnuts are also believed to sweeten the breath. They can be eaten raw in salads, or added to fillings or stir-fries.

Fresh water chestnuts have a short life span and must be eaten within 2–3 weeks of purchase. Cans of peeled and ready-cooked water chestnuts are available in most supermarkets. Once the can is opened, store water chestnuts in water in the refrigerator for up to a week, changing the water daily.

FRUIT

Traditionally, fruit is reserved for the end of a meal to cleanse the palate or aid the digestion, while sweet puddings and cakes are nibbled and indulged in as snacks. A wide variety of tropical fruits are available: take your pick from milky white lychees; sweet pineapples; fragrant red arbutus and the flowery rambutan; aromatic mango and papaya; yellow or green bananas; juicy, brown-skinned longans; star fruit; watermelon-sized jackfruit with its bright yellow segments; guavas; passion fruit; zesty citrus fruits like pomelo; mangosteens; coconuts and custard apples; green dragon fruit; and the infamous, spiky durian, which is considered the "king of fruit" in spite of the fact that it tastes like heaven, but smells like hell!

BANANAS

After coconuts, bananas (*chuoi*) are the most widely used fruit in Vietnam and Cambodia. Many puddings and desserts call for bananas, fresh or fried, while a number of savoury dishes require the leaves or blossom of the banana plant.

Indigenous to South-east Asia, the banana plant looks like a tree but is, in fact, a perennial herb. Every year, it

Right: Tiny Lady Finger bananas, or sugar bananas, are often no more than 7.5cm/3in long.

Right: When very ripe, small apple bananas have a faint taste and aroma of fresh apple.

Above: Banana leaves are not eaten but are often used to wrap food.

grows a new "trunk" and, after it has borne blossom and fruit, it dies back to its roots. The fruit grows in bunches and there are a number of varieties in Vietnam and Cambodia. Most are yellow-skinned and pale-fleshed, but there are some with orange flesh and others with green-striped skins and pink flesh. The sweetest tend to be short and stubby.

Banana leaves

You don't need foil, baking parchment or clear film (plastic wrap) when you've got banana leaves (*la chuoi*). They are versatile and can double up as plates, table mats or be shaped into bowls. In Vietnam and Cambodia, the leaves are most often used as wrappings for pâtés and sweet and savoury sticky rice cakes. Banana leaves are available in Asian and African supermarkets. They are sold both fresh and frozen; the latter need to be thawed and wiped clean before use.

Above: At the heart of the banana flower lies the delicate banana bud.

Banana blossom

The lovely deep purple flower of the banana tree (*bap chuoi*) is enjoyed throughout South-east Asia as a vegetable. Sliced finely and soaked in water with a squeeze of lemon or lime juice to prevent it discolouring, the blossom is usually eaten raw and served in salads.

COCONUT

The coconut (*dua*) is the most commonly used fruit for both sweet and savoury dishes throughout South-east Asia. Both ripe and immature coconuts are used. Ripe fruits are used for cooking and for making coconut milk, whereas the soft, jelly-like flesh of the young ones makes a tasty snack.

Coconut palms grow prolifically in the coastal regions of Vietnam and Cambodia. The whole coconut that we buy is only the stone of the actual fruit; the husk and fibres are removed in the country of origin. The coconut palm leaves are woven into baskets and mats, and the husks and fibres are used as fuel, or for making ropes.

When buying a coconut, the hard shell should be brown and hairy. Shake it and you should hear the sound of the coconut water inside. To extract this liquid, pierce the eyes on top of the coconut and pour it out. The coconut water should be clear and taste sweet.

Above: Coconut is versatile and a valuable crop.

Often, it is drunk to quench the thirst, or it is used to tenderize meat.

To open a coconut, first extract the coconut water. Place the coconut on a flat surface and use a heavy object like a cleaver or hammer to hit it all the way round. Pull the shell apart, pry the flesh out with a knife, and, carefully, peel the brown skin off the flesh so that it is ready to use. If you have difficulty cracking the coconut open, place it in a fairly hot oven for about 15 minutes, until it cracks. The flesh is often easier to extract from the shell, using this method.

Right: Creamed coconut block.

Below: Coconut milk.

Coconut milk

In Vietnam coconut milk (*nuoc dua*) is the main cooking liquid in curries and puddings. It is used to enrich sauces and soups with its creaminess, especially in the southern regions, where the food is sweeter and spicier. Coconut milk is also boiled with sugar to make sweets that are wrapped in rice paper, and it is poured over sticky rice for a moist snack. Coconut milk is made by soaking grated coconut flesh in hot water and then squeezing it to extract the liquid. It doesn't keep well and is usually made daily. Coconut milk is available in cans in Asian markets, health stores and supermarkets.

Coconut cream

From the coconut milk, you can get coconut cream. Once you have squeezed out all the coconut milk, allow it to settle in the bowl and the cream will rise to the top. This can be skimmed off, if you wish to use them separately.

Coconut oil

From coconut cream, you can make coconut oil by boiling it gently in a pan until the milk solids evaporate.

Green coconut water

The coconut water used for cooking is extracted from young, green coconuts. Mild and sweet, it is used in a number of braised dishes. Although you can use the coconut water from ripened coconuts, it is best to look in Asian markets for a young coconut. It will be cylindrical in shape with a conical top and a white, spongy shells as the green skin will have been removed.

Making coconut milk

1 Grate the white flesh from a fresh coconut, or shred it in a food processor.

2 Put the grated flesh into a bowl and pour roughly 600ml/1 pint/ 2½ cups boiling water over it. Stir and leave it to steep for about 30 minutes.

3 Line a sieve with a piece of muslin (cheesecloth) and strain the coconut through it into a bowl. Gather the muslin in your hands and squeeze out any excess liquid. This first pressing is creamy and is used for puddings.

4 For a second, thinner pressing, repeat the process with the same coconut flesh and add it to the first, or keep it separate for soups.

Above: Longans are very common and can often be seen piled high in markets.

Above: Lychees have a sweet flavour.

LYCHEE AND LONGAN

Both lychees (*trai vai*) and longans (*nhan*) are native to the subtropical regions of South-east Asia, as they require heat and high humidity. They belong to the same family, although the smaller and less fleshy longan is sometimes regarded as the inferior relative. Lychees have terracotta-pink, bumpy skins, rather than the smooth, brown ones of longans, but both are easily peeled to reveal a gleaming white, occasionally pink, juicy flesh covering a shiny, coffee-coloured seed. Clusters of fresh lychees and longans are sold on their stalks in the markets of Vietnam and Cambodia. Sweet and fragrant, they are usually eaten as a refreshing snack. Fresh longans can be found in some Asian markets, and lychees are readily

Right: Red-skinned mangoes are eaten as a fruit and green-skinned ones as a vegetable.

available in Asian markets and most supermarkets. They keep well in the refrigerator and are delicious chilled. Lychees are also sold in cans, preserved in their own juice, or in syrup.

PAPAYA

The ripe, yellow-skinned, gourd-like papaya (*du du xanh*), with its sweet, flame-coloured flesh, is eaten as a fruit throughout Vietnam and Cambodia. Also known as paw paw, it is full of vitamins and honey-sweet, often enhanced by a squeeze of lime. However, when a recipe calls for papaya, it is a different variety that is required. Large and round, or pear-shaped, this papaya has a dark green skin with light green flesh and white seeds. High in iron, this tart fruit is enjoyed as a vegetable, peeled and finely sliced, or shredded, in salads. Both types of papaya can be found in Asian markets and some supermarkets. Choose fruit with firm, unblemished skin, not bruised or shrivelled. Ripe papayas do not last very long. Slit them open, scoop out the seeds and enjoy the honeyed flesh with a squeeze of fresh lime.

Right: Papayas, often known as paw paw are one of the most attractive tropical fruits and are eaten as a snack.

Below: Mangosteens have a fragrant, delicate flavour and are best eaten raw.

Above: A durian and its large seeds.

DURIAN

This large fruit, encased in a spiky armour-like skin, is creamy, dense and pungent. If you can put up with the strong, cheesy odour, the yellow flesh is delicious with nut and honey overtones, quite unlike any other fruit. Considered an aphrodisiac, durian (*sau rieng*) is a much sought after fruit during the season, from late spring to late summer. It is an expensive fruit and only available in some Asian markets. Avoid any fruits that have split.

Preparing durian

The prickly shell is split open to reveal large seeds coated in pulp. The pulp is tugged, or sucked, off and the seeds are sucked to extract the cooling water inside.

JACKFRUIT

Large and spiky, the jackfruit (*mit*) shell is similar to a durian. When sliced open, the yellow fruit is delightfully fragrant and resembles a ripe pineapple with lots of seeds. The texture of the flesh is creamy and chewy at the same time; the taste rather like a sweet banana. Packed with vitamins, the fruit is enjoyed on its own as well as mixed with other fruits in a tropical fruit salad. Peel the fruit like a pineapple, cut it into chunks or slices and remove the seeds.

MANGO

Originally from India, several varieties of mango (*xoai*) are popular in Vietnam and Cambodia. The sweetest tend to be large and round with bright yellow skins. Juicy, ripened mangoes are enjoyed as a fruit and the tart green ones are used as a vegetable. Sliced finely, or shredded, the green flesh is added to salads or dipped in the Vietnamese fish sauce. The season for ripe mangoes is short, from March to June, when they are consumed in large quantities, as the sweet, juicy, yellow or orange flesh is thirst-quenching, with a delightful aroma of pine. A good source of vitamin A, different types of mango are available in Asian stores and supermarkets.

Above: The leaves and rind of kaffir limes are valued in Cambodian dishes.

Below: Limes are a very popular flavouring in Vietnamese cooking.

The seeds can be roasted and eaten like pumpkin and melon seeds. Jackfruit is available in some Asian markets.

LIME

In Vietnam and Cambodia, fresh green limes are used frequently for their juice. Tossed in marinades and dressings, the slightly fragrant, citrus taste of the juice enhances the flavour of other ingredients. In Cambodia, kaffir limes feature in many Thai-style dishes. The rind is grated and added to many savoury dishes and the leaves lend a lemony fragrance to soups and stews. Both varieties are available in Asian markets and some supermarkets.

Left: Jackfruit can weigh up to 40kg/88lb.

Below: Pineapples are an important fruit crop in Vietnam and Cambodia.

POMELO

Similar to a large grapefruit, but with thicker skins and denser pith, pomelos (*buoi*) are sweet and mellow. Several varieties are grown, some yellow-skinned, others green, but the best ones are grown along the coast in central Vietnam. Often eaten as a snack, sometimes with a little salt, they are also enjoyed in salads with herbs and spices, or grilled meats. They can be found in some Asian markets and supermarkets.

RAMBUTAN

Shaggy-haired and fiery looking, rambutans (*chom chom*) look like tiny red sea urchins. There are a number of varieties, varying in sweetness and coloured with streaks of gold, orange and green. Easy to open, the hairy shells encase a translucent white fruit with a stone (pit) in the middle, similar to the lychee and longan. Cool and sweet to taste, these fruits are available in some Asian markets.

PINEAPPLE

Grown mainly in the south of Vietnam and Cambodia, pineapples (*dua*) vary in juiciness and sweetness. Often pineapple slices are sold with a little salt and chilli powder to sprinkle on them. Ripe pineapples are mainly eaten as a fruit, although some find their way into hot and sour soups and stews, particularly in Cambodia. Pineapples are readily available; when choosing, look for a firm, puckered skin, with a good orange colouring and a fragrant odour. To prepare fresh pineapple slices, first slice off the leaves, then use a sharp or serrated knife to cut off the skin in vertical strips. Finally, slice the flesh, crossways, into rounds and serve.

Above right: Bright yellow star fruit is also known as carambola.

Right: Rambutans have a distinctive skin covered in soft spiky hairs. They are available fresh and ready prepared in cans.

STAR FRUIT

Also known as carambola, the pretty star-shaped fruit (*khe*) is mildly floral tasting and similar in texture to an Asian pear. In Vietnam and Cambodia, the ripened yellow fruit is enjoyed as a juicy snack. The green immature fruit is sliced finely and served as a tangy vegetable, either as an accompaniment to grilled meats or as part of a table salad.

Left: The largest member of the citrus family, a pomelo can weigh as much as 1kg/2¼lb.

TOFU PRODUCTS

An inexpensive protein food invented by the Chinese, bean curd or tofu is now widely enjoyed throughout the world as an alternative to meat or fish.

TOFU

Soya beans are mainly used to make tofu, also known as bean curd (*dau hu*). It is often referred to as "poor man's meat" in Vietnam and Cambodia. High in protein, incredibly low in calories and devoid of cholesterol, tofu provides essential amino acids, vitamins and minerals for good health. It is made by combining soya bean milk with a coagulant such as gypsum powder to form curds which are then pressed together into blocks.

Highly versatile, it lends itself to stir-frying, grilling (broiling), steaming, smoking or simmering. It is added to many vegetarian dishes for protein and texture, including stir-fries, soups and stuffings. On its own it is bland, but this is the beauty of it, as it has the ability to absorb flavours and is delicious when marinated in Vietnamese flavourings, then stir-fried and served with fresh basil leaves. Fresh tofu, sold in firm blocks packed in water, is available in most health stores. In Asian stores, you may find soft and medium types. Generally, the soft silken texture is better for soups and steamed dishes,

whereas the medium and firm varieties are best in stir-fries and fillings. Tofu is best used straight away, but, if it is kept submerged in water, which is changed daily, it can be stored for 3–4 days in the refrigerator.

Dried tofu

Also known as "bean curd sticks" in Vietnam, this product (*tau hu ky*) is made by simmering soya milk until a thin skin forms on top. Traditionally, a long bamboo stick is used to lift the skin off the milk to be hung on a line to dry. As they dry, the skins shrink a little and stiffen, until they resemble tongs or "sticks". Creamy coloured and delicate tasting, this dried tofu is sold in packages in Asian markets to be used in soups and stews. Before using, it must first be soaked in water for 20–30 minutes. Dried tofu is also available in sheets which can be used as wrappers for salads and other fillings.

Preserved tofu

Cubes of fermented tofu (*chao*) are preserved in salty brine for several months. Before use, the preserved cubes need to be rinsed thoroughly. Strong in flavour, they are used sparingly

Below: Pressed tofu has a firm texture.

Above: Fermented tofu.

when added to stir-fries and soups. Preserved tofu can be found in Asian stores.

Fermented tofu

This is made by fermenting fresh tofu on beds of rice straw, then drying the curd in the sun before marinating wth salt, alcohol and spices. Finally, it is stored in brine in sealed earthenware urns and left to mature for at least six months before being packaged and sold. It is definitely an acquired taste and is traditionally served either on its own with rice congee at breakfast, or used in marinating and cooking. Fermented tofu is available from Southeast Asian markets and, once opened, must be stored in the refrigerator.

Silken tofu

Soft, silken tofu, drizzled with syrup, is sold by vendors as a warm street snack. It is also often used in soups.

Above, clockwise from top: Pressed, silken and firm tofu, all varying in degrees of firmness and suited to stir-fries or soups.

FISH AND SHELLFISH

The Vietnamese and Cambodians are blessed with abundant waters, which is reflected in their diets, as fish and shellfish provide their most important daily source of protein. From their extensive coastlines, they get plentiful supplies of fish, such as grouper, mackerel, shark, red snapper, tuna and sea bass, as well as huge crabs, squid and prawns (shrimp). From their rivers and lakes, they get numerous varieties of carp and catfish, eels, freshwater shrimp and crab, and water-dwelling snails. Most of the fish eaten in Cambodia is of the freshwater variety.

When cooking fish and shellfish in Vietnam and Cambodia, only the freshest is used. It is sold live, at reasonable prices, in the markets and restaurants and is often bought minutes before heading straight for the pot. This is due in part to the lack of refrigeration in most homes, but also because the delicate, sweet flesh of fish and shellfish plucked straight out of the water is much appreciated. To enhance the flavour and texture, many recipes call for a simple infusion with herbs, or steaming with ginger and lemon grass, rather than masking the natural taste with too many spices or strong condiments. The more complex dishes are reserved for special family gatherings or enjoyed when dining out.

Generally, whole fish are steamed with aromatic flavourings; larger steaks might be braised with a caramel sauce, or steamed in coconut milk or beer; and small chunks of fish, or shellfish, are marinated and stir-fried, or grilled over charcoal. In the streets of Ho Chi Minh City and Phnom Penh, the smoky wafts of pungently seasoned fish or shellfish cooking over hot charcoal never fail to make you feel hungry.

Above: Carp is one of the hardiest of all fish. It has meaty flesh that varies in taste according to how the fish is cooked.

With such an abundance of fish and shellfish, methods of preserving it have evolved. Hanging the larger fish up to dry, or salting them, is popular throughout Vietnam and Cambodia, while the smaller varieties are usually pickled. Prawns and squid are so common, they are often salted and dried to be used as flavour enhancers in stocks and noodle dishes.

BARB

There are many types of barb in Vietnam and Cambodia. The silvery white *Puntius altus*, with its black dorsal fin, yellow pectorals and red fins, is farmed in the Mekong Delta. Called *ca he* in Vietnam, it is particularly popular lightly fried and served with *nuoc cham*.

Highly prized by the Khmer is the *Puntius proctozysron*. Called *trey chakeng* in Cambodia, it is mainly silver in colour and angular, almost diamond shaped. All the species that fall into the genus *Barbus* are freshwater fish. They are not that big, so they are often cooked and served whole.

CATFISH

Primarily freshwater fish, catfish are so called because of their barbels, used for feeling along the river beds, which look like whiskers. Free of scales and small bones, catfish are easy to prepare, but the quality of their flesh varies as they are bottom feeders and feed off live and dead prey. Although there are many varieties of catfish, the most popular one in the Mekong is the *Wallagonia attu*, otherwise known as the freshwater shark. Its firm flesh and good flavour make it ideal for grilling (broiling) and stir-frying. In Vietnam, it is called *ca leo*; in Cambodia *trey sanday*.

CARP

In Vietnam and Cambodia, there are numerous species of carp, all of which have different names. Not all carp are good to eat, as some feed in shallow, muddy waters which can affect the taste. One of the most popular types is the *Cirrhinus microlepis*, called *ca roi* in Vietnam and *trey pruol* in Cambodia. A powerful swimmer, it leaps like a salmon and migrates in shoals. Abundant in the Mekong, this delicious carp is much sought after by the Vietnamese and the Khmer.

GOURAMY

There are several types of gouramy, a pond- and lake-dwelling fish that feeds on aquatic plants. Perhaps the most interesting looking, and the most consumed, is the snakeskin gouramy. So called because of its markings, the snakeskin gouramy is primarily greyish-brown in colour with shades of blue and green. Called *ca sat rang* in Vietnam and *trey kantho* in Cambodia, it is delicious grilled or used in soups.

Above: A fierce-looking catfish.

Left: Young eels should be bought alive as they go off very quickly.

EELS

Adult eels are at their plumpest when they have turned silver with almost black backs. Females weigh three times as much as males, so a female silver eel is highly prized. Eels should be bought alive, as they go off quickly once dead. Ask the fishmonger to skin them for you and to chop them into 5cm/2in lengths. The Vietnamese and Cambodians generally eat freshwater eel.

Skinning an eel

You will probably prefer to ask your fishmonger to kill and skin your eel, but if this is not possible, this is how to do it yourself. Grip the eel in a cloth and bang its head sharply on a hard surface to kill it. Put a string noose around the base of the head and hang it firmly on a sturdy hook or door handle. Slit the skin all round the head just below the noose. Pull away the top of the skin, turn it back to make a "cuff", then grip with a cloth or two pairs of pliers and pull the skin down firmly towards the tail. Cut off the head and tail. Alternatively, kill the eel and chop it into sections, leaving the skin on. Grill the pieces, skin up, turning frequently until the skin has puffed up on all sides. When cool enough to handle, peel off the skin.

SNAKEHEAD

With its slim snake-like head, this fish has the ability to survive the dry season by sinking its head in the mud at the bottom of lakes and canals. As long as its breathing apparatus remains moist, it can live off its stores of fat until the rain starts again. Dark mud-coloured and firm-fleshed, it is ideal for steaming, grilling (broiling), stir-fries and curries. The head is usually sold separately for soup. It is called *ca loc* in Vietnam; *trey ros* in Cambodia.

SNAPPER

There are numerous species of this tropical, marine fish, *ca chi vang*. With its long, pointed head and snapping jaw, equipped with canine-like teeth, it is good to eat and in abundant supply. The most common type is the red snapper. When swimming around it is pink in colour with flashes of silver on its scales; once it's dead the body turns red. Red snapper is steamed whole, or filleted for stir-fries and curries.

TUNA

A large oily fish, the tuna (*ca ngu*) has to keep swimming continuously in order to obtain the supply of oxygen it needs, and it swims at very high speeds. All this swimming requires strong muscles, which is the part of the fish that is much sought after. Deep red in colour, the flesh is often cut into steaks that are marinated and pan-fried, grilled (broiled), braised with herbs and spices, or stir-fried, like pieces of meat. In the coastal regions of Vietnam and Cambodia, the most common species of tuna is the yellowfin, *Tuna albacares*.

SEA BASS

One of the finest of all fish, sea bass are as good to look at as they are to eat. They have a sleek shape rather like a salmon, and a beautiful silvery body with a darker back and a white belly. They can grow to a length of 90cm/36in and weigh up to 7kg/15½lb, although the average weight is 1–3kg/ 2¼–6½lb. The firm white flesh is fine-flavoured and is suited to most cooking methods, especially steaming. An excellent way to do this is to marinate the whole fish in spices and wrap it in a banana leaf before cooking.

Below: Sea bass is fleshy and versatile, ideal for stews and curries.

SQUID

An important and plentiful food source, *con muc* or squid are consumed widely in South-east Asia. Along with octopus and cuttlefish, they are members of the cephalopod family. Torpedo-shaped and flanked by two fins, eight arms and two tentacles, the entire body is edible and delicious. Easy to prepare, squid can be cooked in a variety of ways, such as stir-fried with spices.

If stir-frying, slit the prepared sac from top to bottom and turn it inside out. Flatten it on a board and score the inside surface lightly with a knife, pressing just hard enough to make a crisscross pattern. Cut lengthways into ribbons. These will curl when cooked.

Above: Fresh squid is most commonly stir-fried; dried squid is added to stocks.

Preparing squid

1 Grip the head in one hand, the body in the other, and tug the head out of the body sac, pulling most of the innards with it. Grip the top of the backbone and pull it out. Rinse out the inside of the sac and pat dry.

2 Sever the arms and tentacles from the rest of the head and innards and put beside the sac. Discard the rest.

MOLLUSCS

Bivalves, including mussels, clams, oysters and scallops, are widely used in Vietnam and Cambodia. They may be steamed, deep-fried or stir-fred, and are also used in soups.

Like other types of shellfish, molluscs deteriorate rapidly, so you must make sure that they are alive when you cook them. Scallops are an exception, as they are often sold already opened and cleaned. Bivalves such as mussels, clams and oysters should contain plenty of sea water and feel heavy for their size. Do not buy any that have broken shells. If the shells gape, give them a sharp tap on a hard surface. They should snap shut immediately; if they don't, do not buy them, as they will either be dead or moribund.

When buying mussels, clams or similar shellfish, allow approximately 450g/1lb per person, as the shells make up much of the weight. Four or five scallops will serve one person as a good main course.

Mussels, clams and other bivalves must be eaten within one day of purchase, but will keep briefly when stored in the refrigerator. Put them in a large bowl, cover with a damp cloth and keep them in the coldest part of the refrigerator (at 2°C/36°F) until ready to use. Some people advocate sprinkling them with porridge oats and leaving them overnight to fatten up.

Oysters can be kept for a couple of days, thanks to the sea water contained in their shells. Store them cupped side down. Never store shellfish in fresh water, or they will die. Ready-frozen bivalves should not be kept in the freezer for more than 2 months.

The freshwater snail also comes into this category. Popular in Vietnam, it is plucked live from the water straight into the bamboo steamer.

Above: Covering molluscs with a damp cloth will help keep them fresh in the coldest part of the refrigerator.

Preparing molluscs

Scrub bivalves under cold running
water, using a stiff brush or scourer to
remove any dirt or sand. Open them
over a bowl to catch the delicious juice.
This will be gritty, so must be strained
before being used in a sauce or stock.
Cockles usually contain a lot of sand.
They will expel this if left overnight in a
bucket of sea water or salted water.

Cleaning mussels

1 Wash the mussels in cold water,
scrubbing them well. Scrape off
any barnacles with a knife.

2 Give any open mussels a sharp
tap; discard any that fail to close.

3 Pull out and discard the fibrous
"beard" that sprouts between the
two halves of the shell.

CRAB

A member of the crustacean family,
crabs (*cua*) live in fresh water as
well as salt water. Off the coast
of Vietnam and Cambodia,
the saltwater variety can
grow huge, at least 60cm/2ft
in diameter. Crabs are sold
live, so the flesh is firm and
sweet. The whole crab is
steamed with herbs and
aromatics, or it is dropped
into boiling water for a few
minutes to kill it, so that it
can be shelled before using
the meat in recipes.

Preparing crab

Make sure there is no water sloshing
around in the crab. The shell should
neither be soft nor contain any cracks
or holes. If the crab is live, chill it for a
few hours, until it is comatose and no
longer moving, and then cook it. Turn
the crab belly up and remove the
V-shaped flap on the bottom. Hold it
firmly and pull the top shell off the
body. Scoop out the soft, yellowish liver
which is reserved as a delicacy – the
Vietnamese use it to enrich sauces.
Discard the feathery gills and snap off
the legs and claws. You can crack the
legs and claws to extract the tender,
white meat, or leave them intact for
cooking and crack them when eating.
Rinse the body and cut the brown meat
into pieces, according to the recipe.

PRAWNS/SHRIMP

Both marine and freshwater
prawns (*tom*) are popular in
Vietnam and Cambodia. Like
lobsters and crabs, prawns
are crustaceans. The marine
variety is plentiful and
comes in various sizes.
Buy fresh raw prawns
if possible, choosing
specimens that are
a translucent grey
colour tinged with
blue. Prawns are
sweet-flavoured and turn
pink or orange when
they are cooked.

Above: Cooked prawns.

Juicy and meaty, the bigger prawns
are often grilled whole, or added to
stir-fries and curries; the small ones
are dried and added to stocks to
enhance the flavour, or pounded to
make a pungent paste. The small
freshwater ones are more delicate and
are often steamed briefly, or sometimes
eaten alive!

Preparing fresh prawns
Raw freshwater and saltwater
prawns and large shrimp are
peeled before cooking. Raw
prawns must have their intestinal
tracts removed. It is not necessary
to devein small shrimp.

Below: Raw prawns.

DRIED AND FERMENTED FISH PRODUCTS

Pungent dried and fermented fish products play a big role in the flavouring of stocks, stews and stir-fries in Cambodia and Vietnam. Generally, small fish and shellfish are dried whole for texture and flavour.

Dried prawns

Prized for their distinct flavour and chewy texture, dried prawns (shrimp) are used to season a variety of dishes. They are also occasionally eaten as a snack, tossed in lime juice, fish sauce, sugar and chillies. Vibrant orange in colour, having been boiled before being left out in the sun to dry, they should be meaty-looking and springy to touch. They are available in different sizes in Asian markets.

Dried squid

These can be seen hanging above food stalls in the markets of Vietnam and Cambodia. Generally, dried squid are used to add texture to dishes and to season them with their sweet, pungent flavour. Grilled (broiled) or roasted, dried squid lend a smoky sweetness and a strong amber colour to soup stocks. Before using, dried squid should be soaked in warm water for at least 30 minutes, then drained and cleaned in fresh water. They are available in Asian markets.

Above: Dried squid has a subtle fishy aroma, but a strong flavour.

Nuoc mam

The principal ingredient that is quintessentially Vietnamese is *nuoc mam,* which is a fermented fish sauce with a pungent smell. It is a condiment that most Vietnamese can't do without as it is splashed into practically every soup, stir-fry and marinade, as well as serving as a standard dipping sauce.

To make *nuoc mam,* small, silver anchovies are layered with salt and left to ferment in barrels for about three months; the liquid gathered in the base is then drained off and poured back over the fish to ferment for a further three months. The liquid, which by this time is extremely pungent, is then drained and strained into bottles where it is left to mature even further. This is the first pressing, which is of high quality, and is generally used as a table condiment. The second and third pressings are less pungent and are used for cooking. Bottles are available in most Asian stores. Look for a rich, dark colour with the words *ngon* or *thuong hang* on the label as these indicate a superior quality

Preparing dried squid

Dried squid has a long shelf life if kept in a cool, dry place. Dried whole to retain its flavour, it is prized for its aroma and texture.

1 Soak the dried squid in warm water for 30 minutes or so, then drain and wash in fresh water.

2 Score the squid on the inside in a criss-cross fashion, then cut it into small pieces.

Below: Nuoc mam *is a pungent fish sauce used in nearly every savoury Vietnamese dish.*

Above: Dried shrimp.

Above: Shrimp paste, or mam tom, *is pungent and powerful, so use it sparingly.*

Mam tom

The Vietnamese have such a penchant for strong-smelling substances that there is an even more overpowering condiment than *nuoc mam* called *mam tom*, a fermented shrimp paste that is often served with dog meat. It's no wonder that American soldiers nicknamed this paste "Viet Cong tear gas" as one blast of it up the nasal passages can make you positively keel over! *Mam tom* is available in some Asian stores.

Prahoc

Unique to Cambodian cuisine, *prahoc* is a popular fish-based condiment, made by fermenting whole fish, or chunks of fish, with ground rice and salt. Extremely pungent and, perhaps, more offensive-smelling than the Vietnamese *mam tom*, this potent sauce is essential in Cambodian cooking. Once added to dishes, it mellows in odour and enhances the flavour of the other ingredients. The most common fish used to make this condiment are mud fish, grey featherback and gouramy.

Jars of *prahoc* are available in Asian stores. A small jar will go a long way and keep for months. Generally, *prahoc* is not used directly from the jar; a small amount is diluted in boiling water and strained. The strained liquid is called *tuk prahoc*, which is used in practically every Cambodian savoury dish.

Making tuk prahoc

In a small pan, bring 250ml/8fl oz/1 cup water to the boil. Reduce the heat and add roughly 30ml/2 tbsp of *prahoc* from the jar. Simmer gently for 10 minutes, until the fish has broken down and the water is cloudy. Strain the fish through a sieve set over a bowl to extract the liquid, pressing down on the fish. Strain the liquid one more time, through a piece of muslin (cheesecloth), to make sure it is running clear. Leave it to cool and store in an airtight container in a cool place.

Tuk trey

Similar to *nuoc mam*, this is Cambodia's fish sauce. It is made in the same way as *nuoc mam*, by layering small fish and salt in wooden barrels and leaving them to ferment for months until the juices can be extracted and bottled. Bottles of *tuk trey* can be found in some Asian markets. Alternatively, use the Vietnamese fish sauce, *nuoc mam*, or the Thai version, *nam pla*, which are both useful substitutes.

> ### Fish sauce
> It is worth overcoming any aversion to the distinctively pungent fish sauce, as it is an essential part of South-east Asian cooking. Valued for its high protein content, it also enhances the flavour of other ingredients, rather than overpowering them.

Preparing shrimp paste

Shrimp paste can be used straight from the packet if it is to be fried with other ingredients, but it needs to be heated to temper its raw taste before using in sambals, dressings and salads.

1 Cut off a small piece of shrimp paste and shape it into a 1cm/½in cube. Mould the paste on to the end of a metal skewer.

2 Hold the end of the skewer in an oven glove and rotate over a low to medium gas flame, or under an electric grill (broiler), until the paste begins to look dry, but not burnt. This method works well, but gives off a strong smell.

3 Alternatively, to avoid the strong smell, wrap the cube of paste in a piece of foil and dry-fry in a frying pan on a high heat for about 5 minutes, turning it occasionally.

POULTRY AND EGGS

Chickens and ducks are bred all over Vietnam and Cambodia, even in the densely populated neighbourhoods around the major cities. Bicycles with baskets full of cackling chickens and ducks wind their way through the traffic to the markets, where the birds are sold live and killed when selected. The dead birds are then plunged into boiling water to make the feathers easier to pull off so the hungry cook can rush home to the awaiting pot.

Grilling on a spit, or oven roasting, are the most popular methods of cooking poultry and game birds. Symbolizing abundance and prosperity, a whole chicken or duck is cooked for the Vietnamese New Year. Small birds, such as quail and squab, are also common, often spit-roasted and devoured as a snack. The eggs of all these birds are eaten in a variety of ways.

CHICKEN

Chickens in South-east Asia are small and lean, more akin to the free-range variety sold in the West. Many families have their own chickens as they live off insects, worms and kitchen scraps, so they are easy to raise. The eggs are collected and used daily, occasionally added whole to dishes to symbolize fertility, good luck or happiness.

Light, versatile and cheap, chicken is cooked almost as often as pork. In southern Vietnam, chicken frequently ends up in a delicious coconut-milk curry served with chunks of bread; in Cambodia it is stir-fried with lots of ginger. Nothing is wasted in the Vietnamese and Cambodian kitchen, so the wings are deep-fried; the hearts and gizzards are stir-fried with vegetables; the red combs are also stir-fried; the blood is steamed to form solid blocks which are braised; and the carcass is used to make a flavoursome stock for soups. A steaming bowl of chicken broth with ginger is believed to relieve cold symptoms. Chicken portions, such as thighs or drumsticks, are ideal for cooking on the barbecue. Brush them with a marinade spiced with chillies, coriander and ginger, and serve hot with soy sauce or *nuoc cham*.

Left: Every part of the chicken is used in cooking – even the feet.

Jointing a chicken
This method will give you eight good-sized portions of chicken.

1 Place the chicken breast side up on a chopping board. Ease one of the legs away from the body, and using a sharp knife make an incision to reveal the ball of the thighbone as you pull the leg further away from the body. When the thigh socket is visible, cut through the bone to release the drumstick and thigh in one piece. Repeat with the other leg.

2 Trim off the end of the leg bone, then locate the knee joint and cut the leg portion in half at this joint. Repeat with the other chicken leg. Remove any stray feathers.

3 Cut through the breastbone so that the carcass is in two halves. Cut and separate each breast and wing from the backbone.

4 Cut both of the wing and breast pieces into two portions.

COOK'S TIPS
• Use the backbone to make stock, adding onion, celery and a piece of root ginger if appropriate.
• If smaller pieces of chicken are required, for example for stir-fries, the portions can be further divided. Deft Asian cooks will cut the breast and wing portions of chicken into as many as ten pieces, the legs into four pieces and the thighs into six pieces.

Left: Duck is often served
whole in dishes reserved
for festive occasions.

DUCK

Great foragers of food, ducks are also
easy to raise. Like chickens, they live off
insects, worms and kitchen scraps, as
well as other waste, and pretty much
take care of themselves. In South-east
Asia, they are not only valued for their
meat and eggs, but for their feathers
and down, which are used for bedding,
clothing and furnishings.

Duck is often served whole in dishes
reserved for festive occasions, such as
the Vietnamese version of Peking Duck
and the Cambodian speciality of duck
cooked in a clay pot with preserved
limes. In Vietnam, duck's tongues are

*Below: Preserved, salted duck eggs are
a speciality of South-east Asia.*

stir-fried with saté, a spicy
peanut and chilli paste, and their feet
are braised in coconut juice.

The eggs are almost as highly prized
as the duck meat. Following Chinese
tradition, the Vietnamese eat duck eggs
containing under-developed embryos,
which are considered a delicacy as well
as a source of strength. When cooked,
the egg whites are usually so hard that
only the strong-tasting yolks, with their
unusual crunchiness from the bones of
the immature duckling, are eaten.
Large batches of duck eggs are also
preserved in salt, a popular delicacy
throughout South-east Asia.

Preserved duck legs and thighs

Air-cured meats are popular
throughout South-east Asia. Used
primarily for flavouring stocks, or noodle
based soups, the dried duck legs and
thighs give a lovely sweet and meaty
note to the dish. The texture of the
meat, which is slightly chewier than
fresh duck, is much sought after.

Salted duck eggs

Chinese in origin, salted duck eggs are
enjoyed with bland dishes such as
plain noodles and rice porridge.
Their salty flavour is acquired by
coating the eggs in a paste
made of salt and water, and
storing them in rice husks,
or straw, in a cool, dark
place – sometimes
underground – to keep
them fresh while they
absorb the salt through

their shells. Before eating, they are
hard-boiled and then halved to reveal
the polished whites and orange yolks.

QUAILS AND SQUAB

Squab are nestling pigeons, and both
these birds are bred for the pot. Quails
are so popular they are spit-roasted
everywhere you go. Street vendors grill
them to such crispy perfection that you
can hungrily tuck into the tender meat
and munch the whole bird, bones and
all, in a matter of minutes. In Vietnam,
the delicate quail eggs are soft-boiled
and braised in soy sauce. Squab, on the
other hand, is quite expensive and
tends to appear as a treat at banquets
or in restaurants.

FROGS

These are very popular in Vietnam and
Cambodia. For many years, under the
brutal Khmer Rouge regime, frogs,
lizards and insects formed part of the
daily diet for many Cambodians. In
Vietnam, the French influence is more
prevalent and frogs are often cooked in
fairly sophisticated dishes.

*Above: Quail are so small, they are
usually roasted and eaten whole.*

*Below: Squab is roasted for special
occasions or cooked in festive stews.*

PORK AND BEEF

The principal meat in Vietnam and Cambodia is pork. Many families, particularly in the countryside, may own a pig. They are easy and cheap to raise as they live on scraps, they are big enough to feed a family many times over, and every part of them is edible. Displayed in the markets, you will find familiar cuts of pork sitting beside the liver and heart, which are next to the ears, snout, tail and intestines. The fat rendered from pork is on sale too. In Cambodia it is the principal cooking fat; in Vietnam groundnut (peanut), sesame and vegetable oil are used more often.

In Vietnam, the pigs from Hue, the former imperial seat, are held in high esteem. Following traditional methods, they are fed rice and the fruit, leaves and bark of banana trees, which render the meat tender and sweet. A whole suckling pig, spit-roasted over an open wood fire, is a traditional speciality, reserved for wedding banquets and celebratory feasts, in both Vietnam and Cambodia. Depending on whether you are in the northern or southern regions of these countries, the flavour of the spit-roasted pig varies considerably, as the milk-fed meat is rubbed and seasoned with a different local combination of herbs and spices, such

Below: Lean leg steaks, fillet and spare ribs are the preferred cuts of pork.

Above: Vietnamese pot-bellied pigs.

as ginger, garlic, chillies, cinnamon and basil. The traditional slow roasting produces a candy-like, crispy skin, encasing the juiciest, sweetest meat that melts in your mouth like butter.

Beef is enjoyed in Vietnam, but less so in Cambodia. The price of beef does vary, making it a rarity in some homes. In the north of Vietnam, where there is good grazing land, beef is reasonably priced, hence Hanoi's speciality *bo bay mon*, which is a traditional feast of seven distinctly different beef dishes strongly influenced by the indigenous cattle-based agriculture as well as the Mongol invaders, who loved beef. Again, familiar cuts of beef are displayed in the markets, along with the cow's feet and the bull's testicles and penis. Many other meats are available in the markets, such as dog, goat and horse, particularly in the rural regions. Often termed "exotic" in the West, they are not standard fare.

PORK

A light, versatile meat, pork lends itself to every cooking method. It can also be salt- and air-cured and made into special sausages. Cuts of fresh pork are usually eaten as a main dish, often combined with chicken or shellfish. Minced (ground) pork is used for meatballs and fillings and, in Vietnam, steamed in French-inspired pâtés. The cured meat is added to stir-fries and soups for flavour and seasoning. The intestines are used as sausage casings; the heart, liver and kidneys are stir-fried; the gelatinous ears, snout and tail are braised; and the fatty belly and buttocks are roasted or braised.

Preserved pork

The spicy and sweet character of the seasoned and air-cured pork is mainly used to flavour stir-fried dishes. Pork belly is usually seasoned with sugar, soy sauce and spices and hung to cure like bacon, often known as Chinese bacon. The belly and liver are also air-cured with spices in the form of sausages, also referred to as Chinese.

BEEF

In the north of Vietnam, beef is used in stir-fried dishes, braised dishes and noodle soups. Throughout Vietnam, it is the principal ingredient in the national dish, *pho*, a beef and noodle soup, which is eaten at any time of day. In Cambodia, it appears in Khmer dishes, such as *samlaw machou kroeung*, a delicious spicy soup. Both the Vietnamese and the Cambodians prepare a zesty raw-beef salad, where the paper-thin slices of meat are tossed in fish sauce and lime juice. In Vietnam, beef tripe is occasionally used in recipes instead of pork offal but, unlike pork, beef offal is not widely used.

HERBS, SPICES AND FLAVOURINGS

Spices play an essential role in Vietnamese and Cambodian cuisine. Along with the national fish sauces, distinctive combinations of spices and herbs are what give the region's food its unmistakeable character. Many of the spices have been part of the region's culinary history since 166AD, when the Romans first arrived on the spice route, while others only came to the region in the 16th century when the Portuguese introduced vegetables, spices and fruit from the New World.

Herbs also play an important role. In Vietnam they are piled on top of cooked dishes, wrapped around tasty morsels, tucked into rice wrappers, used for garnishing, and served in salads. When the Cambodians cook Vietnamese-style dishes, they use them with the same liberty and flourish. Herbs are also valued for their medicinal qualities, following the ancient Chinese principles of yin and yang. There are, of course, many herbs that grow in the mountains and jungles of Cambodia and Vietnam that are indigenous to those areas and not possible to find elsewhere. Among the available herbs and spices that make up the colourful culinary picture are numerous varieties of mint, dill, coriander, basil, thyme, oregano, chives, lemon grass, ginger, the liquorice-flavoured star anise, turmeric, fresh and dried chillies, galangal, garlic, and Chinese five-spice powder.

Other flavouring ingredients that shape Vietnamese and Cambodian cuisine include tamarind, lotus seeds, tiger lilies, sugar cane, pandanus leaves, dried lily buds, and limes. Peanuts, roasted and crushed, are frequently scattered over dishes for texture and garnish. Spring onions (scallions), which appear in many dishes, are often cut into strips and added raw to soups, spring rolls and stir-fries at the last minute.

BASIL

Seductively aromatic, basil (*rau que*) is used liberally in Vietnamese cuisine, often punctuating it with a unique note. The most common type of basil is the Asian variety with its pointed green leaves and purplish stems. It is sweet and delicately scented with anise. In Vietnam, basil is always used raw, whether it is sprinkled on top of noodle soups or tossed in salads; in Cambodia, basil leaves are added to stir-fries and soups and, sometimes, they are deep-fried for garnishing. The more pungent holy basil, small-leafed lemon basil, liquorice-flavoured basil and other sweet varieties are also grown and used in combination with mint and coriander (cilantro). Asian basil is found in Asian markets, but the sweet Mediterranean basil found in all supermarkets can be used as a substitute.

CORIANDER/CILANTRO

Originally from Central Asia, *rau rau* or coriander found its way into Vietnam and Cambodia through the mountainous regions in the north. A member of the carrot family, coriander plants can grow 60cm/2ft high, or more, with clusters of serrated leaves and white flowers. There is a similar plant, called Vietnamese coriander, *rau ram*, which is indigenous to Vietnam and is often used in the region,

Left: Coriander leaves are used to flavour many savoury dishes and as a popular garnish.

Above: Holy basil is quite pungent with an almost spicy taste.

but it is interchangeable with regular coriander in recipes.

Coriander leaves, seeds and flowers can all be used but, in the cooking of Vietnam and Cambodia, it is mainly the fresh, citrus-flavoured leaves that are required. Freshly chopped, the leaves are tossed in salads and stir-fries and used as a garnish for many soups and noodle dishes. Bunches of fresh leaves are available in Asian stores and supermarkets. They wilt quickly, so treat them like flowers by keeping the stems immersed in water.

MINT

The most commonly used mint (*bac ha*) in Vietnam and Cambodia is similar to the garden mint of the West. It is furry-leafed with a sweet flavour. It is used in salads and as a garnish, often in combination with basil and coriander. There are numerous varieties of mint, including spearmint and peppermint, differing widely in size, shape and flavour. In Cambodia fish-cheek mint, *chi trey*, is the most popular herb to accompany fish; in Vietnam a similar, almost sorrel-like mint with a strong flavour is served as an accompaniment to grilled (broiled) meat and fish. The standard mint leaves sold in supermarkets work well as a substitute.

CHILLIES

The Vietnamese and Cambodians make liberal use of chillies, whether cooked in stir-fries or sliced finely and added raw to the herbs piled on top of soups and noodles. But their fiery pleasure doesn't stop there, as bowls of raw chillies are often passed round for a crunchy bite between mouthfuls. They are also one of the main ingredients in many of the dipping sauces, including the Vietnamese favourite, *nuoc cham*.

The longer a chilli is cooked, the hotter the flavour throughout the dish, and leaving the seeds and membranes in makes it even hotter. Vietnamese and Cambodian cooking methods are such that the chillies are rarely in the pan for long, thus preventing them from distributing the powerful heat they are capable of. Still, some cooks in the southern regions take such a free hand with chillies that many Westerners feel they are exhaling fire like dragons!

Preparing dried chillies

1 Remove the stems and seeds with a knife. Cut into pieces and place in a bowl.

2 Pour over hot water and leave to soak for about 30 minutes. Drain and use according to the recipe.

Right: Red and green Thai bird's eye chillies.

Thai bird chillies

Throughout South-east Asia, the chillies most frequently used are the small red and green Thai varieties (*ot hiem*). Brightly coloured and slender, they are also called finger chillies because of their shape. They are very hot and full of flavour, and you may wish to seed them before use as the seeds are overpoweringly hot. Often, they are simply smashed and added to dipping sauces and stir-fries. Thai bird chillies are available fresh and dried in Asian stores and most supermarkets.

Long chillies

The elongated, red and green chillies are much longer and milder than the Thai bird variety. Resembling cayenne or serrano chillies, they are usually sliced and added to stir-fries, soups and salads. In Vietnam, they are cut into "chilli flowers" for dipping into salt, or for garnishing dishes. Fresh long chillies are available in Asian stores and most supermarkets.

Dried chillies

Numerous types of red chilli are hung up to dry to preserve them as well as to enhance their flavour. Dry-roasting in a heavy frying pan increases the flavour even more. Dried chillies are also used to make chilli oil, by infusing them in palm or grapeseed oil. Dried chillies can be bought whole, or chopped, in Asian stores and some supermarkets. If kept in a dry, cool place, dried chillies have a long shelf life.

Preparing chillies

The seeds and skin of chillies contain capsaicin, which will irritate and burn your eyes and other sensitive parts of your body. Wash your hands after preparing them or wear gloves. Cut off the stalks and halve the chilli lengthways. Scrape out the pith and seeds and chop, or slice, the flesh as required. To seed a chilli without splitting it, slice off the stalk and roll the chilli between your finger and thumb, releasing the seeds with a little pressure. Hold the chilli upside-down, so that the seeds drop out of the opening – but remember it's the pith that is the hottest, and this won't be removed.

Butterflied chillies with lime

This is not suitable for faint-hearted Westeners! In fact it's only popular with masochists who like fire on their tongues and pain in their bellies! Take a handful of green or red chillies, cut them in half lengthways and remove the seeds, then pile them on to a plate. Put some salt at the edge and segments of lime on the plate, too. To eat, take a lime segment and squeeze it over your selected chilli, dip it into the salt and pop it into your mouth. Your Vietnamese and Cambodian dining companions may do this, with neither a tear in their eyes nor sweat on their brows.

Left: Dried chillies.

Above: Butterflied red chillies with salt and lime are extremely hot and should be eaten with caution.

CHILLI PRODUCTS

Fresh and dried chillies are pounded or ground to make a variety of products. Usually intensely hot, these products are served as condiments with practically every dish.

Chilli powder

This deep-red powder is made by finely grinding dried red chillies. Any chilli can be used but the hottest powder is made from the dried Thai bird chillies.

Chilli paste

This is made by grinding seeded red chillies with garlic, salt and soya oil to form a coarse paste (*tuong ot toi*). Versatile and popular, it is used to season sauces and added as a condiment to salads, wrapped dishes and bread. Ready-made chilli paste is sold in jars in Asian markets.

Chilli sauce

This is a smooth, potent sauce (*tuong ot*), made by grinding seeded red chillies with garlic, salt, vinegar and sugar to form a liquid purée. Used as a dipping sauce on its own, or splashed into soups and noodle recipes, it adds fire to any dish. Stored in bottles, it is available ready-made in Asian markets.

Chilli oil

Used for drizzling over soups and noodle dishes, chilli oil can be made by infusing whole dried chillies, or chilli flakes, in grapeseed or palm oil. Heat the oil and infuse the chillies for a few minutes, then strain and store in a glass jar or bottle. Chilli oil is available in Asian markets.

GARLIC

South-east Asian cooks have been using garlic (*toi*) since ancient times. A bulbous perennial of the onion family, it is easy to grow in most conditions. One bulb can contain up to 20 cloves, which should be firm with a pungent aroma and flavour. Chopped or crushed, garlic is added to stir-fries, curries, stews and noodles. It is also used in its raw form to flavour pickles, marinades, sauces and dips. Renowned for its beneficial qualities, garlic is regarded as a great

Above: Cloves of fresh and dried garlic vary in pungency.

cleanser of the blood and gut. It is used to improve blood flow, as well as to remove poisons from the stomach and kidneys. Beyond its culinary use, garlic is believed to ward off evil and demons. Available in Asian stores and all supermarkets, garlic should be stored in a cool, dry place.

Above: Beneficial in cooking as well as in the spirit world, garlic is used liberally in Vietnamese dishes.

GALANGAL

A member of the ginger family, and similar in appearance, galangal (*gio*) is aromatic and pungent. The young rhizomes are creamy white in colour with a lemony flavour; the more mature ones are golden and peppery. It is slightly harder than ginger, but used in much the same way as both fresh and dried ginger, in pastes and marinades as well as in soups and curries. Fresh galangal will keep for about one week if sealed in a plastic bag and kept in the refrigerator. It can also be frozen. Both dried and bottled galangal are available from Asian stores.

Left: Galangal comes in both dried and fresh forms.

GINGER

Indigenous to the Asian jungles, ginger (*gung*) is one of the most important spices in Vietnamese and Cambodian cooking. Knobbly-looking with a smooth, beige skin, it is the rhizome (normally called a root) of a plant that flourishes in sandy soil. It is dug up when young and tender, before it becomes too fibrous. Ginger is an excellent stimulant for the digestion and is believed to be beneficial for the heart, lungs, stomach, spleen and kidneys. Dried ginger also has medicinal properties. Infused in boiling water and drunk, it is used to treat urinary problems.

Fresh ginger root has a pale, yellow flesh that is slightly juicy with a sweet, pungent flavour. Chopped or shredded, it is used liberally in stir-fries, stews, rice, pickles, steamed dishes and puddings. Fresh ginger is readily available in Asian stores and markets. Choose smooth, plump roots and store in a cool, dry place. Fresh ginger can also be frozen and grated ginger keeps well in the refrigerator. Dried ginger is also ground to a powder for use in curry spice mixes and other recipes.

Below: Fresh root ginger, ground ginger and ginger paste.

TURMERIC

Ground turmeric (*bot nghe*) is used extensively in the cooking of Cambodia and southern Vietnam. Fresh turmeric is a knobbly root with fingers, similar in appearance to ginger, but dark brown in colour with a bright orange flesh. The fresh root has a subtle, earthy taste and imparts a vivid yellowy-orange colour to dishes. It is also dried and ground to a deep-yellow powder which imparts both flavour and colour to dishes, marinades, spice mixes, and batters. Both fresh and dried turmeric are available in Asian markets.

LEMON GRASS

A woody, fibrous stalk, lemon grass (*xa*) imparts a sweet, floral, lemony flavour to dishes. It is pale yellowish-green in colour, encased in a paper-like sheath. Once the outer layers have been removed, the lower part of the stalk and the bulb are chopped, pounded or crushed before being added to soups, stir-fries, curries and marinades. Lemon grass is one of the principal ingredients in the Cambodian herbal paste, *kroeung*, which is used for flavouring soups and for rubbing on skewered meat that is to be grilled over hot charcoal. Lemon grass stalks are available fresh and dried in Asian stores and some supermarkets. Fresh lemon should not be used as a substitute.

Above: Ground and fresh turmeric.

Left: Fresh lemon grass stalks.

PANDANUS LEAF

Generally, puddings in Vietnam and Cambodia are sweet and aromatic. Among the flavours used, ginger, coconut, star anise, and pandanus leaf (*la dua*) are the most common. In the markets, coconuts are often sold with pandanus leaves as the two flavours go well together. The long, narrow leaves are tied together and bruised to release their unique flavour before being added to dishes. Fruity-vanilla in taste, the leaves are available fresh or dried in some Asian markets. If you can't find them, you could use vanilla pods (beans) instead.

Above: Pandanus leaves are used in both sweet and savoury dishes.

Left: Star-shaped star anise is used in stocks and medicinal teas.

STAR ANISE

This is the dried, star-shaped fruit of a slender evergreen tree that grows in China and the northern regions of Vietnam and Cambodia. The fruits are reddish-brown with a seed in each of the eight prongs of the star. Not related to aniseed, star anise (*cay hoi*) lends a strong liquorice flavour to soups and stews. Whole, or crushed, star anise is added to stocks to give them a flavour unique to Vietnam and Cambodia. It is also one of the principal spices in Chinese five-spice powder. Star anise is available in Asian stores.

SUGAR CANE

Like bamboo, sugar cane (*mia*) is a giant grass. The stems, which are filled with a sweet, sappy pulp, are often chewed until all the lovely juice has been sucked out and the remaining fibres

Right, from top: Tamarind paste, tamarind pods and dried tamarind slices, used in many savoury dishes to add the much sought-after sour notes.

are then spat on the ground. Chunks of fresh sugar cane skewered on bamboo sticks are a common sight in the markets of Vietnam and Cambodia. Sugar cane is also used as a skewer itself, most famously in the Vietnamese speciality of shrimp paste bound around short lengths of it and grilled. Sugar cane is also pressed to extract the juice, which is used as a sweetener in a variety of savoury and sweet dishes. Fresh sugar cane is available in Asian, African and Caribbean markets.

TAMARIND

The fruit of the tamarind tree (*trai me*) is shaped like a bean pod. Brown in colour, the pod is dry and contains seeds surrounded by a dark, sweet-and-sour pulp. The pulp can easily be extracted and the seeds and pod discarded. The pulp is added to curries and stews for its unique flavour. Cambodian dishes are well known for their sour notes of lime juice and tamarind. You can buy the fresh pods, or packaged fresh and dried pulp, from Asian stores. Easier to find are the tubs of tamarind concentrate, which is added sparingly to dishes, or diluted in water to give the sour fruitiness.

CHINESE FIVE-SPICE POWDER

Based on a mixture of five spices which represent the five basic flavours at the root of Chinese cooking – sweet, sour, bitter, hot and salty – the powder is traditionally made up of star anise, cloves, fennel seeds, cinnamon and Sichuan peppercorns. Adopted from the Chinese, the Vietnamese and Cambodians often adapt

Above: Dried tiger lily buds are prepared by soaking in water for 30 minutes.

this mixture by adding spices such as liquorice root, ginger and cardamom for use in steamed and braised dishes. Designed to be pungent, five-spice powder is used sparingly in northern Vietnam, but more liberally in the southern region and in Cambodia.

TIGER LILY BUDS

Native to Asia, tiger lilies (*kim cham*) grow in almost any type of soil and conditions. Curiously, they produce masses of buds but only flower for one day. Adopted from the Chinese, the Vietnamese have acquired a taste for these buds, which are picked unopened and dried before use. Also known as yellow flower or golden needles, as they are light golden in colour, they are regarded as both a vegetable and a herb. Ranging from 5–10cm/2–4in long, they are crunchy in texture, floral-scented and earthy in flavour with mushroom overtones, and the earthiness intensifies when the buds are dried.

Tiger lily buds are particularly prized for their colour and texture in vegetarian dishes. They are also used in soups and braised dishes of Chinese origin, where they complement ingredients such as bamboo shoots and mushrooms, and they are presented as a delicate garnish for clear broths. Bags of dried, tangled buds are sold in Asian markets. They will keep almost indefinitely if stored in an airtight container, away from strong light, heat or moisture.

STORE-CUPBOARD INGREDIENTS

Flavoured oils, sauces, sugar, salt, agar agar and peanuts are often found in the Vietnamese and Cambodian kitchen.

SESAME OIL

Extracted from sesame seeds, this oil is commonly used in stir-fried dishes. Two types are available: the plain, pale golden oil, which is mildly nutty and is good for frying; and the darker, richer tasting oil made from roasted sesame seeds, which is usually added in small quantities for flavour just before serving.

ANCHOVY SAUCE

Chinese in origin, this pungent, salty sauce is often used in combination with a sweet, fruity ingredient, such as ripe pineapple. Bottles of this thick, light-grey sauce can be found in Asian stores and markets.

OYSTER SAUCE

This thick, brown sauce is made from dried oyster extract, sugar, water and salt. Strongly flavoured and salty, it is used in moderation as a seasoning agent in Chinese-style dishes. It is available in Asian stores.

HOISIN SAUCE

This is a thick, sweet bean sauce of Chinese origin. Primarily made from fermented soya beans, vinegar, sugar and five-spice powder, it is rich in flavour and ideal for marinades and dipping sauces.

Above: Sesame oil (top) and chilli oil are often added to dishes before serving.

It is also used to season noodle soups. Bottles of hoisin sauce are available in most supermarkets.

SOY SAUCE

Probably the most commonly used sauce in South-east Asia is soy sauce, in its various guises. However, in Vietnam and Cambodia, the emphasis is on their own national fish sauces, *nuoc mam* and *tuk trey*; soy sauce is reserved mainly for the vegetarian dishes of the Buddhist communities. Made from fermented soya beans, wheat and yeast, soy sauce is used in Vietnam and Cambodia for seasoning dipping sauces. Naturally fermented soy sauce will not keep forever; it starts to lose its flavour as soon as the bottle is opened. Try to use it up fairly quickly.

Left: Toasted sesame oil imparts a rich flavour to many dishes.

FERMENTED SOYA BEANS

Sometimes called salted beans, this is a salty condiment (*tuong hot*) made from whole beans. Chinese in origin, it is used mainly in Chinese-style dishes as a seasoning ingredient.

BEAN SAUCE

A condiment made from soya beans that have been fermented and puréed. The sauce (*tuong*) is often served on its own, or mixed with other ingredients to form a dip. The Vietnamese salad rolls, *goi cuon*, are traditionally served with a sauce made by mixing *tuong* with sticky

Left: Oyster sauce.

Right: Dark hoisin sauce is ideal for marinades and splashing into soups.

Above: Black bean sauce is made from fermented salted black beans mixed with soy sauce, sugar and spices.

rice, coconut milk, chillies and sugar. In Cambodia a chilli bean sauce is made by combining the fermented bean sauce with garlic and chillies.

PALM SUGAR

Widely used in South-east Asia, palm sugar is extracted from the sap of various palm trees. The sap is collected from incisions made in the trunks of the trees. Palm sugar is golden to toffee-brown in colour with a distinctive flavour. It is usually sold in blocks, often

Below: Palm sugar, also known as jaggery, is sold in blocks, which store well in a cool, dry place.

referred to as jaggery in Asian stores. The sugar palm tree is the symbol of Cambodia, where the sap is used in the production of medicine, wine and vinegar, among other products.

SALT

The sea is the main source of the salt used in South-east Asia. In the cooking of Vietnam and Cambodia, salty flavoured soy sauce and national fish sauces often replace it as a seasoning, but salt is combined in equal amounts with pepper to season deep-fried prawns (shrimp) and squid. It is also commonly used as a last-minute seasoning in the form of a dip. Mixed with Chinese five-spice powder, or chilli powder, a salt dip is often placed on the table to enhance the flavour of roasted or grilled meat and poultry or to sprinkle over a meat stew.

AGAR AGAR

Similar to gelatine, agar agar is a gum that is extracted from dried seaweed and processed into translucent white sticks, or ground to a powder. Once dissolved in boiling water, it turns to jelly and is widely used in the jellied puddings of South-east Asia. Agar agar is available in stick or powder form in Asian stores.

PEANUTS

Important in both Vietnamese and Cambodian cuisine, peanuts are used for richness and texture in a variety of dishes. Boiled and roasted, they are often nibbled as a snack but, primarily, roasted peanuts are used as a garnish, chopped or crushed and scattered over the top of salads, noodles and rice dishes.

Above, clockwise from bottom right: Agar agar is sold in thick and thin strips and as a powder that is used is as a setting agent.

Below: Peanuts may be added whole to salads and noodle dishes, but they are usually roasted and crushed, for use as a garnish.

BEVERAGES

Tea and coffee are the main beverages of Vietnam and Cambodia, along with the juice of the season's fruit. Alcohol is not consumed in vast quantities but is enjoyed on ceremonial occasions.

TEA

As in many parts of Asia, tea in Vietnam plays a significant role in business as well as in the general social life. Whether offered in a home or place of work, in the bank or in the market, it is a gesture of hospitality and it is polite to accept. Everybody drinks tea and the sharing of it is almost ritualistic. It is usually drunk black and, in some homes, its preparation can turn into quite a performance. Weddings, funerals and other celebratory events are also occasions at which to drink tea.

The Thai Binh Province has its own celebration of tea, where enthusiasts set off in boats on ponds and lakes at moonlight when the lotus flowers are in bloom. Each flower is prized open to place a pinch of tea inside, before tying them closed with a piece of string. By dawn the fragrance of the lotus blossom will have permeated the tea, so the dew and tea is gathered to add to teapots.

Below: A woman picking tea from bushes in the Khanh Hoa province.

In Cambodia, the Khmer and Chinese communities enjoy drinking tea too, but without the ritual.

COFFEE

The making of coffee is less ritualistic but no less surprising. First introduced by the French, the Vietnamese have adapted the popular *café au lait* into a unique drink. When you sit down in a café, a glass tumbler with an aluminium pot placed on top will be put before you. Sitting at the bottom of the tumbler is 1cm/½in of sweetened condensed milk, on to which splash little drips of coffee as the water filters through the ground coffee in the aluminium pot. When all the dripping stops there will be a 1cm/½in layer of very strong coffee on top of the sweet condensed milk. As the aroma of fresh coffee rises from the glass, put it to your lips and let the sugary milk mingle with the hot liquid.

This is called *ca phe* or *café vietnamien*. Also influenced by the French, coffee is drunk in Cambodia, where it is generally served black, or as *café au lait*, simply by adding dollops of sweet condensed milk.

SMOOTHIES AND JUICES

Perhaps the most popular drinks of all are smoothies. Smoothie stalls are

Above: Vietnamese coffee made with condensed milk is a unique and utterly delicious drink that should be lingered over in a café.

dotted all over Vietnam and Cambodia, popular with children, who gather to play and quench their thirst with a cool, refreshing drink. Open day and night, smoothie stalls can produce some

Below: The traditional Hue method of making tea involves one large pouring cup and three smaller ones.

Above: Coconut juice is widely enjoyed.

exotic concoctions, such as pineapple, watermelon, coconut and lychee, or strawberry, banana, custard apple and mango, sweetened to your taste with sugar and thickened with a raw egg, if you like. Fresh sugar cane juice, made from the pressed cane, is popular. The juice of unripened coconuts is often drunk straight from the fruit.

BEER AND WINE

There are a number of local beers produced in Vietnam and Cambodia, including the popular Vietnamese "33". Often light golden in colour and taste, similar to European Pilsener lager, beer is refreshing in the tropical heat. The Vietnamese and the Khmer are not great drinkers of alcohol, and foreigners are the main consumers of beer, but it is becoming more popular with the locals.

Since the influence of the French a variety of wines have been produced from locally grown grapes in Vietnam. However, the quality and availability of these wines vary drastically. Rice wine is available in both countries and is more dependable. Made by fermenting rice with sugar, rice wine is more commonly drunk in rural areas. In the more cosmopolitan cities, businessmen can sometimes be seen enjoying rice wine with their lunch, otherwise it is mainly used in religious ceremonies and as an offering of hospitality.

Left: Fresh mango juice.

Above: Sweet soya milk is a very popular drink in Vietnam. High in protein, it is sold hot and cold by street vendors and in cafés and bars. It is often infused with pandanus leaves, ginger or a vanilla pod (bean).

Above: Rice wine, made from fermented rice grains, is quite light with a slightly bitter taste.

EQUIPMENT

The traditional Vietnamese and Cambodian kitchen is basic. Often dark and sparsely kitted out with an open hearth, very little equipment is needed. Food is generally bought daily from the markets, taken home and cooked immediately so, unless you visit the kitchen during the frenzied moments of passionate activity over the hearth, there is little evidence of food or cooking. Without refrigerators, this reliance on fresh produce from the daily markets is vital. For some, two visits to the market are required – in the morning for the ingredients to cook for lunch, and, in the afternoon for the evening meal. Back in the simple kitchen, the activity begins with the scrubbing of vegetables, the plucking and jointing of birds (if it hasn't been done in the markets), the endless chopping and slicing, and the pounding of herbs and spices with a pestle and mortar.

WOK

The wok is the most important utensil for everyday cooking in both Vietnam and Cambodia. Everybody has one. Without a doubt, there is always something delicious being stir-fried in a home or in the streets. However, woks are not only used for stir-frying, they are also used for steaming, deep-frying, braising and soup-making. The most functional, multi-purpose wok should measure approximately 35cm/14in across, large enough for a family meal or to steam a whole fish. The most common wok is double-handled and made of lightweight carbonized steel. This is ideal for deep-frying and steaming but, for stir-frying, you need the single-handled version.

When you first buy a wok, you need to season it before use. Put it over a high heat to blacken the inside – this burns off any dust and factory coating. Leave the wok to cool, then immerse it in hot, soapy water and clean it with an abrasive cloth or stiff brush. Rinse it well and dry over a medium heat. Pour a little cooking oil into the base and, using a piece of kitchen paper, wipe it all around the surface of the wok. Now the wok is ready for use.

After each use, clean the wok with hot water only, dry it over a medium heat, and wipe a thin layer of oil over the surface. This will ensure that it doesn't get rusty. Over time, the wok

Above: A solid mortar and pestle is an essential piece of kitchen equipment.

will acquire a seasoned look – dark and glossy – and should last a lifetime. Woks are sold in all Chinese and Asian markets.

MORTAR AND PESTLE

A big mortar and pestle, made of stone, is of particular value, as it is used not only for grinding spices, chillies and garlic, but also for pounding all the condiments and pastes, as well as the meat for pâtés and savoury balls. Some cooks have several mortar and pestle sets, varying in size according to the activity and ingredient. Coffee grinders and electric blenders can be used as substitutes, but they don't release the oils and flavours of the ingredients in the same way and they produce too smooth a texture. It is worth looking for a solid stone mortar and pestle in Asian markets and kitchen suppliers.

BAMBOO STEAMER

Traditional bamboo steamers come in various sizes. The most practical one is about 30cm/12in wide, as it can be used for rice or a whole fish. Generally, the steamer is set directly over a wok that is filled with boiling water to below the level of the steamer. The food is placed in the steamer, either on a plate, or wrapped in muslin (cheesecloth), or banana leaves. The lid is placed on the steamer and, as the water in the wok is heated, the steam rises under and around the food, cooking it gently. A stainless steel steamer is no substitute

Left: A single-handed wok is good for stir-frying on the hob.

for a bamboo one, which imparts its own delicate fragrance to the dish. Bamboo steamers are available in most Asian stores and some cooking equipment suppliers.

CHOPSTICKS

In Vietnam, chopsticks are used to eat with, as well as for cooking; forks and spoons are more common in Cambodia. Following Chinese methods many Vietnamese cooks will use a set of long chopsticks for stirring, mixing, tasting, and as tongs. Eating chopsticks are traditionally made from bamboo or wood, but more elaborate ones can be made from ivory, bone, gold, silver or jade. For cooking, look for long chopsticks made from bamboo.

CLAY POT

Made from a combination of light-coloured clay and sand, these pots come in all sizes,

Right: Bamboo steamers come in several sizes.

with single or double handles, lids, and glazed interiors. Perhaps the oldest form of cooking vessel, these attractive pots are ideal for slow-cooking, such as braised dishes and soups, as they retain an overall even heat. Generally, they are used on the stove over a low or medium heat, as a high temperature could cause them to crack. When you first buy a clay pot, it needs to be treated for cooking. Fill it with water and place it over a low flame. Gradually increase the heat and let the water boil until it is reduced by half. Rinse the pot and dry thoroughly. Now it is ready for use. Traditional clay pots are available in some Asian markets.

Above: A clay pot can be used in the oven or, with care, on the stove.

Left: Bamboo chopsticks are essential kitchen equipment.

Right: A medium-weight cleaver is a multi-purpose tool.

CLEAVERS

Asian cleavers are the most important tools in the kitchen. There are special blades for the fine chopping of lemon grass and green papaya, heavy blades for opening coconuts, thin ones for shredding spring onions (scallions), and multi-purpose ones for any type of chopping, slicing and crushing. Generally, you use the front, lighter part of the blade for the regular chopping, slicing and shredding; the back, heavier section is for chopping with force through bones; and the flat side is ideal for crushing ginger and garlic, and for transporting the ingredients into the wok.

DRAINING SPOON

Traditional draining spoons are made of wire with a long bamboo handle; more modern ones are made of perforated stainless steel. Both are flat and extremely useful for deep-frying, for blanching noodles and for scooping ingredients out of hot liquid.

Right: Draining spoons are useful for deep-frying and blanching.

COOKING TECHNIQUES

The traditional cooking methods of Vietnam and Cambodia require few culinary tools but a great deal of attention to detail. Fresh ingredients are of the utmost importance, followed by the balance of sharp or mild, salty or sweet, bitter or sour, or a combination of all of these flavours. The layering of ingredients is also important, especially in Vietnamese noodle dishes, where flavours and textures should complement each other but remain separate. Almost every meal is prepared from scratch, starting with the plucking of chickens and grinding of spices, followed by the grilling over charcoal, gentle simmering and steaming, or stir-frying. Armed with the correct equipment, the cooking is fairly easy – most of the work is in the preparation.

Grinding and pounding

Spices, herbs and other ingredients are usually ground and pounded in a large, heavy mortar made of stone. The interior of the mortar should be rough to grip the ingredients and act as an abrasive. The pestle needs to be heavy too, made of the same stone, to provide the right weight for pounding and grinding.

Grinding is most efficient if the herbs, spices and other ingredients are added in the correct order. First the hard seeds or nuts are ground together, then the fresh herbs, ginger and garlic, followed by the oils or pastes. The mixture is then bound and seasoned and ready for use.

DRY-FRYING

Dried spices are often roasted before grinding to release their natural oils and enhance the aroma. This is done by spreading the spices thinly in a heavy frying pan and putting it over a high heat. As the pan begins to heat, shake it so that the spices don't get too brown. Once the spices begin to colour and their aroma fills the air, put them in a mortar and grind to a powder.

BRAISING

The classic method for slow-cooked dishes is braising. Generally, oily fish, duck and red meat are cooked this way, often with pungent herbs, spices and coconut milk or juice. Traditionally, to seal in the moisture, a covered clay pot is used as the cooking vessel. Placed over a medium heat, or in the oven, the cooking process can take anything from 30 minutes to 2 hours, depending on the dish. If you don't have a clay pot, use a heavy-based casserole. The key is in containing the moisture and even heat distribution, so don't use a thin aluminium pot.

1 Put all the ingredients in a clay pot and place in a preheated oven. (It can also be placed over a medium heat on the stove if you prefer.)

GRILLING OVER CHARCOAL

As conventional grills (broilers) don't exist in most homes in Vietnam and Cambodia, grilling is generally done over hot charcoal. This traditional method of cooking not only lends itself to many types of food, it also enhances the taste. Whole fish, pigs or chickens can be cooked this way. Tasty, marinated morsels of food, skewered on bamboo sticks and grilled in the streets, make popular snacks. When cooking over charcoal, light the coals and wait until they have turned red with grey or white ashes. If the charcoal is too hot, the food will just burn.

Wooden and bamboo skewers

If you are using wooden or bamboo skewers, soak them in water for about 30 minutes before using to prevent them from burning.

STEAMING

This is a popular way of preparing delicate-tasting foods, such as fish and shellfish, the French-inspired pork pâtés, and sticky rice cakes wrapped in banana or bamboo leaves. Place the food in a bamboo steamer, which should be lined with leaves if the food isn't wrapped in them. Put the lid on the steamer and set it over a wok that is half-filled with water. Bring the water to the boil, then reduce the heat and steam the food according to the recipe.

STIR-FRYING

Of all the cooking techniques, this is the most important one in Vietnam and Cambodia. The technique is more in the preparation of ingredients than in the cooking process, which only takes minutes. Generally, the ingredients should be cut or shredded into bitesize morsels and laid out in the order in which they are to be cooked. To stir-fry successfully you need a wok, placed over a high heat, and a ladle or spatula to toss the ingredients around, so that they cook but still retain their freshness and crunchy texture.

1 Pour a little oil into the wok and place it over a high heat until hot.

2 Add the spices and aromatics to the oil – it should sizzle on contact – and toss them around to flavour the oil.

3 Add the pieces of meat or fish, and toss them around the wok for a minute or two.

4 Add the sliced or shredded root vegetables or mushrooms and stir-fry for a minute.

5 Add the leafy vegetables or bean-sprouts and toss them around quickly.

6 Finally, toss in the herbs and seasonings and serve immediately. The key is to work quickly and layer the ingredients according to the length of time they require for cooking. Serve hot straight from the wok into warmed bowls and don't leave the food sitting in the wok.

DEEP-FRYING

Use an oil that can be heated to a high temperature, such as groundnut (peanut) oil, and don't put in too much cold food at once, as this will cool the oil down.

1 Pour the oil into a pan or wok (filling it no more than two-thirds full) and heat to about 180°C/350°F. To test the temperature, add a drop of batter or a piece of onion. If it sinks, the oil is not hot enough; if it burns, it is too hot. If it sizzles and rises to the surface, the temperature is perfect.

2 Cook the food in small batches until crisp and lift out with a slotted spoon or wire mesh skimmer when cooked. Drain on a wire rack lined with kitchen paper and serve immediately, or keep warm in the oven until ready to serve.

BLANCHING

This method is often used to cook delicate meat such as chicken breast portions or duck.

1 Place the meat and any flavourings in a pan and add just enough water to cover. Bring to the boil, then remove from the heat and leave to stand, covered, for 10 minutes, then drain.

RECIPES

SOUPS AND BROTHS

In Vietnam and Cambodia, soups and broths are served for breakfast and as snacks throughout the day, as an appetizer to a meal, as accompaniments to steamed rice, and as palate cleansers between courses. At home you may want to serve one of the more substantial soups, such as Hot-and-Sour Fish Soup or Duck and Nut Soup with Jujubes, as a meal in itself, with chunks of fresh bread. Light broths, such as Pork and Lotus Root Broth, make refreshing first courses.

TOFU SOUP WITH MUSHROOMS, TOMATO, GINGER AND CORIANDER

THIS IS A TYPICAL CANH — A CLEAR BROTH FROM THE NORTH OF VIETNAM. IT SHOULD BE LIGHT, TO BALANCE A MEAL THAT MAY INCLUDE SOME HEAVIER MEAT OR POULTRY DISHES. AS THE SOUP IS RELIANT ON A WELL-FLAVOURED, AROMATIC BROTH, THE BASIC STOCK NEEDS TO BE RICH IN TASTE.

SERVES FOUR

INGREDIENTS

    115g/4oz/scant 2 cups dried shiitake
      mushrooms, soaked in water for
      20 minutes
    15ml/1 tbsp vegetable oil
    2 shallots, halved and sliced
    2 Thai chillies, seeded and sliced
    4cm/1½in fresh root ginger, peeled
      and grated or finely chopped
    15ml/1 tbsp *nuoc mam*
    350g/12oz tofu, rinsed, drained
      and cut into bitesize cubes
    4 tomatoes, skinned, seeded and
      cut into thin strips
    salt and ground black pepper
    1 bunch coriander (cilantro),
      stalks removed, finely chopped,
      to garnish
For the stock
    1 meaty chicken carcass or
      500g/1¼lb pork ribs
    25g/1oz dried squid or shrimp,
      soaked in water for 15 minutes
    2 onions, peeled and quartered
    2 garlic cloves, crushed
    7.5cm/3in fresh root ginger, chopped
    15ml/1 tbsp *nuoc mam*
    6 black peppercorns
    2 star anise
    4 cloves
    1 cinnamon stick
    sea salt

1 To make the stock, put the chicken carcass or pork ribs in a deep pan. Drain and rinse the dried squid or shrimp. Add to the pan with the remaining stock ingredients, except the salt, and pour in 2 litres/3½ pints/8 cups water. Bring to the boil, and boil for a few minutes, skim off any foam, then reduce the heat and simmer with the lid on for 1½–2 hours. Remove the lid and continue simmering for a further 30 minutes to reduce. Skim off any fat, season, then strain and measure out 1.5 litres/2½ pints/6¼ cups.

2 Squeeze dry the soaked shiitake mushrooms, remove the stems and slice the caps into thin strips. Heat the oil in a large pan or wok and stir in the shallots, chillies and ginger. As the fragrance begins to rise, stir in the *nuoc mam*, followed by the stock.

3 Add the tofu, mushrooms and tomatoes and bring to the boil. Reduce the heat and simmer for 5–10 minutes. Season to taste and scatter the finely chopped fresh coriander over the top. Serve piping hot.

Per portion Energy 220Kcal/919kJ; Protein 12g; Carbohydrate 26g, of which sugars 4g; Fat 8g, of which saturates 1g; Cholesterol 0mg; Calcium 47.8mg; Fibre 1.1g; Sodium 500mg

WINTER MELON SOUP WITH TIGER LILIES, CORIANDER AND MINT

THIS SOUP USES TWO TRADITIONAL SOUTH-EAST ASIAN INGREDIENTS — WINTER MELON TO ABSORB THE FLAVOURS AND TIGER LILIES TO LIFT THE BROTH WITH A FLORAL SCENT. WHEN CHOOSING TIGER LILIES, MAKE SURE THEY ARE LIGHT GOLDEN IN COLOUR.

SERVES FOUR

INGREDIENTS
- 350g/12oz winter melon
- 25g/1oz light golden tiger lilies, soaked in hot water for 20 minutes
- salt and ground black pepper
- 1 small bunch each coriander (cilantro) and mint, stalks removed, leaves chopped, to serve

For the stock
- 25g/1oz dried shrimp, soaked in water for 15 minutes
- 500g/1¼lb pork ribs
- 1 onion, peeled and quartered
- 175g/6oz carrots, peeled and cut into chunks
- 15ml/1 tbsp *nuoc mam*
- 15ml/1 tbsp soy sauce
- 4 black peppercorns

1 To make the stock, drain and rinse the dried shrimp. Put the pork ribs in a large pan and cover with 2 litres/3½ pints/8 cups water. Bring the water to the boil, skim off any fat, and add the dried shrimp and the remaining stock ingredients. Cover and simmer for 1½ hours, then skim off any foam or fat. Continue simmering, uncovered, for a further 30 minutes. Strain and check the seasoning. You should have about 1.5 litres/2½ pints/6¼ cups.

2 Halve the winter melon lengthways and remove the seeds and inner membrane. Finely slice the flesh into half-moons. Squeeze the soaked tiger lilies dry and tie them in a knot.

3 Bring the stock to the boil in a deep pan or wok. Reduce the heat and add the winter melon and tiger lilies. Simmer for 15–20 minutes, or until the winter melon is tender. Season to taste, and scatter the herbs over the top.

Per portion Energy 46Kcal/198kJ; Protein 2g; Carbohydrate 9g, of which sugars 4g; Fat 0g, of which saturates 0g; Cholesterol 0mg; Calcium 90mg; Fibre 1.4g; Sodium 400mg

BROTH WITH STUFFED CABBAGE LEAVES

The origins of this soup, called canh bap cuon, could be attributed to the French dish chou farci, or to the ancient Chinese tradition of cooking dumplings in a clear broth. This Vietnamese soup is often reserved for special occasions such as the New Year, Tet.

SERVES FOUR

INGREDIENTS
    10 Chinese leaves (Chinese cabbage)
      or Savoy cabbage leaves, halved,
      main ribs removed
    4 spring onions (scallions),
      green tops left whole, white
      part finely chopped
    5–6 dried cloud ear (wood ear)
      mushrooms, soaked in hot water
      for 15 minutes
    115g/4oz minced (ground) pork
    115g/4oz prawns (shrimp), shelled,
      deveined and finely chopped
    1 Thai chilli, seeded and chopped
    30ml/2 tbsp *nuoc mam*
    15ml/1 tbsp soy sauce
    4cm/1½in fresh root ginger, peeled
      and very finely sliced
    chopped fresh coriander (cilantro),
      to garnish
For the stock
    1 meaty chicken carcass
    2 onions, peeled and quartered
    4 garlic cloves, crushed
    4cm/1½in fresh root ginger,
      chopped
    30ml/2 tbsp *nuoc mam*
    30ml/2 tbsp soy sauce
    6 black peppercorns
    a few sprigs of fresh thyme
    sea salt

1 To make the chicken stock, put the chicken carcass into a deep pan. Add all the other stock ingredients except the sea salt and pour over 2 litres/3½ pints/8 cups of water. Bring to the boil, and boil for a few minutes, skim off any foam, then reduce the heat and simmer gently with the lid on for 1½–2 hours.

2 Remove the lid and simmer for a further 30 minutes to reduce the stock. Skim off any fat, season with sea salt, then strain the stock and measure out 1.5 litres/2½ pints/6¼ cups. It is important to skim off any froth or fat, so that the broth is light and fragrant.

3 Blanch the cabbage leaves in boiling water for about 2 minutes, or until tender. Remove with a slotted spoon and refresh under cold water. Add the green tops of the spring onions to the boiling water and blanch for a minute, or until tender, then drain and refresh under cold water. Carefully tear each piece into five thin strips and set aside.

4 Squeeze dry the cloud ear mushrooms, then trim and finely chop and mix with the pork, prawns, spring onion whites, chilli, *nuoc mam* and soy sauce. Lay a cabbage leaf flat on a surface and place a teaspoon of the filling about 1cm/½in from the bottom edge – the edge nearest to you.

5 Fold this bottom edge over the filling, and then fold in the sides of the leaf to seal it. Roll all the way to the top of the leaf to form a tight bundle. Wrap a piece of blanched spring onion green around the bundle and tie it so that it holds together. Repeat with the remaining leaves and filling.

6 Bring the stock to the boil in a wok or deep pan. Stir in the finely sliced ginger, then reduce the heat and drop in the cabbage bundles. Bubble very gently over a low heat for about 20 minutes to ensure that the filling is thoroughly cooked. Serve immediately, ladled into bowls with a sprinkling of fresh coriander leaves.

Per portion Energy 106Kcal/447kJ; Protein 14g; Carbohydrate 9g, of which sugars 1g; Fat 2g, of which saturates 0g; Cholesterol 77mg; Calcium 43mg; Fibre 0.3g; Sodium 1100mg

SPICY TOMATO AND EGG DROP SOUP

POPULAR IN SOUTHERN VIETNAM AND CAMBODIA, THIS SPICY SOUP WITH EGGS IS PROBABLY ADAPTED FROM THE TRADITIONAL CHINESE EGG DROP SOUP. SERVED ON ITS OWN WITH CHUNKS OF CRUSTY BREAD, OR ACCOMPANIED BY JASMINE OR GINGER RICE, THIS IS A TASTY DISH FOR A LIGHT SUPPER.

SERVES FOUR

INGREDIENTS
 30ml/2 tbsp groundnut (peanut) or
   vegetable oil
 3 shallots, finely sliced
 2 garlic cloves, finely chopped
 2 Thai chillies, seeded and
   finely sliced
 25g/1oz galangal, shredded
 8 large, ripe tomatoes, skinned,
   seeded and finely chopped
 15ml/1 tbsp sugar
 30ml/2 tbsp *nuoc mam* or *tuk trey*
 4 lime leaves
 900ml/1½ pints/3¾ cups
   chicken stock
 15ml/1 tbsp wine vinegar
 4 eggs
 sea salt and ground black pepper
For the garnish
 chilli oil, for drizzling
 1 small bunch fresh coriander
   (cilantro), finely chopped
 1 small bunch fresh mint leaves,
   finely chopped

1 Heat the oil in a wok or heavy pan. Stir in the shallots, garlic, chillies and galangal and cook until golden and fragrant. Add the tomatoes with the sugar, *nuoc mam* and lime leaves. Stir until it resembles a sauce. Pour in the stock and bring to the boil. Reduce the heat and simmer for 30 minutes. Season.

VARIATION
The soup is very tasty without the eggs and could be served as a spicy tomato soup on its own.

2 Just before serving, bring a wide pan of water to the boil. Add the vinegar and half a teaspoon of salt. Break the eggs into individual cups or small bowls.

3 Stir the water rapidly to create a swirl and drop an egg into the centre of the swirl. Follow immediately with the others, or poach two at a time, and keep the water boiling to throw the whites up over the yolks. Turn off the heat, cover the pan and leave to poach until firm enough to lift. Poached eggs are traditional, but you could use lightly fried eggs instead.

4 Using a slotted spoon, lift the eggs out of the water and slip them into the hot soup. Drizzle a little chilli oil over the eggs, sprinkle with the coriander and mint, and serve.

Per portion Energy 181Kcal/756kJ; Protein 8g; Carbohydrate 12.3g, of which sugars 11.5g; Fat 11.7g, of which saturates 2.4g; Cholesterol 190mg; Calcium 52mg; Fibre 2.3g; Sodium 280g

HOT-AND-SOUR FISH SOUP

THIS TANGY SOUP, CANH CHUA CA, IS FOUND THROUGHOUT SOUTH-EAST ASIA — WITH THE BALANCE OF HOT, SWEET AND SOUR FLAVOURS VARYING FROM CAMBODIA TO VIETNAM. CHILLIES PROVIDE THE HEAT, TAMARIND PRODUCES THE TARTNESS AND THE DELICIOUS SWEETNESS COMES FROM PINEAPPLE.

SERVES FOUR

INGREDIENTS

  1 catfish, sea bass or red snapper,
    about 1kg/2¼ lb, filleted
  30ml/2 tbsp *nuoc mam*
  2 garlic cloves, finely chopped
  25g/1oz dried squid, soaked in water
    for 30 minutes
  15ml/1 tbsp vegetable oil
  2 spring onions (scallions), sliced
  2 shallots, sliced
  4cm/1½ in fresh root ginger, peeled
    and chopped
  2–3 lemon grass stalks, cut into
    strips and crushed
  30ml/2 tbsp tamarind paste
  2–3 Thai chillies, seeded and sliced
  15ml/1 tbsp sugar
  30–45ml/2–3 tbsp *nuoc mam*
  225g/8oz fresh pineapple, peeled
    and diced
  3 tomatoes, skinned, seeded and
    roughly chopped
  50g/2oz canned sliced bamboo
    shoots, drained
  1 small bunch fresh coriander
    (cilantro), stalks removed, leaves
    finely chopped
salt and ground black pepper
115g/4oz/½ cup beansprouts and
    1 bunch dill, fronds roughly
    chopped, to garnish
  1 lime, cut into quarters, to serve

1 Cut the fish into bitesize pieces, mix with the *nuoc mam* and garlic and leave to marinate. Save the head, tail and bones for the stock. Drain and rinse the soaked dried squid.

2 Heat the oil in a deep pan and stir in the spring onions, shallots, ginger, lemon grass and dried squid. Add the reserved fish head, tail and bones, and sauté them gently for a minute or two. Pour in 1.2 litres/2 pints/5 cups water and bring to the boil. Reduce the heat and simmer for 30 minutes.

3 Strain the stock into another deep pan and bring to the boil. Stir in the tamarind paste, chillies, sugar and *nuoc mam* and simmer for 2–3 minutes. Add the pineapple, tomatoes and bamboo shoots and simmer for a further 2–3 minutes. Stir in the fish pieces and the chopped fresh coriander, and cook until the fish turns opaque.

4 Season to taste and ladle the soup into hot bowls. Garnish with beansprouts and dill, and serve with the lime quarters to squeeze over.

VARIATIONS
• Depending on your mood, or your palate, you can adjust the balance of hot and sour by adding more chilli or tamarind to taste. Enjoyed as a meal in itself, the soup is usually served with plain steamed rice but in Ho Chi Minh City it is served with chunks of fresh baguette, which are perfect for soaking up the spicy, fruity, tangy broth.
• Other fresh herbs, such as chopped mint and basil leaves, also complement this soup.

Per portion Energy 335Kcal/1415kJ; Protein 44g; Carbohydrate 24g, of which sugars 19g; Fat 7g, of which saturates 1g; Cholesterol 108mg; Calcium 138mg; Fibre 2.3g; Sodium 1.2g

CRAB AND ASPARAGUS SOUP WITH NUOC CHAM

IN THIS DELICIOUS SOUP, THE RECIPE HAS CLEARLY BEEN ADAPTED FROM THE CLASSIC FRENCH ASPARAGUS VELOUTÉ TO PRODUCE A MUCH MEATIER VERSION THAT HAS MORE TEXTURE, AND THE VIETNAMESE STAMP OF NUOC CHAM AND NUOC MAM.

SERVES FOUR

INGREDIENTS
15ml/1 tbsp vegetable oil
2 shallots, finely chopped
2 garlic cloves, finely chopped
15ml/1 tbsp rice flour or
  cornflour (cornstarch)
225g/8oz/1⅓ cups cooked crab meat,
  chopped into small pieces
450g/1lb preserved asparagus,
  finely chopped, or 450g/1lb fresh
  asparagus, trimmed and steamed
salt and ground black pepper
basil and coriander (cilantro) leaves,
  to garnish
nuoc cham, to serve
For the stock
1 meaty chicken carcass
25g/1oz dried shrimp, soaked in
  water for 30 minutes, rinsed
  and drained
2 onions, peeled and quartered
2 garlic cloves, crushed
15ml/1 tbsp *nuoc mam*
6 black peppercorns
sea salt

1 To make the stock, put the chicken carcass into a large pan. Add all the other stock ingredients, except the salt, and pour in 2 litres/3½ pints/8 cups water. Bring to the boil, boil for a few minutes, skim off any foam, then reduce the heat and simmer with the lid on for 1½–2 hours. Remove the lid and simmer for a further 30 minutes to reduce the stock. Skim off any fat, season, then strain the stock and measure out 1.5 litres/2½ pints/6¼ cups.

2 Heat the oil in a deep pan or wok. Stir in the shallots and garlic, until they begin to colour. Remove from the heat, stir in the flour, and then pour in the stock. Put the pan back over the heat and bring to the boil, stirring constantly, until smooth.

COOK'S TIP
In households close to the sea, where large crabs – some as large as 60cm/2ft in diameter – can be found in abundance, this soup may be made using a generous quantity of fresh crab. If you have a good supply of fresh crabs, you can increase the quantity of crab meat as much as you like, to make a soup that is very rich and filling.

3 Add the crab meat and asparagus, reduce the heat and leave to simmer for 15–20 minutes. Season to taste with salt and pepper, then ladle the soup into bowls, garnish with fresh basil and coriander leaves, and serve with a splash of *nuoc cham*.

Per portion Energy 143Kcal/593kJ; Protein 45g; Carbohydrate 4g, of which sugars 2g; Fat 7g, of which saturates 1g; Cholesterol 41mg; Calcium 29mg; Fibre 3.5g; Sodium 800mg

CAMBODIAN BAMBOO, FISH AND RICE SOUP

THIS IS A REFRESHING KHMER SOUP MADE WITH FRESHWATER FISH. A SPECIALITY OF PHNOM PENH,
SAMLAW TRAPEANG IS FLAVOURED WITH COCONUT MILK, THE FERMENTED FISH EXTRACT, TUK
PRAHOC, LEMON GRASS AND GALANGAL — SOME OF CAMBODIA'S PRINCIPAL INGREDIENTS.

SERVES FOUR

INGREDIENTS
 75g/3oz/scant ½ cup long grain rice,
  well rinsed
 250ml/8fl oz/1 cup coconut milk
 30ml/2 tbsp *tuk prahoc*
 2 lemon grass stalks, trimmed
  and crushed
 25g/1oz galangal, thinly sliced
 2–3 Thai chillies
 4 garlic cloves, crushed
 15ml/1 tbsp palm sugar
 1 fresh bamboo shoot, peeled,
  boiled in water for 10 minutes,
  and sliced
 450g/1lb freshwater fish fillets,
  such as carp or catfish, skinned
  and cut into bitesize pieces
 1 small bunch fresh basil leaves
 1 small bunch fresh coriander
  (cilantro), chopped, and 1 chilli,
  finely sliced, to garnish
 rice or noodles, to serve
For the stock
 675g/1½lb pork ribs
 1 onion, quartered
 225g/8oz carrots, cut into chunks
 25g/1oz dried squid or dried shrimp,
  soaked in water for 30 minutes,
  rinsed and drained
 15ml/1 tbsp *nuoc mam*
 15ml/1 tbsp soy sauce
 6 black peppercorns
 salt

1 To prepare the stock, put the ribs in a large pan and cover with 2.5 litres/ 4¼ pints/10 cups water. Bring to the boil, skim off any fat, and add the remaining stock ingredients. Cover the pan and simmer for 1 hour, then skim off any foam or fat.

2 Simmer the stock, uncovered, for a further 1–1½ hours, until it has reduced. Check the seasoning and strain the stock into another pan. There should be approximately 2 litres/3½ pints/7¾ cups of stock.

3 Bring the pan of stock to the boil. Stir in the rice and reduce the heat. Add the coconut milk, *tuk prahoc*, lemon grass, galangal, chillies, garlic and sugar. Simmer for about 10 minutes to let the flavours mingle. The rice should be just cooked, with bite to it.

4 Add the sliced bamboo shoot and the pieces of fish. Simmer for 5 minutes, until the fish is cooked. Check the seasoning and stir in the basil leaves. Ladle the soup into bowls, garnish with the chopped coriander and chilli, and serve with the rice or noodles.

Per portion Energy 181Kcal/763kJ; Protein 22.8g; Carbohydrate 19.6g, of which sugars 4.3g; Fat 1.3g, of which saturates 0.2g; Cholesterol 52mg; Calcium 64mg; Fibre 0.9g; Sodium 150mg

SAIGON PORK AND PRAWN SOUP

HU TIEU DO BIEN IS A SPECIALITY OF HO CHI MINH CITY (FORMERLY SAIGON), WHERE THE PORK STOCK IS ENHANCED WITH THE INTENSE SWEET AND SMOKY FLAVOUR OF DRIED SQUID. IT IS ALSO A POPULAR SOUP IN CAMBODIA, WHERE IT IS CALLED K'TIAO.

SERVES FOUR

INGREDIENTS

225g/8oz pork tenderloin
225g/8oz dried rice sticks
   (vermicelli), soaked in lukewarm
   water for 20 minutes
20 prawns (shrimp), shelled and
   deveined
115g/4oz/½ cup beansprouts
2 spring onions (scallions), finely
   sliced
2 green or red Thai chillies, seeded
   and finely sliced
1 garlic clove, finely sliced
1 bunch each coriander (cilantro)
   and basil, stalks removed, leaves
   roughly chopped
1 lime, cut into quarters, and
   nuoc cham, to serve
For the stock
   25g/1oz dried squid
   675g/1½lb pork ribs
   1 onion, peeled and quartered
   225g/8oz carrots, peeled and cut
      into chunks
   15ml/1 tbsp *nuoc mam*
   15ml/1 tbsp soy sauce
   6 black peppercorns
   salt

1 To make the stock, soak the dried squid in water for 30 minutes, rinse and drain. Put the ribs in a large pan and cover with approximately 2.5 litres/4½ pints/10 cups water. Bring to the boil, skim off any fat, and add the dried squid with the remaining stock ingredients. Cover the pan and simmer for 1 hour, then skim off any foam or fat and continue to simmer, uncovered, for a further 1½ hours.

2 Strain the stock and check the seasoning. You should have roughly 2 litres/3½ pints/8 cups.

COOK'S TIP
To serve the soup on its own, add bitesize pieces of soaked dried shiitake mushrooms or cubes of firm tofu.

3 Pour the stock into a wok or deep pan and bring to the boil. Reduce the heat, add the pork tenderloin and simmer for 25 minutes. Lift the tenderloin out of the stock, place it on a board and cut it into thin slices. Meanwhile, keep the stock simmering gently over a low heat.

4 Bring a pan of water to the boil. Drain the rice sticks and add to the water. Cook for about 5 minutes, or until tender, separating them with chopsticks if they stick together. Drain the rice sticks and divide them among four warm bowls.

5 Drop the prawns into the simmering stock for 1 minute. Lift them out with a slotted spoon and layer them with the slices of pork on top of the rice sticks. Ladle the hot stock over them and sprinkle with beansprouts, spring onions, chillies, garlic and herbs. Serve each bowl of soup with a wedge of lime to squeeze over it and *nuoc cham* to splash on top.

Per portion Energy 319Kcal/1339kJ; Protein 22g; Carbohydrate 50g, of which sugars 1g; Fat 3g, of which saturates 0g; Cholesterol 49mg; Calcium 91mg; Fibre 0.6g; Sodium 500mg

BEEF NOODLE SOUP

SOME WOULD SAY THAT THIS CLASSIC NOODLE SOUP, PHO, IS VIETNAM IN A BOWL. MADE WITH BEEF (PHO BO) OR CHICKEN (PHO GA), IT IS VIETNAMESE FAST FOOD, STREET FOOD, WORKING MEN'S FOOD AND FAMILY FOOD. IT IS NUTRITIOUS AND FILLING, AND MAKES AN INTENSELY SATISFYING MEAL.

SERVES SIX

INGREDIENTS
  250g/9oz beef sirloin
  500g/1¼lb dried noodles, soaked in
    lukewarm water for 20 minutes
  1 onion, halved and finely sliced
  6–8 spring onions (scallions),
    cut into long pieces
  2–3 red Thai chillies, seeded and
    finely sliced
  115g/4oz/½ cup beansprouts
  1 large bunch each fresh coriander
    (cilantro) and mint, stalks removed,
    leaves chopped
  2 limes, cut in wedges, and hoisin
    sauce, *nuoc mam* or *nuoc cham*
    to serve
For the stock
  1.5kg/3lb 5oz oxtail, trimmed of fat
    and cut into thick pieces
  1kg/2¼lb beef shank or brisket
  2 large onions, peeled and quartered
  2 carrots, peeled and cut into chunks
  7.5cm/3in fresh root ginger,
    cut into chunks
  6 cloves
  2 cinnamon sticks
  6 star anise
  5ml/1 tsp black peppercorns
  30ml/2 tbsp soy sauce
  45–60ml/3–4 tbsp *nuoc mam*
  salt

1 To make the stock, put the oxtail into a large, deep pan and cover it with water. Bring it to the boil and blanch the meat for about 10 minutes. Drain the meat, rinsing off any scum, and clean out the pan. Put the blanched oxtail back into the pan with the other stock ingredients, apart from the *nuoc mam* and salt, and cover with about 3 litres/5¼ pints/12 cups water. Bring it to the boil, reduce the heat and simmer, covered, for 2–3 hours.

2 Remove the lid and simmer for another hour, until the stock has reduced to about 2 litres/3½ pints/ 8 cups. Skim off any fat and then strain the stock into another pan.

3 Cut the beef sirloin across the grain into thin pieces, the size of the heel of your hand. Bring the stock to the boil once more, stir in the *nuoc mam*, season to taste, then reduce the heat and leave the stock simmering until ready to use.

4 Meanwhile, bring a pan filled with water to the boil, drain the rice sticks and add to the water. Cook for about 5 minutes or until tender – you may need to separate them with a pair of chopsticks if they look as though they are sticking together.

5 Drain the noodles and divide them equally among six wide soup bowls. Top each serving with the slices of beef, onion, spring onions, chillies and beansprouts.

6 Ladle the hot stock over the top of these ingredients, top with the fresh herbs and serve with the lime wedges to squeeze over. Pass around the hoisin sauce, *nuoc mam* or *nuoc cham* for those who like a little sweetening, fish flavouring or extra fire.

COOK'S TIPS
• The key to *pho* is a tasty, light stock flavoured with ginger, cinnamon, cloves and star anise, so it is worth cooking it slowly and leaving it to stand overnight to allow the flavours to develop fully.
• To enjoy this dish, use your chopsticks to lift the noodles through the layers of flavouring and slurp them up. This is the essence of Vietnam.

Per portion Energy 391Kcal/1635kJ; Protein 16g; Carbohydrate 74g, of which sugars 3g; Fat 2g, of which saturates 1g; Cholesterol 21mg; Calcium 62mg; Fibre 0.8g; Sodium 600mg

SPICY BEEF AND AUBERGINE SOUP

A WONDERFUL KHMER DISH, THIS SOUP, SAMLAW MACHOU KROEUNG, IS SWEET, SPICY AND TANGY. THE FLAVOUR IS MAINLY DERIVED FROM THE CAMBODIAN HERBAL CONDIMENT, KROEUNG, AND THE FERMENTED FISH EXTRACT, TUK TREY.

SERVES SIX

INGREDIENTS
   4 dried New Mexico chillies
   15ml/1 tbsp vegetable oil
   75ml/5 tbsp *kroeung*
   2–3 fresh or dried red Thai chillies
   75ml/5 tbsp tamarind extract
   15–30ml/1–2 tbsp *tuk trey*
   30ml/2 tbsp palm sugar
   12 Thai aubergines (eggplants), with
     stems removed and cut into
     bitesize chunks
   1 bunch watercress or rocket
     (arugula), trimmed and chopped
   1 handful fresh curry leaves
   sea salt and ground black pepper
For the stock
   1kg/2¼lb beef shanks or brisket
   2 large onions, quartered
   2–3 carrots, cut into chunks
   90g/3½oz fresh root ginger, sliced
   2 cinnamon sticks
   4 star anise
   5ml/1 tsp black peppercorns
   30ml/2 tbsp soy sauce
   45–60ml/3–4 tbsp *tuk trey*

1 To make the stock, put the beef shanks into a deep pan with all the other stock ingredients, apart from the soy sauce and *tuk trey*. Cover with 3 litres/5 pints/12 cups water and bring it to the boil. Reduce the heat and simmer, covered, for 2–3 hours.

COOK'S TIP
For a greater depth of flavour, you can dry-roast the New Mexico chillies before soaking them in water.

2 Soak the New Mexico chillies in water for 30 minutes. Split them open, remove the seeds and scrape out the pulp with a spoon.

3 Take the lid off the stock and stir in the remaining two ingredients. Simmer, uncovered, for another hour, until the stock has reduced to about 2 litres/3½ pints/7¾ cups. Skim off any fat, strain the stock into a bowl and put aside. Lift the meat on to a plate, tear it into thin strips and put half of it aside for the soup.

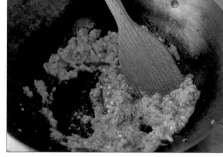

4 Heat the oil in a wok or heavy pan. Stir in the *kroeung* along with the pulp from the New Mexico chillies and the whole Thai chillies. Stir the spicy paste as it sizzles, until it begins to darken. Add the tamarind extract, *tuk trey*, sugar and the reserved stock. Stir well and bring to the boil.

5 Reduce the heat and add the reserved beef, aubergines and watercress or rocket. Continue cooking for about 20 minutes to allow the flavours to mingle.

6 Meanwhile, dry-fry the curry leaves. Heat a small, heavy pan over a high heat, add the curry leaves and cook them until they begin to crackle. Transfer them to a plate and set aside.

6 Season the soup to taste. Stir in half the curry leaves and ladle the soup into individual bowls. Scatter the remaining curry leaves over the top and serve.

Per portion Energy 303Kcal/1276kJ; Protein 37g; Carbohydrate 16.5g, of which sugars 14.5g; Fat 10.6g, of which saturates 4.2g; Cholesterol 90mg; Calcium 35mg; Fibre 2.4g; Sodium 300mg

SOUR BROTH WITH WATER SPINACH AND BEEF

WATER SPINACH IS A POPULAR VEGETABLE IN VIETNAM. WHEN COOKED, THE STEMS REMAIN CRUNCHY WHILE THE LEAVES SOFTEN, LENDING A DELIGHTFUL CONTRAST OF TEXTURE TO THE DISH. SERVED AS AN APPETIZER, THIS IS A LIGHT SOUP WITH TENDER BITES OF BEEF AND SOUR NOTES OF LEMON JUICE.

SERVES FOUR TO SIX

INGREDIENTS

    30ml/2 tbsp *nuoc mam*
    5ml/1 tsp sugar
    175g/6oz beef fillet, finely
      sliced across the grain into
      2.5cm/1in strips
    1.2 litres/2 pints/5 cups beef or
      chicken stock
    175g/6oz water spinach, trimmed,
      rinsed, leaves and stalks separated
    juice of 1 lemon
    ground black pepper
    1 red or green chilli, seeded and
      finely sliced, to garnish

1 In a bowl, stir the *nuoc mam* with the sugar until it has dissolved. Toss in the beef strips and leave to marinate for 30 minutes. Pour the stock into a pan and bring it to the boil. Reduce the heat and add the water spinach. Stir in the lemon juice and season with pepper.

2 Place the meat strips in individual bowls and ladle the hot broth over the top. Garnish with chillies and serve.

VARIATION
You can sprinkle coriander and mint or fried garlic and ginger over the top.

Per portion Energy 61Kcal/254kJ; Protein 7.4g; Carbohydrate 1.2g, of which sugars 1.1g; Fat 3g, of which saturates 1.1g; Cholesterol 17mg; Calcium 51mg; Fibre 0.6g; Sodium 600mg

PORK AND LOTUS ROOT BROTH

THIS VIETNAMESE SOUP IS FROM THE CENTRAL REGION OF THE COUNTRY WHERE THE LOTUS, A TYPE OF WATER LILY, IS USED IN MANY DISHES. IN THIS CLEAR BROTH, WHICH IS SERVED AS AN APPETIZER, THE THIN, ROUND SLICES OF FRESH LOTUS ROOT LOOK LIKE DELICATE FLOWERS FLOATING IN WATER.

SERVES FOUR TO SIX

INGREDIENTS
  450g/1lb fresh lotus root, peeled and
    thinly sliced
  ground black pepper
  1 red chilli, seeded and finely sliced,
    and 1 small bunch basil leaves,
    to garnish
For the stock
  450g/1lb pork ribs
  1 onion, quartered
  2 carrots, cut into chunks
  25g/1oz dried squid or dried shrimp,
    soaked in water for 30 minutes,
    rinsed and drained
  15ml/1 tbsp *nuoc mam*
  15ml/1 tbsp soy sauce
  6 black peppercorns
  sea salt

1 Put the ribs into a pan and cover with 1.5 litres/2½ pints/6¼ cups water. Bring to the boil, skim off any fat, and add the other ingredients. Reduce the heat, cover, and simmer for 2 hours.

2 Take off the lid and simmer for a further 30 minutes to reduce the stock. Strain the stock and shred the meat off the pork ribs.

3 Pour the stock back into the pan and bring it to the boil. Reduce the heat and add the lotus root. Partially cover the pan and simmer gently for 30–40 minutes, until the lotus root is tender.

4 Stir in the shredded meat and season the broth with salt and pepper. Ladle the soup into bowls and garnish with the chilli and basil leaves.

Per portion Energy 181Kcal/756kJ; Protein 23.8g; Carbohydrate 4g, of which sugars 3.1g; Fat 7.8g, of which saturates 2.7g; Cholesterol 74mg; Calcium 65mg; Fibre 1.4g; Sodium 270mg

CHICKEN RICE SOUP WITH LEMON GRASS

SHNOR CHROOK IS CAMBODIA'S ANSWER TO THE CHICKEN NOODLE SOUP THAT IS POPULAR IN THE WEST. LIGHT AND REFRESHING, IT IS THE PERFECT CHOICE FOR A HOT DAY, AS WELL AS A GREAT PICK-ME-UP WHEN YOU ARE FEELING LOW OR TIRED.

SERVES FOUR

INGREDIENTS
  2 lemon grass stalks, trimmed,
    cut into 3 pieces, and lightly
    bruised
  15ml/1 tbsp fish sauce, such as
    nam pla
  90g/3½oz/½ cup short grain
    rice, rinsed
  1 small bunch coriander (cilantro)
    leaves, finely chopped, and 1 green
    or red chilli, seeded and cut into
    thin strips, to garnish
  1 lime, cut in wedges, to serve
  sea salt
  ground black pepper
For the stock
  1 small chicken or 2 meaty
    chicken legs
  1 onion, quartered
  2 cloves garlic, crushed
  25g/1oz fresh root ginger, sliced
  2 lemon grass stalks, cut in half
    lengthwise and bruised
  2 dried red chillies
  30ml/2 tbsp *nuoc mam*

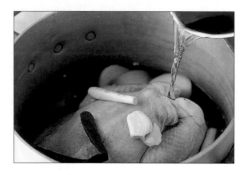

1 Put the chicken into a deep pan. Add all the other stock ingredients and pour in 2 litres/3½ pints/7¾ cups water. Bring to the boil for a few minutes, then reduce the heat and simmer gently with the lid on for 2 hours.

2 Skim off any fat from the stock, strain and reserve. Remove the skin from the chicken and shred the meat. Set aside.

4 Ladle the piping hot soup into warmed individual bowls, garnish with chopped coriander and the thin strips of chilli and serve with lime wedges to squeeze over.

COOK'S TIPS
• The fresh, citrus aroma of lemon grass and lime, combined with the warmth of the chillies, is invigorating and awakens the senses. However, many Vietnamese and Cambodians often spike the soup with additional chillies as a garnish, or served on the side.
• Variations of this soup crop up all over Cambodia and Vietnam, where it is often served as a meal in itself.

3 Pour the stock back into the deep pan and bring to the boil. Reduce the heat and stir in the lemon grass stalks and fish sauce. Stir in the rice and simmer, uncovered, for about 40 minutes. Add the shredded chicken and season to taste.

Per portion Energy 147Kcal/615kJ; Protein 12.8g; Carbohydrate 19.8g, of which sugars 1.4g; Fat 1.7g, of which saturates 0.4g; Cholesterol 53mg; Calcium 37mg; Fibre 0.8g; Sodium 320mg

DUCK AND PRESERVED LIME SOUP

THIS RICH CAMBODIAN SOUP, SAMLAW TIAH, ORIGINATES IN THE CHIU CHOW REGION OF SOUTHERN CHINA. THIS RECIPE CAN BE MADE WITH CHICKEN STOCK AND LEFTOVER DUCK MEAT FROM A ROASTED DUCK, OR BY ROASTING A DUCK, SLICING OFF THE BREAST AND THIGH MEAT FOR THE SOUP.

SERVES FOUR TO SIX

INGREDIENTS
 1 lean duck, approximately
   1.5kg/3lb 5oz
 2 preserved limes
 25g/1oz fresh root ginger,
   thinly sliced
 sea salt and ground black pepper
For the garnish
 vegetable oil, for frying
 25g/1oz fresh root ginger,
   thinly sliced into strips
 2 garlic cloves, thinly sliced
   into strips
 2 spring onions (scallions),
   finely sliced

COOK'S TIPS
• With the addition of noodles, this soup could be served as a meal in itself.
• Preserved limes have a distinct bitter flavour. Look for them in Asian markets.

1 Place the duck in a large pan with enough water to cover. Season with salt and pepper and bring the water to the boil. Reduce the heat, cover the pot, and simmer for 1½ hours.

2 Add the preserved limes and ginger. Continue to simmer for another hour, skimming off the fat from time to time, until the liquid has reduced a little and the duck is so tender that it almost falls off the bone.

3 Meanwhile heat some vegetable oil in a wok. Stir in the ginger and garlic strips and fry until gold and crispy. Drain well on kitchen paper and set aside for garnishing.

4 Remove the duck from the broth and shred the meat into individual bowls. Check the broth for seasoning, then ladle it over the duck in the bowls. Scatter the spring onions with the fried ginger and garlic over the top and serve.

Per portion Energy 124Kcal/520kJ; Protein 19.8g; Carbohydrate 0.3g, of which sugars 0.3g; Fat 6.5g, of which saturates 1.3g; Cholesterol 110mg; Calcium 19mg; Fibre 0g; Sodium 100mg

DUCK AND NUT SOUP WITH JUJUBES

This northern Vietnamese dish is satisfying and delicious. Packed with nuts and sweetened with jujubes (dried Chinese red dates), it resembles neither a soup nor a stew, but something in between. Served on its own, or with rice and pickles, it is a meal in itself.

SERVES FOUR

INGREDIENTS

30–45ml/2–3 tbsp vegetable oil
4 duck legs, split into thighs
 and drumsticks
juice of 1 coconut
60ml/4 tbsp *nuoc mam*
4 lemon grass stalks, bruised
12 chestnuts, peeled
90g/3½oz unsalted cashew nuts,
 roasted
90g/3½oz unsalted almonds, roasted
90g/3½oz unsalted peanuts, roasted
12 jujubes
sea salt and ground black pepper
1 bunch fresh basil leaves, to garnish

VARIATION

Replace the jujubes with dates if you cannot find them.

1 Heat the oil in a wok or heavy pan. Brown the duck legs in the oil and drain on kitchen paper.

2 Bring 2 litres/3½ pints/7¾ cups water to the boil. Reduce the heat and add the coconut juice, *nuoc mam*, lemon grass and duck legs. Cover the pan and simmer over a gentle heat for 2–3 hours. Skim off any fat.

3 Add the nuts and jujubes and cook for 40 minutes, until the chestnuts are soft and the duck is very tender. Skim off any fat, season to taste and scatter the basil leaves over the top to serve.

COOK'S TIP

To extract the coconut juice, pierce the eyes on top and turn the coconut upside down over a bowl.

Per portion Energy 604Kcal/2512kJ; Protein 44g; Carbohydrate 9g, of which sugars 3.6g; Fat 44g, of which saturates 9.2g; Cholesterol 165mg; Calcium 49mg; Fibre 3.1g; Sodium 230mg

AROMATIC BROTH WITH ROAST DUCK, PAK CHOI AND EGG NOODLES

SERVED ON ITS OWN, THIS CHINESE-INSPIRED SOUP, MI VIT TIM, MAKES A DELICIOUS AUTUMN OR WINTER MEAL. IN A VIETNAMESE HOUSEHOLD, A BOWL OF WHOLE FRESH OR MARINATED CHILLIES MIGHT BE PRESENTED AS A FIERY SIDE DISH TO CHEW ON.

SERVES FOUR

INGREDIENTS
15ml/1 tbsp vegetable oil
2 shallots, thinly sliced
4cm/1½ in fresh root ginger,
    peeled and sliced
15ml/1 tbsp soy sauce
5ml/1 tsp five-spice powder
10ml/2 tsp sugar
175g/6oz pak choi (bok choy)
450g/1lb fresh egg noodles
350g/12oz roast duck, thinly sliced
sea salt
For the stock
1 chicken or duck carcass
2 carrots, peeled and quartered
2 onions, peeled and quartered
4cm/1½ in fresh root ginger, peeled
    and cut into chunks
2 lemon grass stalks, chopped
30ml/2 tbsp *nuoc mam*
15ml/1 tbsp soy sauce
6 black peppercorns
For the garnish
4 spring onions (scallions), sliced
1–2 red Serrano chillies, seeded and
    finely sliced
1 bunch each coriander (cilantro) and
    basil, stalks removed, leaves
    chopped

1 To make the stock, put the chicken or duck carcass into a deep pan. Add all the other stock ingredients and pour in 2.5 litres/4½ pints/10¼ cups water. Bring to the boil, and boil for a few minutes, skim off any foam, then reduce the heat and simmer gently with the lid on for 2–3 hours. Remove the lid and continue to simmer for a further 30 minutes to reduce the stock. Skim off any fat, season with salt, then strain the stock. Measure out 2 litres/3½ pints/8 cups.

2 Heat the oil in a wok or deep pan and stir in the shallots and ginger. Add the soy sauce, five-spice powder, sugar and stock and bring to the boil. Season with a little salt, reduce the heat and simmer for 10–15 minutes.

3 Meanwhile, cut the pak choi diagonally into wide strips and blanch in boiling water to soften them. Drain and refresh under cold running water to prevent them cooking any further. Bring a large pan of water to the boil, then add the fresh noodles. Cook for 5 minutes, then drain well.

4 Divide the noodles among four soup bowls, lay some of the pak choi and sliced duck over them, and then ladle over generous amounts of the simmering broth. Garnish with the spring onions, chillies and herbs, and serve immediately.

COOK'S TIP
If you can't find fresh egg noodles, you can use dried instead. Soak them in lukewarm water for 20 minutes, then cook, one portion at a time, in a sieve (strainer) lowered into the boiling water. Use a chopstick to untangle them as they soften. Ready-cooked egg noodles are also available in supermarkets.

Per portion Energy 673Kcal/2836kJ; Protein 37g; Carbohydrate 86g, of which sugars 22g; Fat 6g, of which saturates 1g; Cholesterol 81mg; Calcium 4mg; Fibre 0.7g; Sodium 700mg

SAVOURY SNACKS

The Vietnamese and Cambodians are keen snackers. Life is busy on the streets, and wherever you go there are small restaurants, cafés and makeshift stalls, made out of bamboo, cooking and selling every type of sweet or savoury snack. Cities such as Ho Chi Minh City and Phnom Penh are abuzz with the sounds, sights and aromatic smells of cooking and eating. Savoury snacks such as Vietnamese Spring Rolls and Sizzling Spiced Crêpes will be equally popular as snacks at home.

CRUNCHY SUMMER ROLLS

THESE DELIGHTFUL RICE PAPER ROLLS FILLED WITH CRUNCHY RAW SUMMER VEGETABLES AND FRESH HERBS ARE LIGHT AND REFRESHING, EITHER AS A SNACK OR AN APPETIZER TO A MEAL, AND ARE ENJOYED ALL OVER VIETNAM AND CAMBODIA.

SERVES FOUR

INGREDIENTS
   12 round rice papers
   1 lettuce, leaves separated and
      ribs removed
   2–3 carrots, cut into julienne strips
   1 small cucumber, peeled, halved
      lengthways and seeded, and cut
      into julienne strips
   3 spring onions (scallions), trimmed
      and cut into julienne strips
   225g/8oz mung beansprouts
   1 bunch fresh mint leaves
   1 bunch coriander (cilantro) leaves
   dipping sauce, to serve
      (see Cook's Tips)

1 Pour some lukewarm water into a shallow dish. Soak the rice papers, 2–3 at a time, for about 5 minutes until they are pliable. Place the soaked papers on a clean dishtowel and cover with a second dishtowel to keep them moist.

2 Work with one paper at a time. Place a lettuce leaf towards the edge nearest to you, leaving about 2.5cm/1in to fold over. Place a mixture of the vegetables on top, followed by some mint and coriander leaves.

3 Fold the edge nearest to you over the filling, tuck in the sides, and roll tightly to the edge on the far side. Place the filled roll on a plate and cover with clear film (plastic wrap), so it doesn't dry out. Repeat with the remaining rice papers and vegetables. Serve with a dipping sauce of your choice. If you are making these summer rolls ahead of time, keep them in the refrigerator under a damp dishtowel, so that they remain moist.

COOK'S TIPS
• In Vietnam, these crunchy filled rolls are often served with a light peanut dipping sauce. In Cambodia, they are accompanied by a dipping sauce called *tuk trey* (also the name of the national fish sauce), which is similar to the Vietnamese dipping sauce, *nuoc cham*, except that it has chopped peanuts in it. They are, in fact, delicious with any dipping sauce.
• Rice papers can be bought in Chinese and South-east Asian markets.

VARIATION
This recipe only uses vegetables, which are cut into equal lengths, but you can also add pre-cooked shredded pork, chicken or prawns to summer rolls.

Per portion 106Kcal/445kJ; Protein 3.5g; Carbohydrate 21.2g, of which sugars 4.7g; Fat 0.7g, of which saturates 0.2g; Cholesterol 0mg; Calcium 44mg; Fibre 2.2g; Sodium 10mg

CURRIED SWEET POTATO BALLS

THESE SWEET POTATO BALLS FROM CAMBODIA ARE DELICIOUS DIPPED IN A FIERY SAUCE, SUCH AS NUOC CHAM, FRIED BLACK CHILLI SAUCE OR HOT PEANUT DIPPING SAUCE. SIMPLE TO MAKE, THEY ARE IDEAL FOR SERVING AS A NIBBLE WITH A DRINK.

SERVES FOUR

INGREDIENTS

450g/1lb sweet potatoes or taro root, boiled or baked, and peeled
30ml/2 tbsp sugar
15ml/1 tbsp Indian curry powder
25g/1oz fresh root ginger, peeled and grated
150g/5oz/1¼ cups glutinous rice flour or plain (all-purpose) flour
salt
sesame seeds or poppy seeds
vegetable oil, for deep-frying
dipping sauce, to serve

1 In a bowl, mash the cooked sweet potatoes or taro root. Beat in the sugar, curry powder, and ginger. Add the rice flour (sift it if you are using plain flour) and salt, and work into a stiff dough – add more flour if necessary.

2 Pull off lumps of the dough and mould them into small balls – you should be able to make roughly 24 balls. Roll the balls on a bed of sesame seeds or poppy seeds until they are completely coated.

3 Heat enough oil for deep-frying in a wok. Fry the sweet potato balls in batches, until golden. Drain on kitchen paper. Serve the balls with wooden skewers to make it easier to dip them into a dipping sauce of your choice.

Per portion Energy 354Kcal/1495kJ; Protein 5g; Carbohydrate 61g, of which sugars 14.8g; Fat 11.8g, of which saturates 1.5g; Cholesterol 0mg; Calcium 84mg; Fibre 3.9g; Sodium 50mg

VIETNAMESE SPRING ROLLS

ONE OF THE MOST POPULAR FOODS THROUGHOUT VIETNAM IS THE SPRING ROLL, WHICH MAKES AN IDEAL QUICK SNACK. THEY ARE CALLED CHA GIO IN THE SOUTH AND NEM RAN IN THE NORTH, AND THEIR FILLINGS VARY FROM REGION TO REGION.

MAKES ABOUT 30

INGREDIENTS
    30 dried rice wrappers
    vegetable oil, for deep-frying
    1 bunch fresh mint, stalks removed,
        and *nuoc cham*, to serve
For the filling
    50g/2oz dried bean thread
        (cellophane) noodles, soaked in
        warm water for 20 minutes
    25g/1oz dried cloud ear (wood ear)
        mushrooms, soaked in warm water
        for 15 minutes
    2 eggs
    30ml/2 tbsp *nuoc mam*
    2 garlic cloves, crushed
    10ml/2 tsp sugar
    1 onion, finely chopped
    3 spring onions (scallions),
        finely sliced
    350g/12oz/1½ cups minced
        (ground) pork
    175g/6oz/1¾ cups cooked crab meat
        or raw prawns (shrimp)
    salt and ground black pepper

1 To make the filling, squeeze dry the soaked noodles and chop them into small pieces. Squeeze dry the soaked dried cloud ear mushrooms and chop them.

2 Beat the eggs in a bowl. Stir in the *nuoc mam*, garlic and sugar. Add the onion, spring onions, noodles, mushrooms, pork and crab meat or prawns. Season well with salt and ground black pepper.

COOK'S TIP
These spring rolls filled with rice noodles are typically Vietnamese, but you can substitute beansprouts for the noodles to create rolls more akin to the Chinese version. Fresh mint leaves give these rolls a refreshing bite, but fresh coriander (cilantro), basil or flatleaf parsley work just as well and give an interesting flavour. Dipped into a piquant sauce of your choice, they are very moreish.

3 Have ready a damp dishtowel, some clear film (plastic wrap) and a bowl of water. Dip a rice wrapper in the water and place it on the damp towel. Spoon about 15ml/1 tbsp of the spring roll filling on to the side nearest to you, just in from the edge. Fold the nearest edge over the filling, fold over the sides, tucking them in neatly, and then roll the whole wrapper into a tight cylinder. Place the roll on a plate and cover with clear film to keep it moist. Continue making spring rolls in the same way, using the remaining wrappers and filling.

4 Heat the vegetable oil in a wok or heavy pan for deep-frying. Make sure it is hot enough by dropping in a small piece of bread; it should foam and sizzle. Cook the spring rolls in batches, turning them in the oil so that they become golden all over. Drain them on kitchen paper and serve immediately with mint leaves to wrap around them and *nuoc cham* for dipping.

Per portion Energy 63Kcal/236kJ; Protein 2g; Carbohydrate 5g, of which sugars 1g; Fat 4g, of which saturates 1g; Cholesterol 20mg; Calcium 10mg; Fibre 0.3g; Sodium 60mg

SIZZLING SPICED CRÊPES

FRENCH IN STYLE, BUT VIETNAMESE IN FLAVOUR, THESE DELIGHTFULLY CRISPY, TASTY CRÊPES, MADE WITH COCONUT MILK AND FILLED WITH PRAWNS, MUSHROOMS AND BEANSPROUTS, ARE OUT OF THIS WORLD. YOU CAN MAKE EIGHT SMALL CRÊPES, RATHER THAN FOUR SMALL ONES, IF YOU PREFER.

SERVES FOUR

INGREDIENTS

- 115g/4oz/½ cup minced (ground) pork
- 15ml/1 tbsp *nuoc mam*
- 2 garlic cloves, crushed
- 175g/6oz/⅔ cup button (white) mushrooms, finely sliced
- about 60ml/4 tbsp vegetable oil
- 1 onion, finely sliced
- 1–2 green or red Thai chillies, seeded and finely sliced
- 115g/4oz prawns (shrimp), shelled and deveined
- 225g/8oz/1 cup beansprouts
- 1 small bunch fresh coriander (cilantro), stalks removed, leaves roughly chopped
- salt and ground black pepper
- *nuoc cham*, to serve

For the batter

- 115g/4oz/1 cup rice flour
- 10ml/2 tsp ground turmeric
- 10ml/2 tsp curry powder
- 5ml/1 tsp sugar
- 2.5ml/½ tsp salt
- 300ml/½ pint/1¼ cups canned coconut milk
- 4 spring onions (scallions), trimmed and finely sliced

1 To make the batter, beat the rice flour, spices, sugar and salt with the coconut milk and 300ml/½ pint/1¼ cups water, until smooth and creamy. Stir in the spring onions and then leave to stand for 30 minutes.

2 In a bowl, mix the pork with the *nuoc mam*, garlic and seasoning and knead well. Lightly sauté the sliced mushrooms in 15ml/1 tbsp of the oil and set aside.

3 Heat 10ml/2 tsp of the oil in a non-stick pan. Stir in a quarter of the onion and the chillies, then add a quarter each of the pork and the prawns. Pour in 150ml/¼ pint/⅔ cup of the batter, swirling the pan so that it spreads over the pork and prawns right to the edges.

4 Pile a quarter of the beansprouts and mushrooms on one side of the crêpe, just in from the middle. Reduce the heat and cover the pan for 2–3 minutes, or until the edges pull away from the sides. Remove the lid and cook the crêpe for another 2 minutes; gently lift up an edge of the crêpe with a spatula to see if it's brown underneath.

5 Once it is nicely browned, scatter some chopped coriander over the empty side of the crêpe and fold it over the beansprouts and mushrooms. Slide the crêpe on to a plate and keep warm while you make the remaining crêpes in the same way. Serve with *nuoc cham* for dipping, or drizzle with chilli sauce and serve fresh red or green chillies on the side.

Per portion Energy 379Kcal/1581kJ; Protein 18g; Carbohydrate 37g, of which sugars 9g; Fat 18g, of which saturates 3g; Cholesterol 77mg; Calcium 119mg; Fibre 3.2g; Sodium 50mg

RICE NOODLES WITH FRESH HERBS

BUN IS THE WORD USED TO DESCRIBE THE THIN, WIRY NOODLES KNOWN AS RICE STICKS OR RICE VERMICELLI. HOWEVER, WHEN THE VIETNAMESE TALK ABOUT A DISH CALLED BUN, THEY ARE USUALLY REFERRING TO THIS RECIPE, WHICH COULD BE DESCRIBED AS A NOODLE SALAD.

SERVES FOUR

INGREDIENTS
half a small cucumber
225g/8oz dried rice sticks (vermicelli)
4–6 lettuce leaves, shredded
115g/4oz/½ cup beansprouts
1 bunch mixed basil, coriander
   (cilantro), mint and oregano, stalks
   removed, leaves shredded
juice of half a lime
nuoc mam or *nuoc cham*, to drizzle

COOK'S TIP
In the street stalls and cafés of Hanoi, different types of mint, ginger leaves, oregano and thyme provide the herb bedding for this dish, giving it a really distinctive, fragrant flavour.

1 Peel the cucumber, cut it in half lengthways, remove the seeds, and cut into matchsticks.

2 Add the rice sticks to a pan of boiling water, loosening them gently, and cook for 3–4 minutes, or until *al dente*. Drain, rinse under cold water, and drain again.

3 In a bowl, toss the shredded lettuce, beansprouts, cucumber and herbs together. Add the noodles and lime juice and toss together. Drizzle with a little *nuoc mam* or *nuoc cham* for seasoning, and serve immediately on its own, or with stir-fried seafood or chicken as a complete meal.

Per portion Energy 221Kcal/926kJ; Protein 4g; Carbohydrate 48g, of which sugars 1g; Fat 0g, of which saturates 0g; Cholesterol 0mg; Calcium 44mg; Fibre 0.8g; Sodium 10mg

GRILLED PRAWNS WITH LEMON GRASS

NEXT TO EVERY FISH STALL IN EVERY MARKET IN VIETNAM AND CAMBODIA, THERE IS BOUND TO BE SOMEONE COOKING UP FRAGRANT, CITRUS-SCENTED SNACKS FOR YOU TO EAT AS YOU WANDER AROUND THE MARKET. THE AROMATIC SCENT OF LEMON GRASS IS HARD TO RESIST.

SERVES FOUR

INGREDIENTS

    16 king prawns (jumbo shrimp),
      cleaned, with shells intact
    120ml/4fl oz/½ cup *nuoc mam*
    30ml/2 tbsp sugar
    15ml/1 tbsp vegetable or sesame oil
    3 lemon grass stalks, trimmed and
      finely chopped

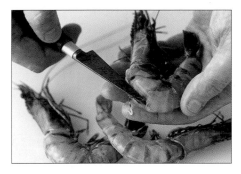

1 Using a small sharp knife, carefully slice open each king prawn shell along the back and pull out the black vein, using the point of the knife. Try to keep the rest of the shell intact. Place the deveined prawns in a shallow dish and set aside.

2 Put the *nuoc mam* in a small bowl with the sugar, and beat together until the sugar has dissolved completely. Add the oil and lemon grass and mix well.

COOK'S TIP
Big, juicy king prawns (jumbo shrimp) are best for this recipe, but you can use smaller ones if the large king prawns are not available.

3 Pour the marinade over the prawns, using your fingers to rub it all over the prawns and inside the shells too. Cover the dish with clear film (plastic wrap) and chill for at least 4 hours.

4 Cook the prawns on a barbecue or under a conventional grill (broiler) for 2–3 minutes each side. Serve with little bowls of water for rinsing sticky fingers.

Per portion Energy 174Kcal/726kJ; Protein 13g; Carbohydrate 11g, of which sugars 3g; Fat 9g, of which saturates 1g; Cholesterol 169mg; Calcium 30mg; Fibre 0.3g; Sodium 30mg

FRIED SQUID WITH SALT AND PEPPER

COOKING SQUID COULDN'T BE SIMPLER. SALT AND PEPPER ARE USED TO SEASON, AND THAT'S IT. A CHINESE TRADITION FOR ALL SORTS OF FISH AND SHELLFISH, THIS IS A VIETNAMESE AND CAMBODIAN FAVOURITE TOO. IDEAL SNACK AND FINGER FOOD, THE TENDER SQUID CAN BE SERVED ON ITS OWN.

SERVES FOUR

INGREDIENTS

    450g/1lb baby or medium squid
    30ml/2 tbsp coarse salt
    15ml/1 tbsp ground black pepper
    50g/2oz/½ cup rice flour or
      cornflour (cornstarch)
    vegetable oil, for deep-frying
    2 limes, halved

1 Prepare the squid by pulling the head away from the body. Sever the tentacles from the rest and trim them. Reach inside the body sac and pull out the backbone, then clean the squid inside and out, removing any skin. Rinse well in cold water.

2 Using a sharp knife, slice the squid into rings and pat them dry with kitchen paper. Put them in a dish with the tentacles. Combine the salt and pepper with the rice flour or cornflour, add it to the squid and toss well, making sure it is evenly coated.

3 Heat the oil for deep-frying in a wok or heavy pan. Cook the squid in batches, until the rings turn crisp and golden. Drain on kitchen paper and serve with limes to squeeze over. This dish can also be served with noodles, or with chunks of baguette and fresh chillies.

Per portion Energy 339Kcal/1405kJ; Protein 14g; Carbohydrate 5g, of which sugars 0g; Fat 29g, of which saturates 4g; Cholesterol 146mg; Calcium 70mg; Fibre 0g; Sodium 140mg

DEEP-FRIED SWEET POTATO PATTIES

THIS DISH, BANH TOM, IS A HANOI SPECIALITY. THE STREET SELLERS IN THE CITY AND THE CAFÉS ALONG THE BANKS OF WEST LAKE ARE WELL KNOWN FOR THEIR VARIED AND DELICIOUS BANH TOM. TRADITIONALLY, THE PATTIES ARE SERVED WITH HERBS AND LETTUCE LEAVES FOR WRAPPING.

SERVES FOUR

INGREDIENTS

   50g/2oz/½ cup plain
     (all-purpose) flour
   50g/2oz/½ cup rice flour
   4ml/scant 1 tsp baking powder
   10ml/2 tsp sugar
   2.5cm/1in fresh root ginger,
     peeled and grated
   2 spring onions (scallions),
     finely sliced
   175g/6oz small fresh prawns
     (shrimp), peeled and deveined
   1 slim sweet potato, about
     225g/8oz, peeled and cut into
     fine matchsticks
   vegetable oil, for deep-frying
   salt and ground black pepper
   chopped fresh coriander (cilantro),
     to garnish
   lettuce leaves *and nuoc cham* or
     other dipping sauce, to serve

1 Sift the plain and rice flour and baking powder into a bowl. Add the sugar and about 2.5ml/½ tsp each of salt and pepper. Gradually stir in 250ml/8fl oz/1 cup water, until thoroughly combined. Add the grated ginger and sliced spring onions and leave to stand for 30 minutes. Add extra ginger if you like a strong flavour.

COOK'S TIP

Banh tom made with sweet potato are particularly popular in Hanoi, but they are also very good made with strips of winter melon or courgette (zucchini), beansprouts or bamboo shoots, or finely sliced cabbage leaves. Simply replace the sweet potato with the vegetable of your choice, add a little chilli, if you like, shape into patties and cook as before. You can make the patties any size: small for a snack or first course, or large for a main course; simply adjust the amount you spoon on to the spatula before frying. Serve the patties with a piquant or tangy dipping sauce of your own choice.

2 Add the prawns and sweet potato to the batter and fold them in, making sure they are well coated. Heat enough oil for deep-frying in a wok. Place a heaped tablespoon of the mixture on to a metal spatula. Lower it into the oil, pushing it off the spatula so that it floats in the oil. Fry for 2–3 minutes, turning it over so that it is evenly browned. Drain on kitchen paper. Continue with the rest of the batter, frying the patties in batches.

3 Arrange the patties on lettuce leaves, garnish with coriander, and serve immediately with *nuoc cham* or another dipping sauce of your choice.

Per portion Energy 276Kcal/1159kJ; Protein 11g; Carbohydrate 35g, of which sugars 6g; Fat 11g, of which saturates 1g; Cholesterol 85mg; Calcium 83mg; Fibre 81g; Sodium 200mg

GRILLED SHRIMP PASTE ON SUGAR CANE SKEWERS

THIS DISH, KNOWN AS CHAO TOM *IN VIETNAM, IS A CLASSIC. ORIGINALLY CREATED BY THE INGENIOUS COOKS OF THE IMPERIAL KITCHENS IN HUE, IT HAS BECOME A NATIONAL TREASURE. TO APPRECIATE ITS FULL IMPACT, IT IS BETTER TO SIMPLY GRILL IT AND EAT IT BY ITSELF, ENJOYING EVERY SINGLE BITE, RIGHT DOWN TO THE SWEET, SMOKY FLAVOURS OF THE SUGAR CANE.*

SERVES FOUR

INGREDIENTS
   50g/2oz pork fat
   7.5ml/1½ tsp vegetable oil
   1 onion, finely chopped
   2 garlic cloves, crushed
   1 egg
   15ml/1 tbsp fish sauce
   15ml/1 tbsp raw cane or
      dark brown sugar
   15ml/1 tbsp cornflour (cornstarch)
   350g/12oz raw prawns (shrimp),
      peeled and deveined
   a piece of fresh sugar cane,
      about 20cm/8in long
   salt and ground black pepper

1 Place the pork fat in a large pan of boiling water and boil for 2–3 minutes. Drain well and chop using a sharp knife. Set aside.

COOK'S TIP
Although canned sugar cane can be used for this recipe, it is no substitute for fresh. Fresh sugar cane is often available in African, Caribbean and Asian markets, as well as in some supermarkets. When cooked in the Vietnamese home, this dish is usually served with the traditional accompaniments of salad, rice wrappers and a dipping sauce. The grilled shrimp paste is pulled off the sugar cane, wrapped in a rice paper and dipped in sauce. The stripped sugar cane can then be chewed.

2 Heat the oil in a heavy pan and stir in the onion and garlic. Just as they begin to colour, remove from the heat and transfer them to a bowl. Beat in the egg, fish sauce and sugar, until the sugar has dissolved. Season with a little salt and plenty of black pepper, and then stir in the cornflour.

3 Add the pork fat and prawns to the mixture, and mix well. Grind in a mortar using a pestle, or process to a slightly lumpy paste in a food processor.

VARIATION
At home, this dish makes a fascinating appetizer or an interesting addition to a barbecue spread. To savour the wonderful tastes, it is best served by itself, straight from the hot grill. There is nothing quite like it!

4 Divide the paste into eight portions. Using a strong knife or cleaver, cut the sugar cane in half and then cut each half into quarters lengthways. Take a piece of sugar cane in your hand and mould a portion of the paste around it, pressing it gently so the edges are sealed. Place the coated sticks on an oiled tray, while you make the remaining skewers in the same way.

5 For the best flavour, cook the shrimp paste skewers over a barbecue for 5–6 minutes, turning them frequently until they are nicely browned all over.

6 Alternatively, cook the skewers under a conventional grill (broiler). Serve immediately, while still hot.

Per portion Energy 256Kcal/1066kJ; Protein 18g; Carbohydrate 12g, of which sugars 4.8g; Fat 15.7g, of which saturates 5.7g; Cholesterol 239mg; Calcium 85mg; Fibre 0.2g; Sodium 192mg

DEEP-FRIED PRAWN SANDWICHES

IN THE BUSY STREET MARKETS OF PHNOM PENH, THERE IS ALWAYS SOMETHING INTERESTING BEING COOKED. NEXT TO THE STALL SELLING DEEP-FRIED FURRY, BLACK SPIDERS, YOU MIGHT COME ACROSS THE LESS ALARMING SNACK OF DEEP-FRIED PRAWN SANDWICHES.

SERVES FOUR

INGREDIENTS
  3–4 shallots, roughly chopped
  4 garlic cloves, roughly chopped
  25g/1oz fresh root ginger, peeled
    and chopped
  1 lemon grass stalk, trimmed
    and chopped
  1 Thai chilli, seeded and chopped
  10ml/2 tsp sugar
  225g/8oz fresh prawns (shrimp),
    shelled and deveined
  30ml/2 tbsp *tuk trey*
  1 egg, beaten
  12 thin slices of day-old baguette
  vegetable oil, for deep-frying
  ground black pepper
  chilli oil, for drizzling

1 Using a large mortar and pestle, pound the chopped shallots, garlic, ginger, lemon grass, chilli and sugar. Add the shelled prawns and pound them too to make a paste. Mix well and bind all the ingredients with the *tuk trey* and beaten egg. Season with ground black pepper.

2 Spread the mixture on each piece of bread, patting it down firmly. In a wok, heat enough oil for deep-frying. Using a slotted spoon, lower the sandwiches, prawn side down, into the oil. Cook in batches, flipping them over so they turn golden on both sides. Drain on kitchen paper and serve hot with chilli oil.

Per portion Energy 489Kcal/2065kJ; Protein 22.5g; Carbohydrate 70.6g, of which sugars 6.3g; Fat 15g, of which saturates 2g; Cholesterol 157mg; Calcium 202mg; Fibre 3.1g; Sodium 860mg

STEAMED EGGS WITH SHRIMP PASTE

THROUGHOUT VIETNAM AND CAMBODIA, THERE ARE VARIATIONS OF THIS TYPE OF STEAMED OMELETTE COOKED AS A SNACK AT ANY TIME OF DAY. CUT INTO STRIPS AND THEN SPLASHED WITH CHILLI OIL, OR DIPPED IN A SPICY OR PUNGENT SAUCE, IT IS VERY TASTY.

<u>SERVES TWO TO FOUR</u>

INGREDIENTS
 5 eggs
 115g/4oz small, fresh prawns
  (shrimp), shelled and deveined
 a handful of beansprouts
 2 spring onions (scallions), trimmed
  and finely sliced
 10ml/2 tsp shrimp paste
 1 bunch coriander (cilantro), chopped
 15ml/1 tbsp vegetable oil
 chilli oil, for drizzling
 sea salt and ground black pepper
 fresh coriander leaves, to garnish
 dipping sauce, to serve

VARIATION
Alternatively, you could fry the omelette in a non-stick pan.

1 Beat the eggs in a bowl. Stir in the prawns, beansprouts, spring onions, shrimp paste and coriander. Season.

2 Fill a pan one-third full with water and bring to the boil. Lightly oil a shallow, heatproof dish and place on top of the pan. Pour in the egg mixture and steam for 5–10 minutes, until the eggs are firm.

3 Cut the steamed omelette into strips and place them on a plate. Drizzle a little chilli oil over them and garnish with coriander leaves.

4 Serve the omelette strips with a dipping sauce, such as the Vietnamese shrimp sauce or *nuoc cham*.

Per portion Energy 146Kcal/606kJ; Protein 13.5g; Carbohydrate 0.9g, of which sugars 0.6g; Fat 10g, of which saturates 2.3g; Cholesterol 294mg; Calcium 64mg; Fibre 0.4g; Sodium 140mg

CHILLI AND HONEY-CURED DRIED BEEF

WHEN IT COMES TO INGREDIENTS, THE VIETNAMESE WILL DRY ALMOST ANYTHING — FISH, CHILLIES, MUSHROOMS, SNAKE, MANGOES, PIGS' EARS AND BEEF ARE JUST SOME OF THEM. SOME DRIED GOODS ARE DESTINED FOR STEWS, SOUPS AND MEDICINAL PURPOSES, WHEREAS OTHERS ARE JUST FOR CHEWING ON.

SERVES FOUR

INGREDIENTS

450g/1lb beef sirloin
2 lemon grass stalks, trimmed
  and chopped
2 garlic cloves, chopped
2 dried Serrano chillies, seeded
  and chopped
30–45ml/2–3 tbsp honey
15ml/1 tbsp *nuoc mam*
30ml/2 tbsp soy sauce
rice wrappers, fresh herbs and
  dipping sauce, to serve (optional)

1 Trim the beef and cut it across the grain into thin, rectangular slices, then set aside.

2 Using a mortar and pestle, grind the chopped lemon grass, garlic and chillies to a paste. Stir in the honey, *nuoc mam* and soy sauce. Put the beef into a bowl, add the paste and rub it into the meat. Spread out the meat on a wire rack and place it in the refrigerator, uncovered, for 2 days, or until dry and hard.

3 Cook the dried beef on the barbecue or under a conventional grill (broiler), and serve it as a snack on its own or with rice wrappers, fresh herbs and a dipping sauce.

COOK'S TIP
Drying is an ancient method of preserving food, which also intensifies the flavour or potency of most ingredients. In hot countries beef can be dried quickly in the sun, but in cooler areas it dries more slowly, so needs to be put in the refrigerator to prevent it going off.

VARIATION
This recipe also works well with venison. Cut the meat into thin strips and you have a South-east Asian version of the South African *biltong*.

Per portion Energy 138Kcal/581kJ; Protein 18g; Carbohydrate 9g, of which sugars 8g; Fat 3g, of which saturates 2g; Cholesterol 38mg; Calcium 7mg; Fibre 0.1g; Sodium 40mg

BACON-WRAPPED BEEF ᴏɴ SKEWERS

IN NORTHERN VIETNAM, BEEF OFTEN FEATURES ON THE STREET MENU. GRILLED, STIR-FRIED, OR SITTING MAJESTICALLY IN A STEAMING BOWL OF PHO, BEEF IS USED WITH PRIDE. IN CAMBODIA AND SOUTHERN VIETNAM, SNACKS LIKE THIS ONE WOULD NORMALLY BE MADE WITH PORK OR CHICKEN.

SERVES FOUR

INGREDIENTS
    225g/8oz beef fillet or rump, cut
      across the grain into 12 strips
    12 thin strips of streaky (fatty) bacon
    ground black pepper
    4 bamboo skewers, soaked in water
    nuoc cham, for dipping
For the marinade
    15ml/1 tbsp groundnut (peanut) oil
    30ml/2 tbsp *nuoc mam*
    30ml/2 tbsp soy sauce
    4–6 garlic cloves, crushed
    10ml/2 tsp sugar

1 To make the marinade, mix all the marinade ingredients in a large bowl until the sugar dissolves. Season generously with black pepper. Add the beef strips, coating them in the marinade, and set aside for about an hour.

2 Preheat a griddle pan over a high heat. Roll up each strip of beef and wrap it in a slice of bacon. Thread the rolls on to the skewers, so that you have three on each one.

3 Cook the bacon-wrapped rolls for 4–5 minutes, turning once, until the bacon is golden and crispy. Serve immediately, with a bowl of *nuoc cham* for dipping

Per portion Energy 279Kcal/1155kJ; Protein 21.7g; Carbohydrate 1.0g, of which sugars 1.0g; Fat 21.3g, of which saturates 7.1g; Cholesterol 69mg; Calcium 6mg; Fibre 0g; Sodium 750mg

DRY-COOKED PORK STRIPS

THIS CAMBODIAN DISH IS QUICK AND LIGHT ON A HOT DAY. PORK, CHICKEN, PRAWNS (SHRIMP) AND SQUID CAN ALL BE COOKED THIS WAY. WITH THE LETTUCE AND HERBS, IT'S A VERY FLAVOURSOME SNACK, BUT YOU CAN SERVE IT WITH A DIPPING SAUCE, IF YOU LIKE.

SERVES TWO TO FOUR

INGREDIENTS
  15ml/1 tbsp groundnut (peanut) oil
  30ml/2 tbsp *tuk trey*
  30ml/2 tbsp soy sauce
  5ml/1 tsp sugar
  225g/8oz pork fillet, cut into thin,
    bitesize strips
  8 lettuce leaves
  chilli oil, for drizzling
  fresh coriander (cilantro) leaves
  a handful of fresh mint leaves

VARIATION
Try basil, flat leaf parsley, spring onions
or sliced red onion in these parcels.

1 In a wok or heavy pan, heat the oil, *tuk trey* and soy sauce with the sugar. Add the pork and stir-fry over a medium heat, until all the liquid has evaporated. Cook the pork until it turns brown, almost caramelized, but not burnt.

2 Drop spoonfuls of the cooked pork into lettuce leaves, drizzle a little chilli oil over the top, add a few coriander and mint leaves, wrap them up and serve immediately.

Per portion Energy 96Kcal/401kJ; Protein 12.2g; Carbohydrate 0.4g, of which sugars 0.4g; Fat 5g, of which saturates 1.1g; Cholesterol 35mg; Calcium 7mg; Fibre 0.1g; Sodium 300mg

PORK PÂTÉ IN A BANANA LEAF

This pâté, cha lua, has a Vietnamese twist: it is steamed in banana leaves and has a slightly springy texture and delicate flavour. Baguettes are a common sight alongside the noodles and vegetables in southern markets and frequently eaten smeared with pâté.

SERVES SIX

INGREDIENTS

- 45ml/3 tbsp *nuoc mam*
- 30ml/2 tbsp vegetable or sesame oil
- 15ml/1 tbsp sugar
- 10ml/2 tsp five-spice powder
- 2 shallots, peeled and finely chopped
- 2 garlic cloves, crushed
- 750g/1lb 10oz/3¼ cups minced (ground) pork
- 25g/1oz/¼ cup potato starch
- 7.5ml/1½ tsp baking powder
- 1 banana leaf, trimmed into a strip 25cm/10in wide
- vegetable oil, for brushing
- salt and ground black pepper
- *nuoc cham* and a baguette or salad, to serve

1 In a bowl, beat the *nuoc mam* and oil with the sugar and five-spice powder. Once the sugar has dissolved, stir in the shallots and garlic. Add the minced pork and seasoning, and knead well until thoroughly combined. Cover and chill for 2–3 hours.

2 Knead the mixture again, thumping it down into the bowl to remove any air. Add the potato starch and baking powder and knead until smooth and pasty. Mould the pork mixture into a fat sausage, about 18cm/7in long, and place it on an oiled dish.

COOK'S TIP

You can find banana leaves in African, Caribbean and Asian markets. To prepare them, trim the leaves to fit the steamer, using a pair of scissors, making sure that there is enough to fold over the pâté. If you cannot find banana leaves, you can use large spring green (collard) leaves, or several Savoy cabbage leaves instead.

VARIATION

This pâté can also be added to soups and stir-fried dishes, in which it is complemented by fresh herbs and spices, or it can be fried with eggs.

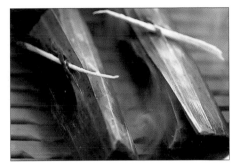

3 Lay the banana leaf on a flat surface, brush it with a little vegetable oil, and place the pork sausage across it. Lift up the edge of the banana leaf nearest to you and fold it over the sausage mixture, tuck in the sides, and roll it up into a firm, tight bundle. Secure the bundle with a piece of string, so that it doesn't unravel during the cooking process.

4 Fill a wok one-third full with water. Balance a bamboo steamer, with its lid on, above the level of the water. Bring to the boil, lift the lid and place the banana leaf bundle on the rack, being careful not to burn yourself. Re-cover and steam for 45 minutes. Leave the pâté to cool in the leaf, open it up and cut it into slices. Drizzle with *nuoc cham*, and serve with a baguette or salad.

Per portion Energy 234Kcal/978kJ; Protein 28g; Carbohydrate 8g, of which sugars 3g; Fat 10g, of which saturates 2g; Cholesterol 79mg; Calcium 46mg; Fibre 0.4g; Sodium 700mg

SINGAPORE NOODLES

THE VIETNAMESE HAVE PUT THEIR OWN PARTICULARLY DELICIOUS STAMP ON SINGAPORE NOODLES, WHICH ARE POPULAR THROUGHOUT SOUTH-EAST ASIA. IN HO CHI MINH CITY, THE NOODLES ARE STANDARD STREET AND CAFÉ FOOD, AN IDEAL SNACK FOR ANYONE FEELING A LITTLE PECKISH.

SERVES FOUR

INGREDIENTS

   30ml/2 tbsp sesame oil
   1 onion, finely chopped
   3 garlic cloves, finely chopped
   3–4 green or red Thai chillies,
     seeded and finely chopped
   4cm/1½in fresh root ginger,
     peeled and finely chopped
   6 spring onions (scallions),
     finely chopped
   1 skinless chicken breast fillet,
     cut into bitesize strips
   90g/3½oz pork, cut into bitesize
     strips
   90g/3½oz prawns (shrimp), shelled
   2 tomatoes, skinned, seeded
     and chopped
   30ml/2 tbsp tamarind paste
   15ml/1 tbsp *nuoc mam*
   grated rind and juice of 1 lime
   10ml/2 tsp sugar
   150ml/¼ pint/⅔ cup water or
     fish stock
   225g/8oz fresh rice sticks
     (vermicelli)
   salt and ground black pepper
   1 bunch each fresh basil and mint,
     stalks removed, and *nuoc cham*,
     to serve

1 Heat a wok or heavy pan and add the oil. Stir in the onion, garlic, chillies and ginger, and cook until they begin to colour. Add the spring onions and cook for 1 minute, add the chicken and pork, and cook for 1–2 minutes, then stir in the prawns.

2 Add the tomatoes, followed by the tamarind paste, *nuoc mam*, lime rind and juice, and sugar. Pour in the water or fish stock, and cook gently for 2–3 minutes. Bubble up the liquid to reduce it.

VARIATIONS
• At the Singapore noodle stalls, batches of cold, cooked noodles are kept ready to add to the delicious concoction cooking in the wok. At home, you can make this dish with any kind of noodles – egg or rice, fresh or dried.
• Cured Chinese sausage and snails, or strips of squid, are sometimes added to the mixture to ring the changes.

3 Meanwhile, toss the noodles in a large pan of boiling water and cook for a few minutes until tender.

4 Drain the noodles and add to the chicken and prawn mixture. Season with salt and ground black pepper.

5 Serve immediately, with basil and mint leaves scattered over the top, and drizzled with spoonfuls of *nuoc cham*.

COOK'S TIP
It's important to serve this dish immediately once the noodles have been added, otherwise they will go soft.

Per portion Energy 420Kcal/1756kJ; Protein 23g; Carbohydrate 59g, of which sugars 9g; Fat 10g, of which saturates 2g; Cholesterol 86mg; Calcium 119mg; Fibre 1.3g; Sodium 500mg

FISH AND SHELLFISH

With Vietnam's long coastline, Cambodia's huge lake, the Tonlé
Sap, and many rivers including the mighty Mekong that they
share, both countries enjoy an abundance of varied saltwater
and freshwater fish and shellfish. Marinated, or cooked, in
coconut milk, with liberal quantities of ginger, garlic and
chillies, as well as aromatic herbs, recipes such as Sea Bass
Steamed in Coconut Milk with Ginger, Cashew Nuts and Basil
are easy to prepare at home.

HANOI FRIED FISH <u>WITH</u> DILL

THE NORTH OF VIETNAM IS WELL KNOWN FOR ITS USE OF PUNGENT HERBS, SO MUCH SO THAT A DISH OF NOODLES CAN BE SERVED PLAIN, DRESSED ONLY WITH CORIANDER AND BASIL. IN THIS POPULAR DISH FROM HANOI, CHA CA HANOI, THE DILL COMPLEMENTS THE FISH BEAUTIFULLY.

SERVES FOUR

INGREDIENTS
- 75g/3oz/⅔ cup rice flour
- 7.5ml/1½ tsp ground turmeric
- 500g/1¼ lb white fish fillets, such as cod, skinned and cut into chunks
- vegetable oil, for deep-frying
- 1 large bunch fresh dill
- 15ml/1 tbsp groundnut (peanut) oil
- 30ml/2 tbsp roasted peanuts
- 4 spring onions (scallions), cut into bitesize pieces
- 1 small bunch fresh basil, stalks removed, leaves chopped
- 1 small bunch fresh coriander (cilantro), stalks removed
- cooked rice, 1 lime, cut into wedges, and *nuoc cham*, to serve

1 Mix the flour with the ground turmeric and toss the chunks of fish in it until they are well coated. Heat the oil in a wok or a large heavy pan and cook the fish in batches until crisp and golden. Use a perforated ladle to remove the fish from the oil, and drain on kitchen paper.

2 Scatter some of the dill fronds on a serving dish, arrange the fish on top and keep warm. Chop some of the remaining dill fronds and set aside for the garnish.

3 Heat the groundnut oil in a small wok or frying pan. Stir in the peanuts and cook for 1 minute, then add the spring onions, the remaining dill fronds, basil and coriander. Stir-fry for no more than 30 seconds, then spoon the herbs and peanuts over the fish. Garnish with the chopped dill and serve with lime wedges and *nuoc cham* to drizzle over the top.

Per portion Energy 350Kcal/1458kJ; Protein 27g; Carbohydrate 17g, of which sugars 1g; Fat 19g, of which saturates 3g; Cholesterol 85mg; Calcium 112mg; Fibre 1.2g; Sodium 200mg

CATFISH COOKED IN A CLAY POT

WONDERFULLY EASY AND TASTY, THIS SOUTHERN-STYLE VIETNAMESE AND CAMBODIAN DISH, CALLED CA KHO TO, IS A CLASSIC. IN THE SOUTH OF VIETNAM, CLAY POTS ARE REGULARLY USED FOR COOKING AND THEY ENHANCE BOTH THE LOOK AND TASTE OF THIS TRADITIONAL DISH.

SERVES FOUR

INGREDIENTS
30ml/2 tbsp sugar
15ml/1 tbsp sesame or vegetable oil
2 garlic cloves, crushed
45ml/3 tbsp *nuoc mam*
350g/12oz catfish fillets, cut
  diagonally into 2 or 3 pieces
4 spring onions (scallions), cut
  into bitesize pieces
ground black pepper
chopped fresh coriander (cilantro),
  to garnish
fresh bread, to serve

1 Place the sugar in a clay pot or heavy pan, and add 15ml/1 tbsp water to wet it. Heat the sugar until it begins to turn golden brown, then add the oil and crushed garlic.

2 Stir the *nuoc mam* into the caramel mixture and add 120ml/4fl oz/¹/2 cup boiling water, then toss in the catfish pieces, making sure they are well coated with the sauce. Cover the pot, reduce the heat and simmer for about 5 minutes.

3 Remove the lid, season with ground black pepper and gently stir in the spring onions. Simmer for a further 3–4 minutes to thicken the sauce, garnish with fresh coriander, and serve immediately straight from the pot with chunks of fresh bread.

Per portion Energy 126Kcal/533kJ; Protein 16g; Carbohydrate 10g, of which sugars 8g; Fat 3g, of which saturates 0g; Cholesterol 40mg; Calcium 25mg; Fibre 0.2g; Sodium 600mg

SOUR CARP WITH TAMARIND, GALANGAL, BASIL AND CORIANDER

THIS RIVER CARP DISH IS POPULAR IN BOTH CAMBODIA AND VIETNAM. IF YOU WANT TO MAKE A SLIGHTLY SIMPLER VERSION, YOU COULD JUST TOSS THE COOKED FISH IN THE HERBS AND SERVE IT WITH NOODLES OR RICE AND A SALAD.

SERVES FOUR

INGREDIENTS
- 500g/1¼lb carp fillets, cut into 3 or 4 pieces
- 30ml/2 tbsp sesame or vegetable oil
- 10ml/2 tsp ground turmeric
- 1 small bunch each fresh coriander (cilantro) and basil, stalks removed
- 20 lettuce leaves or rice wrappers
- *nuoc mam* or other dipping sauce, to serve

For the marinade
- 30ml/2 tbsp tamarind paste
- 15ml/1 tbsp soy sauce
- juice of 1 lime
- 1 green or red Thai chilli, finely chopped
- 2.5cm/1in galangal root, peeled and grated
- a few sprigs of fresh coriander (cilantro) leaves, finely chopped

1 Prepare the marinade by mixing together all the marinade ingredients in a bowl. Toss the fish pieces in the marinade, cover with clear film (plastic wrap) and chill in the refrigerator for at least 6 hours, or overnight.

COOK'S TIP
Any freshwater fish can be used for this recipe but, because it is stirred in a wok, you will need one with firm, thick flesh, such as catfish or barb. Allow plenty of time for the fish to marinate and soak up the flavours.

2 Lift the pieces of fish out of the marinade and lay them on a plate. Heat a wok or heavy pan, add the oil and stir in the turmeric. Working quickly, so that the turmeric doesn't burn, add the fish pieces, gently moving them around the wok for 2–3 minutes. Add any remaining marinade to the pan and cook for a further 2–3 minutes, or until the pieces of fish are cooked through.

3 To serve, divide the fish among four plates, sprinkle with the coriander and basil, and add some of the lettuce leaves or rice wrappers and a small bowl of dipping sauce to each serving. To eat, tear off a bitesize piece of fish, place it on a wrapper with a few herb leaves, fold it up into a roll, then dip it into the sauce.

Per portion Energy 298Kcal/1246kJ; Protein 24g; Carbohydrate 19g, of which sugars 5g; Fat 14g, of which saturates 2g; Cholesterol 121mg; Calcium 120mg; Fibre 0g; Sodium 300mg

EEL BRAISED IN A CARAMEL SAUCE WITH BUTTERNUT SQUASH

ALTHOUGH THIS DISH IS FOUND IN MANY PARTS OF VIETNAM, IT IS TRADITIONALLY A NORTHERN DISH AND IT IS THERE, IN THE HIGHLANDS, THAT IT IS BEST SAMPLED. THE EELS ARE CAUGHT IN THE RED, BLACK AND SONG MA RIVERS, AND THE LOCAL NAME OF THE DISH IS "THREE RIVERS EEL".

SERVES FOUR

INGREDIENTS
    45ml/3 tbsp raw cane sugar
    30ml/2 tbsp soy sauce
    45ml/3 tbsp *nuoc mam*
    2 garlic cloves, crushed
    2 dried chillies
    2–3 star anise
    4–5 black peppercorns
    350g/12oz eel on the bone, skinned,
        cut into 2.5cm/1in-thick chunks
    200g/7oz butternut squash, cut into
        bitesize chunks
    4 spring onions (scallions), cut into
        bitesize pieces
    30ml/2 tbsp sesame or vegetable oil
    5cm/2in fresh root ginger, peeled
        and cut into matchsticks
    salt
    cooked rice or noodles,
        to serve

2 Add the eel chunks, squash and spring onions, making sure the fish is well coated in the sauce, and season with salt. Reduce the heat, cover the pan and simmer gently for about 20 minutes, until the eel and vegetables are tender.

3 Meanwhile, heat a small wok, pour in the oil and stir-fry the ginger until crisp and golden. Remove and drain on kitchen paper.

4 Serve with rice or noodles, with the crispy ginger sprinkled on top.

1 Put the sugar in a wok or heavy pan with 30ml/2 tbsp water, and gently heat it until it turns golden. Remove the pan from the heat and stir in the soy sauce and *nuoc mam* with 120ml/4fl oz/½ cup water. Add the garlic, chillies, star anise and peppercorns and return to the heat.

COOK'S TIP
If you can't find eel, use mackerel for this dish. The fat rendered from these fish melts into the caramel sauce, making it deliciously velvety. It is often served with chopped fresh coriander (cilantro) on top.

Per portion Energy 204Kcal/857kJ; Protein 11g; Carbohydrate 20g, of which sugars 14g; Fat 10g, of which saturates 1g; Cholesterol 0mg; Calcium 76mg; Fibre 1g; Sodium 110mg

JUNGLE FISH COOKED IN BANANA LEAVES

STEAMING FRESHWATER FISH IN BANANA LEAVES OVER HOT CHARCOAL IS A TRADITIONAL METHOD OF COOKING IN THE JUNGLE. BANANA LEAVES ARE LARGE AND TOUGH, AND SERVE AS BASIC COOKING VESSELS AND WRAPPERS FOR ALL SORTS OF FISH AND MEAT.

SERVES FOUR

INGREDIENTS
    350g/12oz freshwater fish fillets,
      such as trout, cut into
      bitesize chunks
    6 banana leaves
    vegetable oil, for brushing
    sticky rice, noodles or salad, to serve
For the marinade
    2 shallots
    5cm/2in turmeric root, peeled
      and grated
    2 spring onions (scallions),
      finely sliced
    2 garlic cloves, crushed
    1–2 green Thai chillies, seeded
      and finely chopped
    15ml/1 tbsp *nuoc mam*
    2.5ml/½ tsp raw cane sugar
    salt and ground black pepper

1 To make the marinade, grate the shallots into a bowl, then combine with the other marinade ingredients, Season with salt and pepper. Toss the chunks of fish in the marinade, then cover and chill for 6 hours, or overnight.

VARIATION
This dish can be made with any of the catfish or carp family, or even talapia.

2 Prepare a barbecue. Place one of the banana leaves on a flat surface and brush it with oil. Place the marinated fish on the banana leaf, spreading it out evenly, then fold over the sides to form an envelope. Place this envelope, fold side down, on top of another leaf and fold that one in the same manner. Repeat with the remaining leaves until they are all used up.

3 Secure the last layer of banana leaf with a piece of bendy wire. Place the banana leaf packet on the barbecue. Cook for about 20 minutes, turning it over from time to time to make sure it is cooked on both sides – the outer leaves will burn. Carefully untie the wire (it will be hot) and unravel the packet. Check that the fish is cooked and serve with sticky rice, noodles or salad.

COOK'S TIP
Banana leaves are available in some African and Asian stores and markets. If you can't find them, wrap the fish in vine leaves that have been soaked in cold water, or large flexible cabbage leaves. You can also use foil.

Per portion Energy 155Kcal/648kJ; Protein 18g; Carbohydrate 4g, of which sugars 2g; Fat 8g, of which saturates 1g; Cholesterol 59mg; Calcium 36mg; Fibre 0.7g; Sodium 200mg

FISH ᴵᴺ COCONUT CUSTARD

THIS IS A KHMER CLASSIC. RICH AND SUMPTUOUS, AMOK TREY CROPS UP ALL OVER CAMBODIA. IN PHNOM PENH, THERE ARE RESTAURANTS THAT SPECIALIZE IN IT. THE FISH IS STEAMED IN A CUSTARD, MADE WITH COCONUT MILK AND FLAVOURED WITH THE CAMBODIAN HERBAL PASTE, KROEUNG.

SERVES FOUR

INGREDIENTS
  2 x 400ml/14oz cans coconut milk
  3 eggs
  80ml/3fl oz *kroeung*
  15ml/1 tbsp *tuk trey*
  10ml/2 tsp palm sugar or honey
  1 kg/2¼ lb fresh, skinned white fish
    fillets, cut into 8 pieces
  1 small bunch chopped fresh
    coriander (cilantro), plus a few
    whole sprigs, to garnish
  jasmine rice or crusty bread and
    salad, to serve

VARIATION
If you don't have a big enough steamer, this dish can be cooked in the oven in a bain marie. Cook at 160°C/325°F/Gas 3 for about 50 minutes.

1 Half fill a wok or large pan with water. Set a bamboo or stainless steel steamer over it and put the lid on. Bring the water to the boil.

2 In a bowl, beat the coconut milk with the eggs, *kroeung*, *tuk trey* and sugar or honey, until it is well blended and the sugar has dissolved.

3 Place the fish fillets in a heatproof dish that will fit in the steamer. Pour the coconut mixture over the fish and place the dish in the steamer. Put the lid back on the steamer and reduce the heat so that the custard won't curdle. Steam over gently simmering water until the fish is cooked. Garnish with coriander and serve immediately with jasmine rice or crusty bread and salad.

Per portion Energy 309Kcal/1304kJ; Protein 51.1g; Carbohydrate 12.4g, of which sugars 12.4g; Fat 6.5g, of which saturates 1.8g; Cholesterol 258mg; Calcium 103mg; Fibre 0g; Sodium 400mg

GRILLED EEL WRAPPED IN BACON WITH LEMON GRASS AND GINGER

WITH SO MANY RIVERS IN VIETNAM AND CAMBODIA, FRESHWATER EEL IS JUST AS POPULAR AS CATFISH AND CARP. FIRM-FLESHED AND RICH IN FLAVOUR, EEL IS DELICIOUS GRILLED, BRAISED, OR STIR-FRIED. THIS RECIPE IS BEST SERVED WITH A DIPPING SAUCE, A CRUNCHY SALAD, AND JASMINE RICE.

SERVES FOUR TO SIX

INGREDIENTS

    2 lemon grass stalks, trimmed
      and chopped
    25g/1oz fresh root ginger, peeled
      and chopped
    2 garlic cloves, chopped
    2 shallots, chopped
    15ml/1 tbsp palm sugar
    15ml/1 tbsp vegetable or groundnut
      (peanut) oil
    30ml/2 tbsp *nuoc mam* or *tuk trey*
    1.2kg/2½lb fresh eel, skinned and
      cut into 2.5cm/1in pieces
    12 slices streaky (fatty) bacon
    freshly ground black pepper
    a small bunch of fresh coriander
      (cilantro) leaves, to garnish
    nuoc cham, for dipping

1 Using a mortar and pestle, pound the lemon grass, ginger, garlic and shallots with the sugar to form a paste. Add the oil and *nuoc mam* or *tuk trey*, mix well and season with black pepper. Put the eel pieces in a dish and smear them thoroughly in this paste. Cover and place in the refrigerator for 2–3 hours to marinate.

2 Wrap each piece of marinated eel in a strip of bacon, gathering up as much of the marinade as possible.

3 To cook the eel parcels, you can use a conventional grill, a well-oiled griddle pan, or a barbecue. If grilling over charcoal, you can skewer the eel parcels; otherwise, spread them over the grill (broiler) or griddle pan. Cook the eel parcels until nice and crispy, roughly 2–3 minutes on each side. Serve with fresh coriander leaves and *nuoc cham* for dipping.

COOK'S TIP

When buying fresh eel, it's worth asking the fishmonger to gut it, cut off the head, bone it, skin it and slice it for you – it makes life easier!

Per portion Energy 460Kcal/1911kJ; Protein 39.3g; Carbohydrate 0.8g, of which sugars 0.6g; Fat 33.3g, of which saturates 9g; Cholesterol 324mg; Calcium 43mg; Fibre 0.1g; Sodium 650mg

CHARCOAL-GRILLED FISH CAMBODIAN-STYLE

A WHOLE FISH GRILLED OVER CHARCOAL IS KNOWN AS TREI AING *AND IT IS USUALLY SERVED WITH SALAD LEAVES, HERBS, CHOPPED PEANUTS, AND A STRONG-FLAVOURED SAUCE. CHUNKS OF THE COOKED FISH ARE WRAPPED IN THE LEAVES AND DIPPED IN THE SAUCE.*

SERVES TWO TO FOUR

INGREDIENTS

1 good-sized fish, such as trout, snakehead, barb or carp, gutted and rinsed, head removed, if you like
225g/8oz mung beansprouts
1 bunch each fresh basil, coriander (cilantro) and mint, stalks removed, leaves chopped
1 lettuce, broken into leaves
30ml/2 tbsp roasted unsalted peanuts, finely chopped
steamed rice, to serve

For the sauce
3 garlic cloves, chopped
2 red Thai chillies, seeded and chopped
25g/1oz fresh root ginger, peeled and chopped
15ml/1 tbsp palm sugar
45ml/3 tbsp *tuk trey*
juice of 1 lime
juice of 1 coconut

3 Lay out the beansprouts, herbs and lettuce leaves on a large plate and place the peanuts in a bowl. Put everything in on the table, including the cooked fish, sauce and rice. Using chopsticks, if you like, lift up the charred skin and tear off pieces of fish. Place each piece on a lettuce leaf, sprinkle with beansprouts, herbs and peanuts, wrap it up and dip it into the sauce.

1 First prepare the sauce. Using a mortar and pestle, grind the garlic, chillies and ginger with the sugar to form a paste. Add the *tuk trey*, lime juice and coconut juice and bind well. Pour the sauce into a serving bowl.

2 Prepare the barbecue. Place the fish over the charcoal and grill it for 2–3 minutes each side, until cooked right through. Alternatively, use a conventional grill (broiler).

Per portion Energy 231Kcal/971kJ; Protein 41.2g; Carbohydrate 4.1g, of which sugars 2.5g; Fat 5.6g, of which saturates 0.9g; Cholesterol 92mg; Calcium 101mg; Fibre 3g; Sodium 130mg

SPICY PAN-SEARED TUNA WITH CUCUMBER, GARLIC AND GINGER

THIS POPULAR DISH, WHICH CAN BE FOUND ALL OVER VIETNAM IN RESTAURANTS OR AT FOOD STALLS, IS MADE WITH MANY TYPES OF THICK-FLESHED FISH. TUNA IS PARTICULARLY SUITABLE BECAUSE IT IS DELICIOUS PAN-SEARED AND SERVED A LITTLE RARE.

SERVES FOUR

INGREDIENTS
   1 small cucumber
   10ml/2 tsp sesame oil
   2 garlic cloves, crushed
   4 tuna steaks
For the dressing
   4cm/1½in fresh root ginger, peeled
     and roughly chopped
   1 garlic clove, roughly chopped
   2 green Thai chillies, seeded and
     roughly chopped
   45ml/3 tbsp raw cane sugar
   45ml/3 tbsp *nuoc mam*
   juice of 1 lime
   60ml/4 tbsp water

1 To make the dressing, grind the ginger, garlic and chillies to a pulp with the sugar, using a mortar and pestle. Stir in the *nuoc mam*, lime juice and water, and mix well. Leave the dressing to stand for 15 minutes.

2 Cut the cucumber in half lengthways and remove the seeds. Cut the flesh into long, thin strips. Toss the cucumber in the dressing and leave to soak for at least 15 minutes.

3 Wipe a heavy pan with the oil and rub the garlic around it. Heat the pan and add the tuna steaks. Sear for a few minutes on both sides, so that the outside is slightly charred but the inside is still rare. Lift the steaks on to a warm serving dish. Using tongs or chopsticks, lift the cucumber strips out of the dressing and arrange them around the steaks. Drizzle the dressing over the tuna, and serve immediately.

Per portion Energy 262Kcal/1103kJ; Protein 31g; Carbohydrate 16g, of which sugars 13g; Fat 8g, of which saturates 2g; Cholesterol 35mg; Calcium 44mg; Fibre 0.5g; Sodium 150mg

SEA BASS STEAMED IN COCONUT MILK WITH GINGER, CASHEW NUTS AND BASIL

THIS IS A DELICIOUS RECIPE FOR ANY WHOLE WHITE FISH, SUCH AS SEA BASS OR COD, OR FOR LARGE CHUNKS OF TROUT OR SALMON. YOU WILL NEED A STEAMER LARGE ENOUGH TO FIT THE WHOLE FISH OR, IF USING FISH CHUNKS, YOU CAN USE A SMALLER STEAMER AND FIT THE FISH AROUND THE BASE.

SERVES FOUR

INGREDIENTS
200ml/7fl oz coconut milk
10ml/2 tsp raw cane or muscovado (molasses) sugar
about 15ml/1 tbsp vegetable oil
2 garlic cloves, finely chopped
1 red Thai chilli, seeded and finely chopped
4cm/1½in fresh root ginger, peeled and grated
750g/1lb 10oz sea bass, gutted and skinned on one side
1 star anise, ground
1 bunch fresh basil, stalks removed
30ml/2 tbsp cashew nuts
sea salt and ground black pepper
rice and salad, to serve

1 Heat the coconut milk with the sugar in a small pan, stirring until the sugar dissolves, then remove from the heat. Heat the oil in a small frying pan and stir in the garlic, chilli and ginger. Cook until they begin to brown, then add the mixture to the coconut milk and mix well to combine.

2 Place the fish, skin side down, on a wide piece of foil and tuck up the sides to form a boat-shaped container. Using a sharp knife, cut several diagonal slashes into the flesh on the top and rub with the ground star anise. Season with salt and pepper and spoon the coconut milk over the top, making sure that the fish is well coated.

3 Scatter half the basil leaves over the top of the fish and pull the foil packet almost closed. Lay the packet in a steamer. Cover the steamer, bring the water to the boil, reduce the heat and simmer for 20–25 minutes, or until just cooked. Alternatively, place the foil packet on a baking tray and cook in a preheated oven at 180°C/350°F/Gas 4.

4 Roast the cashew nuts in the frying pan, adding extra oil if necessary. Drain the nuts on kitchen paper, then grind them to crumbs. When the fish is cooked, lift it out of the foil and transfer it to a serving dish. Spoon the cooking juices over, sprinkle with the cashew nut crumbs and garnish with the remaining basil leaves. Serve with rice and a salad.

Per portion Energy 235Kcal/983kJ; Protein 26g; Carbohydrate 8g, of which sugars 6g; Fat 11g, of which saturates 2g; Cholesterol 100mg; Calcium 217mg; Fibre 0.3g; Sodium 300mg

BABY SQUID STUFFED with PORK, MUSHROOMS, TIGER LILY BUDS and DILL

In Vietnam and Cambodia, squid is often stir-fried or stuffed. Variations of this dish can be served as an appetizer or a main course. This recipe calls for the tender baby squid to be stuffed with a dill-flavoured pork mixture. The squid can be grilled or fried.

SERVES FOUR

INGREDIENTS
- 3 dried cloud ear (wood ear) mushrooms
- 10 dried tiger lily buds
- 25g/1oz bean thread (cellophane) noodles
- 8 baby squid
- 350g/12oz minced (ground) pork
- 3–4 shallots, finely chopped
- 4 garlic cloves, finely chopped
- 1 bunch dill fronds, finely chopped
- 30ml/2 tbsp *nuoc mam*
- 5ml/1 tsp palm sugar
- ground black pepper
- vegetable or groundnut (peanut) oil, for frying
- coriander (cilantro) leaves, to garnish
- *nuoc cham*, for drizzling

2 Meanwhile, prepare the squid one at a time. Hold the body sac in one hand, hold the head with the other and pull it off. Pull out the backbone and rinse out the body sac. Peel off the outer membrane, pat the body sac dry, and put aside. Sever the tentacles from the head. Discard the head and chop the tentacles. Repeat with the other squid.

4 In a small bowl, stir the *nuoc mam* with the sugar, until it dissolves completely. Add it to the mixture in the bowl and mix well. Season with ground black pepper.

1 Soak the mushrooms, tiger lily buds and bean thread noodles in lukewarm water for about 15 minutes, until they have softened.

3 Drain the soaked tree ear mushrooms, tiger lily buds and bean thread noodles. Squeeze them in kitchen paper to get rid of any excess water, then chop them finely and put them in a bowl. Add the chopped tentacles, minced pork, shallots, garlic and three-quarters of the dill. Mix well.

COOK'S TIPS
- Instead of frying the squid, you can cook them over a charcoal or conventional grill (broiler).
- Served on a platter, these baby squid are an impressive sight at parties.

5 Using your fingers, stuff the pork mixture into each squid, packing it in firmly. Leave a little gap at the end to sew together with a needle and cotton thread or to skewer with a cocktail stick (toothpick) so that the filling doesn't spill out on cooking.

6 Heat some oil in a large wok or heavy pan, and fry the squid for about 5 minutes, turning them from time to time. Pierce each one several times to release any excess water – this will cause the oil to spit, so take care when doing this; you may wish to use a spatterproof lid. Continue cooking for a further 10 minutes, until the squid are nicely browned. Serve whole or thinly sliced, garnished with the remaining dill and coriander, and drizzled with *nuoc cham*.

Per portion Energy 315Kcal/1311kJ; Protein 25g; Carbohydrate 7.9g, of which sugars 1.9g; Fat 20.4g, of which saturates 4.6g; Cholesterol 170mg; Calcium 18mg; Fibre 0.2g; Sodium 110mg

GRIDDLED SQUID AND TOMATOES IN A TAMARIND DRESSING

THIS IS A LOVELY VIETNAMESE DISH — SWEET, CHARRED SQUID SERVED IN A TANGY DRESSING MADE WITH TAMARIND, LIME AND NUOC MAM. IT IS BEST MADE WITH BABY SQUID BECAUSE THEY ARE TENDER AND SWEET. THE TOMATOES AND HERBS ADD WONDERFUL FRESH FLAVOURS.

2 Heat a ridged griddle, wipe the pan with a little oil, and griddle the tomatoes until lightly charred on both sides. Transfer them to a board, chop into bitesize chunks, and place in a bowl.

3 Clean the griddle, then heat it up again and wipe with a little more oil. Griddle the squid for 2–3 minutes each side, pressing them down with a spatula, until nicely browned. Transfer to the bowl with the tomatoes, add the herbs and the dressing and toss well. Serve immediately.

SERVES FOUR

INGREDIENTS
vegetable oil, for greasing
2 large tomatoes, skinned, halved
    and seeded
500g/1¼lb fresh baby squid
1 bunch each fresh basil, coriander
    (cilantro) and mint, stalks removed,
    leaves chopped
For the dressing
15ml/1 tbsp tamarind paste
juice of half a lime
30ml/2 tbsp *nuoc mam*
15ml/1 tbsp raw cane sugar
1 garlic clove, crushed
2 shallots, halved and finely sliced
2 Serrano chillies, seeded and sliced

1 Put the dressing ingredients in a bowl and stir until well mixed. Set aside.

VARIATION
Traditionally, the squid are steamed for this dish: you can steam them for 10–15 minutes, if you prefer.

COOK'S TIPS
• To prepare squid yourself, get a firm hold of the head and pull it from the body. Reach down inside the body sac and pull out the transparent backbone, as well as any stringy parts. Rinse the body sac inside and out and pat dry. Cut the tentacles off above the eyes and add to the pile of squid you're going to cook. Discard everything else.
• Griddled scallops and prawns (shrimp) are also delicious in this tangy dressing.

Per portion Energy 165Kcal/701kJ; Protein 22g; Carbohydrate 15g, of which sugars 10g; Fat 3g, of which saturates 1g; Cholesterol 281mg; Calcium 105mg; Fibre 1g; Sodium 500mg

PRAWN AND CAULIFLOWER CURRY WITH FENUGREEK, COCONUT AND LIME

THIS IS A BASIC FISHERMAN'S CURRY FROM THE SOUTHERN COAST OF VIETNAM. SIMPLE TO MAKE, IT WOULD USUALLY BE EATEN FROM A COMMUNAL BOWL, OR FROM THE WOK ITSELF, AND SERVED WITH NOODLES, RICE OR CHUNKS OF BAGUETTE TO MOP UP THE DELICIOUSLY FRAGRANT, CREAMY SAUCE.

SERVES FOUR

INGREDIENTS

- 450g/1lb raw tiger prawns (jumbo shrimp), shelled and cleaned
- juice of 1 lime
- 15ml/1 tbsp sesame or vegetable oil
- 1 red onion, roughly chopped
- 2 garlic cloves, roughly chopped
- 2 Thai chillies, seeded and chopped
- 1 cauliflower, broken into florets
- 5ml/1 tsp sugar
- 2 star anise, dry-fried and ground
- 10ml/2 tsp fenugreek, dry-fried and ground
- 450ml/¾ pint/2 cups coconut milk
- 1 bunch fresh coriander (cilantro), stalks removed, leaves chopped, to garnish
- salt and ground black pepper

1 In a bowl, toss the prawns in the lime juice and set aside. Heat a wok or heavy pan and add the oil. Stir in the onion, garlic and chillies. As they brown, add the cauliflower. Stir-fry for 2–3 minutes.

VARIATION
Other popular combinations include prawns with butternut squash or pumpkin.

2 Toss in the sugar and spices. Add the coconut milk, stirring to make sure it is thoroughly combined. Reduce the heat and simmer for 10–15 minutes, or until the liquid has reduced and thickened a little. Add the prawns and lime juice and cook for 1–2 minutes, or until the prawns turn opaque. Season to taste, and sprinkle with coriander. Serve hot.

Per portion Energy 232Kcal/971kJ; Protein 25g; Carbohydrate 13g, of which sugars 12g; Fat 10g, of which saturates 2g; Cholesterol 219mg; Calcium 167mg; Fibre 2.2g; Sodium 500mg

MUSSELS STEAMED WITH CHILLI, GINGER LEAVES AND LEMON GRASS

THIS DISH, CALLED SO HAP XA, IS VIETNAM'S VERSION OF THE FRENCH CLASSIC, MOULES MARINIÈRE. HERE THE MUSSELS ARE STEAMED OPEN IN A HERB-INFUSED STOCK WITH LEMON GRASS AND CHILLI INSTEAD OF WINE AND PARSLEY.

SERVES FOUR

INGREDIENTS
    600ml/1 pint/2½ cups chicken stock
       or beer, or a mixture of the two
    1 Thai chilli, seeded and chopped
    2 shallots, finely chopped
    3 lemon grass stalks,
       finely chopped
    1 bunch ginger or basil leaves
    1kg/2¼lb fresh mussels, cleaned and
       bearded
    salt and ground black pepper

COOK'S TIP
Aromatic ginger leaves are hard to find outside Asia. If you can't find them, basil or coriander (cilantro) will work well.

1 Pour the stock or beer into a deep pan. Add the chilli, shallots, lemon grass and most of the ginger or basil leaves, retaining a few leaves for the garnish Bring to the boil. Cover and simmer for 10–15 minutes, then season to taste.

2 Discard any mussels that remain open when tapped, then add the remaining mussels to the stock. Stir well, cover and cook for 2 minutes, or until the mussels have opened. Discard any that remain closed. Ladle the mussels and cooking liquid into individual bowls.

Per portion Energy 73Kcal/311kJ; Protein 11g; Carbohydrate 3g, of which sugars 1g; Fat 2g, of which saturates 0g; Cholesterol 36mg; Calcium 37mg; Fibre 0.7g; Sodium 700mg

SHELLFISH CURRY <u>WITH</u> COCONUT MILK <u>AND</u> BASIL

THIS RECIPE IS MADE WITH PRAWNS, SQUID AND SCALLOPS BUT YOU COULD USE ANY COMBINATION OF SHELLFISH, OR EVEN ADD CHUNKS OF FILLETED FISH. SERVE WITH STEAMED RICE OR BAGUETTES BROKEN INTO CHUNKS, WITH A FEW EXTRA CHILLIES TO MUNCH ON THE SIDE.

SERVES FOUR

INGREDIENTS

    4cm/1½ in fresh root ginger, peeled
      and roughly chopped
    3 garlic cloves, roughly chopped
    45ml/3 tbsp groundnut (peanut) oil
    1 onion, finely sliced
    2 lemon grass stalks, finely sliced
    2 green or red Thai chillies, seeded
      and finely sliced
    15ml/1 tbsp raw cane sugar
    10ml/2 tsp shrimp paste
    15ml/1 tbsp *nuoc mam*
    30ml/2 tbsp curry powder or
      garam masala
    550ml/18fl oz/2½ cups coconut milk
    grated rind and juice of 1 lime
    4 medium-sized squid, cleaned
      and cut diagonally into 3 or 4
      pieces
    12 king or queen scallops, shelled
    20 large raw prawns (shrimp), shelled
      and deveined
    1 small bunch fresh basil,
      stalks removed
    1 small bunch fresh coriander
      (cilantro), stalks removed, leaves
      finely chopped, to garnish
    salt

1 Using a mortar and pestle, grind the ginger with the garlic until it almost resembles a paste. Heat the oil in a flameproof clay pot, wok or heavy pan and stir in the onion. Cook until it begins to turn brown, then stir in the garlic and ginger paste.

2 Once the fragrant aromas begin to rise, add the sliced lemon grass, sliced chillies and raw cane sugar. Cook briefly before adding the Vietnamese or Thai shrimp paste, *nuoc mam* and curry powder or garam masala. Mix thoroughly with a wooden spoon and stir-fry gently for 1–2 minutes.

3 Add the coconut milk, lime rind and juice. Mix well and bring to the boil. Cook, stirring, for 2–3 minutes. Season to taste with salt.

4 Gently stir in the squid, scallops and prawns and bring to the boil once more. Reduce the heat and cook gently until the shellfish turns opaque. Stir in the basil leaves and sprinkle the chopped coriander over the top. Serve immediately from the pot.

COOK'S TIP

To devein the prawns, first peel off the shells, then make a shallow cut down the centre of the curved back of each prawn. Carefully pull out the black vein with a cocktail stick (toothpick) or your fingers, then rinse the deveined prawns well.

Per portion Energy 528Kcal/2225kJ; Protein 68g; Carbohydrate 24g, of which sugars 14g; Fat 18g, of which saturates 4g; Cholesterol 699mg; Calcium 250mg; Fibre 2.5g; Sodium 1300mg

BAKED STUFFED CRAB SHELLS

THE VIETNAMESE HAVE MADE THIS FRENCH-INSPIRED DISH THEIR OWN WITH A COMBINATION OF BEAN THREAD NOODLES AND CLOUD EAR MUSHROOMS. IT IS TIME-CONSUMING TO COOK THE CRABS YOURSELF, SO USE FRESHLY COOKED CRAB MEAT FROM YOUR FISHMONGER OR SUPERMARKET.

SERVES FOUR

INGREDIENTS

 25g/1oz dried bean thread
  (cellophane) noodles
 6 dried cloud ear (wood ear)
  mushrooms
 450g/1lb fresh crab meat
 15ml/1 tbsp vegetable oil
 10ml/2 tsp *nuoc mam*
 2 shallots, finely chopped
 2 garlic cloves, finely chopped
 2.5cm/1in fresh root ginger, peeled
  and grated
 1 small bunch coriander (cilantro),
  stalks removed, leaves chopped
 1 egg, beaten
 25g/1oz/2 tbsp butter
 salt and ground black pepper
 fresh dill fronds,
  to garnish
 nuoc cham, to serve

1 Preheat the oven to 180°C/350°F/ Gas 4. Soak the bean thread noodles and cloud ear mushrooms separately in bowls of lukewarm water for 15 minutes. Squeeze them dry and chop finely.

2 In a bowl, mix together the noodles and mushrooms with the crab meat. Add the oil, *nuoc mam*, shallots, garlic, ginger and coriander. Season, then stir in the beaten egg.

3 Spoon the mixture into four small crab shells or use individual ovenproof dishes, packing it in tightly, and dot the top of each one with a little butter. Place the shells on a baking tray and cook for about 20 minutes, or until the tops are nicely browned.

4 Garnish with dill and serve immediately with a little *nuoc cham* to drizzle over the top.

Per portion Energy 289Kcal/1206kJ; Protein 26g; Carbohydrate 8g, of which sugars 2g; Fat 17g, of which saturates 5g; Cholesterol 145mg; Calcium 39mg; Fibre 24g; Sodium 800mg

LOBSTER AND CRAB STEAMED IN BEER

IN SPITE OF ITS APPEARANCE ON MENUS IN RESTAURANTS THAT SPECIALIZE IN THE COMPLEX AND REFINED IMPERIAL DISHES OF HUE, THIS RECIPE IS VERY EASY TO MAKE. IT MAY BE EXPENSIVE, BUT IT'S A WONDERFUL DISH FOR A SPECIAL OCCASION.

SERVES FOUR

INGREDIENTS

4 uncooked lobsters, about
  450g/1lb each
4 uncooked crabs, about
  225g/8oz each
600ml/1 pint/2½ cups beer
4 spring onions (scallions), trimmed
  and chopped into long pieces
4cm/1½in fresh root ginger, peeled
  and finely sliced
2 green or red Thai chillies, seeded
  and finely sliced
3 lemon grass stalks, finely sliced
1 bunch fresh dill, fronds chopped
1 bunch each fresh basil and
  coriander (cilantro), stalks removed,
  leaves chopped
about 30ml/2 tbsp *nuoc mam*, plus
  extra for serving
juice of 1 lemon
salt and ground black pepper

3 Add the remaining flavouring ingredients to the beer with the *nuoc mam* and lemon juice, Pour into a dipping bowl and serve immediately with the hot lobsters and crabs, with extra splashes of *nuoc mam*, if you like.

COOK'S TIP
Whether you cook the lobsters and crabs at the same time depends on the number of people you are cooking for and the size of your steamer. However, they don't take long to cook so it is easy to steam them in batches. In the markets and restaurants of Vietnam, you can find crabs that are 60cm/24in in diameter, which may feed several people but require a huge steamer. Depending on the size and availability of the lobsters and crabs, you can make this recipe for as many people as you like, because the quantities are simple to adjust. For those who like their food fiery, splash a little chilli sauce into the beer broth.

1 Clean the lobsters and crabs thoroughly and rub them with salt and pepper. Place them in a large steamer and pour the beer into the base.

2 Scatter half the spring onions, ginger, chillies, lemon grass and herbs over the lobsters and crabs, and steam for about 10 minutes, or until the lobsters turn red. Lift them on to a warmed serving dish.

VARIATION
Prawns (shrimp) and mussels are also delicious cooked this way.

Per portion Energy 264Kcal/1112kJ; Protein 48g; Carbohydrate 4g, of which sugars 1g; Fat 7g, of which saturates 1g; Cholesterol 210mg; Calcium 185mg; Fibre 0.5g; Sodium 130mg

VIETNAMESE LEMON GRASS SNAILS

THE LIVE SNAILS SOLD IN VIETNAMESE MARKETS ARE USUALLY DESTINED FOR THIS POPULAR DELICACY. SERVED STRAIGHT FROM THE BAMBOO STEAMER, THESE LEMON GRASS-INFUSED MORSELS ARE SERVED AS AN APPETIZER, OR AS A SPECIAL SNACK, DIPPED IN NUOC CHAM.

SERVES FOUR

INGREDIENTS
24 fresh snails in their shells
225g/8oz lean minced (ground) pork,
  passed through the mincer twice
3 lemon grass stalks, trimmed
  and finely chopped or ground
  (reserve the outer leaves)
2 spring onions (scallions),
  finely chopped
25g/1oz fresh root ginger, peeled and
  finely grated
1 red Thai chilli, seeded and
  finely chopped
10ml/2 tsp sesame or groundnut
  (peanut) oil
sea salt and ground black pepper
nuoc cham or other sauce,
  for dipping

1 Pull the snails out of their shells and place them in a colander. Rinse the snails thoroughly in plenty of cold water and pat dry with kitchen paper. Rinse the shells and leave to drain.

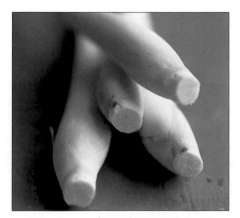

2 Chop the snails finely and put them in a bowl. Add the minced pork, lemon grass, spring onions, ginger, chilli and oil. Season with salt and pepper and mix all the ingredients together.

3 Select the best of the lemon grass leaves and tear each one into thin ribbons, roughly 7.5cm/3in long. Bend each ribbon in half and put it inside a snail shell, so that the ends are poking out. The idea is that each diner pulls the ends of the lemon grass ribbon to gently prize the steamed morsel out of its shell.

COOK'S TIP
The idea of eating snails may have come from the French, but the method of cooking them in Vietnam is very different. Fresh snails in their shells are available in South-east Asian markets, and in some supermarkets and delicatessens. If you ask for snails in a Vietnamese restaurant, they are likely to be cooked this way.

4 Using your fingers, stuff each shell with the snail and pork mixture, gently pushing it between the lemon grass ends to the back of the shell so that it fills the shell completely.

5 Fill a wok or large pan a third of the way up with water and bring it to the boil. Arrange the snail shells, open side up, in a steamer that fits the wok or pan.

6 Place the lid on the steamer and steam for about 10 minutes, until the mixture is cooked. Serve hot with *nuoc cham* or another strong-flavoured dipping sauce of your choice, such as soy sauce spiked with chopped chillies.

Per portion Energy 136Kcal/573kJ; Protein 24.1g; Carbohydrate 0.2g, of which sugars 0.2g; Fat 4.3g, of which saturates 1.1g; Cholesterol 70mg; Calcium 9mg; Fibre 0.1g; Sodium 700mg

POULTRY AND FROG'S LEGS

Chickens and ducks are bred throughout Vietnam and Cambodia. They are sold live in the markets, so that they are fresh for the pot. Containers of hopping frogs are also a familiar sight. All these creatures can be cooked in a variety of ways, including spit-roasting, grilling, stir-frying and stewing, and are usually richly spiced, like sumptuous Chicken and Sweet Potato Curry with Coconut and Caramel Sauce, or fiery hot Curried Frog's Legs.

CHICKEN AND SWEET POTATO CURRY WITH COCONUT AND CARAMEL SAUCE

HO CHI MINH CITY IS HOME TO MANY STALLS SPECIALIZING IN CHICKEN OR SEAFOOD CURRIES. THE ONE THING COMMON TO ALL IS THE USE OF INDIAN CURRY POWDER AND COCONUT MILK. SERVE THIS CURRY WITH BAGUETTES FOR MOPPING UP THE SAUCE, OR STEAMED FRAGRANT RICE OR NOODLES.

SERVES FOUR

INGREDIENTS
   45ml/3 tbsp Indian curry powder or
      garam masala
   15ml/1 tbsp ground turmeric
   500g/1¼lb skinless chicken thighs
      or chicken portions
   25ml/1½ tbsp raw cane sugar
   30ml/2 tbsp sesame oil
   2 shallots, chopped
   2 garlic cloves, chopped
   4cm/1½in galangal, peeled
      and chopped
   2 lemon grass stalks, chopped
   10ml/2 tsp chilli paste or dried
      chilli flakes
   2 medium sweet potatoes, peeled
      and cubed
   45ml/3 tbsp *nuoc mam*
   600ml/1 pint/2½ cups coconut milk
   1 small bunch each fresh basil
      and coriander (cilantro),
      stalks removed
   salt and ground black pepper

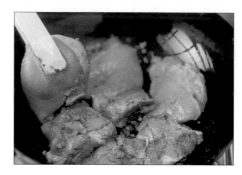

3 Heat a wok or heavy pan and add the oil. Stir-fry the shallots, garlic, galangal and lemon grass. Stir in the rest of the turmeric and curry powder with the chilli paste or flakes, followed by the chicken, and stir-fry for 2–3 minutes.

4 Add the sweet potatoes, then the *nuoc mam*, caramel sauce, coconut milk and 150ml/¼ pint/⅔ cup water, mixing thoroughly to combine the flavours. Bring to the boil, reduce the heat and cook for about 15 minutes until the chicken is cooked through. Season and stir in half the basil and coriander. Garnish with the remaining herbs and serve immediately.

VARIATION
This curry is equally good made with pork or prawns (shrimp), or a combination of the two. Galangal is available in Asian stores, but you can use fresh root ginger if you prefer.

1 In a small bowl, mix together the curry powder or garam masala and the turmeric. Put the chicken in a bowl and coat with half of the spice. Set aside.

2 To make the caramel sauce, heat the sugar in a small pan with 7.5ml/1½ tsp water, until the sugar dissolves and the syrup turns golden. Remove from the heat and set aside.

Per portion Energy 387Kcal/1632kJ; Protein 31g; Carbohydrate 38g, of which sugars 19g; Fat 14g, of which saturates 3g; Cholesterol 131mg; Calcium 1.8mg; Fibre 1g; Sodium 1000mg

STIR-FRIED CHICKEN <u>WITH</u> CHILLIES <u>AND</u> LEMON GRASS

THIS IS GOOD HOME COOKING. THERE ARE VARIATIONS OF THIS DISH, USING PORK OR SEAFOOD, THROUGHOUT SOUTH-EAST ASIA SO, FOR A SMOOTH INTRODUCTION TO THE COOKING OF THE REGION, THIS IS A GOOD PLACE TO START. SERVE WITH A SALAD, RICE WRAPPERS AND A DIPPING SAUCE.

SERVES FOUR

INGREDIENTS
  15ml/1 tbsp sugar
  30ml/2 tbsp sesame or groundnut
    (peanut) oil
  2 garlic cloves, finely chopped
  2–3 green or red Thai chillies,
    seeded and finely chopped
  2 lemon grass stalks, finely sliced
  1 onion, finely sliced
  350g/12oz skinless chicken breast
    fillets, cut into bitesize strips
  30ml/2 tbsp soy sauce
  15ml/1 tbsp *nuoc mam*
  1 bunch fresh coriander (cilantro),
    stalks removed, leaves chopped
  salt and ground black pepper
  nuoc cham, to serve

1 To make a caramel sauce, put the sugar into a pan with 5ml/1 tsp water. Heat gently until the sugar has dissolved and turned golden. Set aside.

2 Heat a large wok or heavy pan and add the sesame or groundnut oil. Stir in the chopped garlic, chillies and lemon grass, and stir-fry until they become fragrant and golden. Add the onion and stir-fry for 1 minute, then add the chicken strips.

3 When the chicken is cooked through, add the soy sauce, *nuoc mam* and caramel sauce. Stir to mix and heat through, then season with a little salt and pepper. Toss the coriander into the chicken and serve with *nuoc cham* to drizzle over it.

Per portion Energy 202Kcal/847kJ; Protein 22g; Carbohydrate 9g, of which sugars 7g; Fat 9g, of which saturates 1g; Cholesterol 61mg; Calcium 32mg; Fibre 0.6g; Sodium 800mg

CAMBODIAN CHICKEN <u>WITH</u> YOUNG GINGER

GINGER PLAYS A BIG ROLE IN CAMBODIAN COOKING, PARTICULARLY IN THE STIR-FRIED DISHES. WHENEVER POSSIBLE, THE JUICIER AND MORE PUNGENT YOUNG GINGER IS USED. THIS IS A SIMPLE AND DELICIOUS WAY TO COOK CHICKEN, PORK OR BEEF.

<u>SERVES FOUR</u>

INGREDIENTS
    30ml/2 tbsp groundnut (peanut) oil
    3 garlic cloves, finely sliced
       in strips
    50g/2oz fresh young root ginger,
       finely sliced in strips
    2 Thai chillies, seeded and finely
       sliced in strips
    4 chicken breasts or 4 boned
       chicken legs, skinned and cut
       into bitesize chunks
    30ml/2 tbsp *tuk prahoc*
    10ml/2 tsp sugar
    1 small bunch coriander (cilantro)
       stalks removed, roughly chopped
    ground black pepper
    jasmine rice and crunchy salad or
       baguette, to serve

1 Heat a wok or heavy pan and add the oil. Add the garlic, ginger and chillies, and stir-fry until fragrant and golden. Add the chicken and toss it around the wok for 1–2 minutes.

COOK'S TIP
Young ginger is available in Chinese and South-east Asian markets.

2 Stir in the *tuk prahoc* and sugar, and stir-fry for a further 4–5 minutes until cooked. Season with pepper and add some of the fresh coriander. Transfer the chicken to a serving dish and garnish with the remaining coriander. Serve hot with jasmine rice and a crunchy salad with fresh herbs, or with chunks of freshly baked baguette.

Per portion Energy 222Kcal/935kJ; Protein 36.4g; Carbohydrate 3g, of which sugars 2.9g; Fat 7.3g, of which saturates 1.1g; Cholesterol 105mg; Calcium 32mg; Fibre 0.6g; Sodium 100mg

CARAMELIZED CHICKEN WINGS <u>WITH</u> GINGER

COOKED IN A WOK OR IN THE OVEN, THESE CARAMELIZED WINGS ARE DRIZZLED WITH CHILLI OIL AND EATEN WITH THE FINGERS, AND EVERY BIT OF TENDER MEAT IS SUCKED OFF THE BONE. OFTEN SERVED WITH RICE AND PICKLES, VARIATIONS OF THIS RECIPE CAN BE FOUND IN VIETNAM AND CAMBODIA.

SERVES TWO TO FOUR

INGREDIENTS
  75ml/5 tbsp sugar
  30ml/2 tbsp groundnut (peanut) oil
  25g/1oz fresh root ginger, peeled and
    finely shredded or grated
  12 chicken wings, split in two
  chilli oil, for drizzling
  mixed pickled vegetables,
    to serve

1 To make a caramel sauce, gently heat the sugar with 60ml/4 tbsp water in a small, heavy pan until it turns golden, Set aside.

2 Heat the oil in a wok or heavy pan. Add the ginger and stir-fry until fragrant Add the chicken wings and toss them around the wok to brown.

3 Pour in the caramel sauce and make sure the chicken wings are coated in it. Reduce the heat, cover the wok or pan, and cook for about 30 minutes, until tender, and the sauce has caramelized.

4 Drizzle chilli oil over the wings and serve from the wok or pan with mixed pickled vegetables.

Per portion Energy 393Kcal/1641kJ; Protein 30.5g; Carbohydrate 14.4g, of which sugars 14.4g; Fat 24g, of which saturates 6.3g; Cholesterol 134mg; Calcium 16mg; Fibre 0g; Sodium 100mg

STIR-FRIED GIBLETS WITH GARLIC AND GINGER

As almost every part of the bird is used in Vietnam and Cambodia, there are specific recipes to which they are destined. Apart from being tossed into the stockpot, the giblets are often quickly stir-fried with garlic and ginger and served with rice.

SERVES TWO TO FOUR

INGREDIENTS
  30ml/2 tbsp groundnut (peanut) oil
  2 shallots, halved and finely sliced
  2 garlic cloves, finely chopped
  1 Thai chilli, seeded and finely sliced
  25g/1oz fresh root ginger, peeled
    and shredded
  225g/8oz chicken livers, trimmed
    and finely sliced
  115g/4oz mixed giblets, finely sliced
  15–30ml/1–2 tbsp *nuoc mam*
  1 small bunch coriander (cilantro),
    finely chopped
  ground black pepper
  steamed rice, to serve

1 Heat the oil in a wok or heavy pan. Stir in the shallots, garlic, chilli and ginger, and stir-fry until golden. Add the chicken livers and mixed giblets and stir-fry for a few minutes more, until browned.

2 Stir in the *nuoc mam*, adjusting the quantity according to taste, and half the chopped coriander. Season with ground black pepper and garnish with the rest of the coriander. Serve hot, with steamed fragrant rice.

Per portion Energy 134Kcal/556kJ; Protein 15g; Carbohydrate 1.5g, of which sugars 1.1g; Fat 7.4g, of which saturates 1.3g; Cholesterol 290mg; Calcium 12mg; Fibre 0.2g; Sodium 360mg

CAMBODIAN CHICKEN AND VEGETABLE STEW

SAMLAA KAKO *IS ONE OF THE MOST POPULAR* CAMBODIAN *DISHES ON RESTAURANT MENUS AND IT IS COOKED DAILY IN PEOPLE'S HOMES. THERE ARE MANY DIFFERENT VERSIONS, DEPENDING ON THE AREA AND WHICH VEGETABLES ARE IN SEASON, BUT IT IS ALWAYS DELICIOUS.*

SERVES FOUR TO SIX

INGREDIENTS
  30ml/2 tbsp groundnut (peanut) oil
  4 garlic cloves, halved and crushed
  25g/1oz galangal, peeled and
    finely sliced
  2 chillies
  30ml/2 tbsp *kroeung*
  15ml/1 tbsp palm sugar
  12 chicken thighs
  30ml/2 tbsp *tuk prahoc*
  a handful kaffir lime leaves
  600ml/1 pint/2½ cups coconut milk
  350g/12oz pumpkin flesh, seeded
    and cut into bitesize chunks
  1 long Asian or Mediterranean
    aubergine (eggplant), quartered
    lengthways, each quarter cut into 3
  115g/4oz long beans, trimmed and
    cut into 5cm/2in lengths
  3 tomatoes, skinned, quartered,
    and seeded
  a handful morning glory or spinach
    leaves, washed and trimmed
  a small bunch basil leaves
  sea salt and ground black pepper
  1 small bunch each fresh coriander
    (cilantro) and mint, stalks removed,
    coarsely chopped, to garnish
  jasmine rice, to serve

COOK'S TIP
A meal in itself, a big pot of *samlaa kako* is placed in the middle of the table and everyone helps themselves. Sometimes it includes rice cooked in it, at other times it is served with jasmine rice.

1 Heat the groundnut oil in a wok or heavy pan. Add the garlic, galangal and whole chillies and stir-fry until fragrant and golden. Stir in the *kroeung* and sugar, until it has dissolved. Add the chicken, tossing it well, and stir in the *tuk prahoc*, kaffir lime leaves and coconut milk. Reduce the heat and simmer for 10 minutes.

2 Add the pumpkin, aubergine and snake beans and simmer until tender. If you need to add more liquid, stir in a little water. Add the tomatoes and morning glory or spinach, and the basil leaves. Cook for a further 2 minutes, then season to taste with salt and pepper. Garnish with coriander and mint and serve hot with jasmine rice.

Per portion Energy 418Kcal/1747kJ; Protein 31g; Carbohydrate 15g, of which sugars 14.3g; Fat 26.4g, of which saturates 6.7g; Cholesterol 160mg; Calcium 127mg; Fibre 3g; Sodium 350mg

VIETNAMESE ROAST DUCK

THIS DISH, VIT QUAY, IS VIETNAM'S ANSWER TO PEKING DUCK, ALTHOUGH HERE THE SUCCULENT, CRISPY BIRD IS ENJOYED IN ONE COURSE. IN A VIETNAMESE HOME, THE DUCK IS SERVED WITH PICKLED VEGETABLES OR A SALAD, SEVERAL DIPPING SAUCES, AND A FRAGRANT STEAMED RICE.

2 Preheat the oven to 220°C/425°F/ Gas 7. Stuff the ginger, garlic, lemon grass and spring onions into the duck's cavity and tie the legs with string. Using a bamboo or metal skewer, poke holes in the skin, including the legs.

3 Place the duck, breast side down, on a rack over a roasting pan and cook it in the oven for 45 minutes, basting from time to time with the juices that have dripped into the pan. After 45 minutes, turn the duck over so that it is breast side up. Baste it generously and return it to the oven for a further 45 minutes, basting it every 15 minutes. The duck is ready once the juices run clear when the bird is pierced with a skewer.

4 Serve immediately, pulling at the skin and meat with your fingers, rather than neatly carving it. Serve with ginger dipping sauce, *nuoc mam gung*, pickled vegetables and salad leaves for wrapping up the morsels.

COOK'S TIP
Leaving the duck uncovered in the refrigerator for 24 hours will allow the skin to dry out thoroughly, ensuring that it becomes succulent and crispy when cooked.

SERVES FOUR TO SIX

INGREDIENTS
    1 duck, about 2.25kg/5lb
    90g/3½oz fresh root ginger, peeled, roughly chopped and lightly crushed
    4 garlic cloves, peeled and crushed
    1 lemon grass stalk, halved and bruised
    4 spring onions (scallions), halved and crushed
    ginger dipping sauce, *nuoc mam gung*, pickled vegetables and salad leaves, to serve
For the marinade
    80ml/3fl oz *nuoc mam*
    30ml/2 tbsp soy sauce
    30ml/2 tbsp honey
    15ml/1 tbsp five-spice powder
    5ml/1 tsp ground ginger

1 In a bowl, beat the ingredients for the marinade together until well blended. Rub the skin of the duck lightly to loosen it, until you can get your fingers between the skin and the meat. Rub the marinade all over the duck, inside its skin and out, then place the duck on a rack over a tray and put it in the refrigerator for 24 hours.

Per portion Energy 228Kcal/960kJ; Protein 27g; Carbohydrate 13g, of which sugars 7g; Fat 8g, of which saturates 3g; Cholesterol 131mg; Calcium 69mg; Fibre 0.3g; Sodium 140mg

DUCK IN A SPICY ORANGE SAUCE

THE VIETNAMESE AND CAMBODIAN DISHES OF DUCK COOKED WITH PINEAPPLE, AND DUCK WITH ORANGE, ARE INSPIRED BY THE FRENCH DUCK Á L'ORANGE, BUT THE USE OF SPICES, LEMON GRASS AND CHILLIES MAKES THEM QUITE DIFFERENT. SERVE WITH STEAMED RICE AND A VEGETABLE DISH.

SERVES FOUR

INGREDIENTS

    4 duck legs
    4 garlic cloves, crushed
    50g/2oz fresh root ginger, peeled and
      finely sliced
    2 lemon grass stalks, trimmed,
      cut into 3 pieces and crushed
    2 dried whole red Thai chillies
    15ml/1 tbsp palm sugar
    5ml/1 tsp five-spice powder
    30ml/2 tbsp *nuoc cham* or *tuk trey*
    900ml/1½ pints/3¾ cups fresh
      orange juice
    sea salt and ground black pepper
    1 lime, cut into quarters

3 Stir in the orange juice and place the duck legs back in the pan. Cover the pan and gently cook the duck for 1–2 hours, until the meat is tender and the sauce has reduced. Season and serve with lime wedges to squeeze over it.

1 Place the duck legs, skin side down, in a large heavy pan or flameproof clay pot. Cook them on both sides over a medium heat for about 10 minutes, until browned and crispy. Transfer them to a plate and set aside.

2 Stir the garlic, ginger, lemon grass and chillies into the fat left in the pan, and cook until golden. Add the sugar, five-spice powder and *nuoc cham* or *tuk trey*.

Per portion Energy 280Kcal/1181kJ; Protein 31g; Carbohydrate 23.8g, of which sugars 23.8g; Fat 10g, of which saturates 2g; Cholesterol 165mg; Calcium 48mg; Fibre 0.4g; Sodium 250mg

GARLIC-ROASTED QUAILS WITH HONEY

THIS IS A GREAT INDO-CHINESE FAVOURITE MADE WITH QUAILS OR POUSSINS. CRISPY, TENDER AND JUICY, THEY ARE SIMPLE TO PREPARE AND DELICIOUS TO EAT. ROAST THEM IN THE OVEN OR GRILL OVER A BARBECUE. SERVE WITH FRAGRANT STEAMED RICE.

1 In a bowl, beat the mushroom soy sauce with the honey and sugar until the sugar has dissolved. Stir in the garlic, crushed peppercorns and sesame oil. Open out and skewer the quails or poussins, put them in a dish and rub the marinade over them. Cover and chill for at least 4 hours.

2 Preheat the oven to 230°C/450°F/ Gas 8. Place the quails breast side down in a roasting pan or on a wire rack set over a baking tray, then put them in the oven for 10 minutes.

3 Take them out and turn them over so they are breast side up, baste well with the juices and return them to the oven for a further 15–20 minutes until cooked through. Serve immediately with *nuoc cham* for dipping or drizzling.

COOK'S TIP
The quails can be roasted whole, or split down the backbone, opened out and secured with skewers. For the New Year, Tet, whole chickens are marinated in similar garlicky flavourings and cooked over charcoal or in the oven.

SERVES FOUR

INGREDIENTS
150ml/¼ pint/⅔ cup mushroom
    soy sauce
45ml/3 tbsp honey
15ml/1 tbsp sugar
8 garlic cloves, crushed
15ml/1 tbsp black peppercorns,
    crushed
30ml/2 tbsp sesame oil
8 quails or poussins
nuoc cham, to serve

Per portion Energy 649Kcal/2701kJ; Protein 51g; Carbohydrate 17g, of which sugars 3g; Fat 43g, of which saturates 11g; Cholesterol 250mg; Calcium 61mg; Fibre 0.2g; Sodium 200mg

DUCK WITH PINEAPPLE AND CORIANDER

THIS RECIPE TAKES ADVANTAGE OF THE ABUNDANCE OF PINEAPPLES THAT GROW IN VIETNAM AND CAMBODIA. SERVE WITH STEAMED RICE AND A CRUNCHY SALAD FOR A DELICIOUS MEAL. REMEMBER TO ALLOW PLENTY OF TIME FOR THE DUCK TO MARINATE.

SERVES FOUR TO SIX

INGREDIENTS

1 small duck, skinned, trimmed
    and jointed
1 pineapple, skinned, cored and
    cut in half crossways
45ml/3 tbsp sesame or vegetable oil
4cm/1½in fresh root ginger, peeled
    and finely sliced
1 onion, sliced
salt and ground black pepper
1 bunch fresh coriander (cilantro),
    stalks removed, to garnish

For the marinade

3 shallots
45ml/3 tbsp soy sauce
30ml/2 tbsp *nuoc mam*
10ml/2 tsp five-spice powder
15ml/1 tbsp sugar
3 garlic cloves, crushed
1 bunch fresh basil, stalks removed,
    leaves finely chopped

1 To make the marinade, grate the shallots into a bowl, then add the remaining marinade ingredients and beat together until the sugar has dissolved. Place the duck in a wide dish and rub with the marinade. Cover and chill for 6 hours or overnight.

2 Take one of the pineapple halves and cut into 4–6 slices, and then again into half-moons, and set aside. Take the other pineapple half and chop it to a pulp. Using your hands, squeeze all the juice from the pulp into a bowl. Discard the pulp and reserve the juice.

3 Heat 30ml/2 tbsp of the oil in a wide pan. Stir in the ginger and the onion. When they begin to soften, add the duck to the pan and brown on both sides. Pour in the pineapple juice and any remaining marinade, then add water so that the duck is just covered. Bring to the boil, reduce the heat and simmer for about 25 minutes.

4 Meanwhile, heat the remaining oil in a heavy pan and sear the pineapple slices on both sides – you may have to do this in two batches. Add the seared pineapple to the duck, season to taste with salt and black pepper and cook for a further 5 minutes, or until the duck is tender. Arrange on a warmed serving dish, garnish with the coriander leaves and serve.

COOK'S TIP

This is quite a fancy dish and a little more time-consuming than some to prepare, so it might be one reserved for celebrations. You can find this dish in Vietnamese and Cambodian restaurants listed as *duck à l'ananas*, demonstrating the French influence on the cuisine.

Per portion Energy 356Kcal/1489kJ; Protein 28g; Carbohydrate 19g, of which sugars 13g; Fat 20g, of which saturates 4g; Cholesterol 131mg; Calcium 122mg; Fibre 2g; Sodium 150mg

CAMBODIAN STIR-FRIED FROG'S LEGS

FROG'S LEGS ARE POPULAR THROUGHOUT SOUTH-EAST ASIA. SOLD LIVE IN THE MARKETS, PLUMP FROGS ARE BEHEADED, SKINNED AND CLEANED FOR KEEN COOKS, AS THE WHOLE FROG IS EDIBLE. THIS IS ONE OF THE MOST DELICIOUS WAYS OF COOKING FROG'S LEGS WITH RICHLY FRAGRANT KROEUNG.

SERVES THREE TO FOUR

INGREDIENTS
    15ml/1 tbsp groundnut
      (peanut) oil
    2 garlic cloves, finely chopped
    2 Thai chillies, seeded and
      finely chopped
    30ml/2 tbsp *kroeung*
    15ml/1 tbsp *tuk prahoc*
    15ml/1 tbsp palm sugar
    4 fresh kaffir lime leaves
    6 pairs of frog's legs, separated
      into 12 single legs, rinsed and
      dabbed dry
    chilli oil, for drizzling

VARIATION
You can garnish the frog's legs with chopped fresh herbs, such as coriander (cilantro) or basil, if you like.

1 Heat the oil in a wok or heavy pan. Stir in the garlic and chillies, until they become fragrant. Add the *kroeung, tuk prahoc* and sugar and stir-fry until it begins to colour. Add the lime leaves and frog's legs, tossing them around the wok to make sure they are coated in the sauce. Arrange the legs against the base and sides of the wok to fry on both sides, until brown and crisp.

2 Transfer the frog's legs to a warmed serving dish and drizzle with chilli oil. Serve with garlic and ginger rice and a salad.

COOK'S TIP
Frog's legs, often sold in pairs, can be bought fresh and frozen in Asian markets. They are prized for stir-fries, where they are cooked with garlic and herbs.

Per portion Energy 113Kcal/475kJ; Protein 12.4g; Carbohydrate 8.5g, of which sugars 8.2g; Fat 3.4g, of which saturates 0.5g; Cholesterol 35mg; Calcium 22mg; Fibre 0.5g; Sodium 480mg

CURRIED FROG'S LEGS

FROG'S LEGS COOKED WITH HOT INDIAN SPICES AND COCONUT MILK ARE POPULAR IN SOUTHERN VIETNAM AND CAMBODIA. THIS DISH IS FIERY HOT, BUT IT IS OFTEN SERVED WITH EXTRA CHILLIES ON THE SIDE, FOR SERIOUS LOVERS OF SPICY HEAT.

SERVES TWO TO FOUR

INGREDIENTS

  4 pairs of frog's legs, well rinsed
  30ml/2 tbsp vegetable oil
  2 shallots, halved and sliced
  300ml/½ pint/1¼ cups
    coconut milk
  sea salt and ground black pepper
  1 small bunch fresh coriander
    (cilantro), stalks removed,
    to garnish
  steamed or boiled noodles or rice, and
    fruit-based salad, green chillies,
    seeded and cut into quarters
    lengthways (optional), to serve
For the curry paste
  2 dried red chillies, soaked in warm
    water for 30 minutes
  2 garlic cloves, chopped
  1 lemon grass stalk, trimmed and
    roughly chopped
  25g/1oz fresh root ginger, peeled
    and roughly chopped
  10ml/2 tsp sugar
  15ml/1 tbsp Indian curry powder
  15ml/1 tbsp vegetable oil
  2.5ml/½ tsp sea salt

1 First make the curry paste. Split the dried chillies in half, remove the seeds and scrape out the flesh with a teaspoon. Using a mortar and pestle, pound the chilli flesh with the chopped garlic, lemon grass, ginger and sugar, until it forms a paste. Stir in the curry powder with the salt and bind with the oil.

2 Rub the curry paste all over the frog's legs. Put them in a dish, cover, and leave to stand for an hour.

3 Heat the oil in a wok or heavy pan. Add the shallots and stir-fry until they turn golden and fragrant. Add the frog's legs and brown on both sides. Add the coconut milk, reduce the heat and cook gently for about 25 minutes, until the frog's legs are cooked.

4 Season with sea salt and ground black pepper. Garnish with sprigs of coriander and serve with noodles or rice and a tangy fruit-based salad and, if you like, a bowl of quartered red or green chillies on the side.

Per portion Energy 146Kcal/609kJ; Protein 9.4g; Carbohydrate 7.5g, of which sugars 7.1g; Fat 8.9g, of which saturates 1.2g; Cholesterol 26mg; Calcium 29mg; Fibre 0.2g; Sodium 110mg

BEEF AND PORK

Beef is eaten frequently in northern Vietnam, but used more
sparingly in other regions where it is more expensive. Pork is
the principal meat of both Vietnam and Cambodia. Many rural
families keep a pig, and every bit is put to good use. Combined
with sharp, tangy flavourings, dishes such as Beef Saté and
Caramelized Pork in Bamboo never fail to be exciting.

BEEF STEW WITH STAR ANISE AND BASIL

THE VIETNAMESE PRIZE THIS DISH FOR BREAKFAST, AND ON CHILLY MORNINGS PEOPLE QUEUE UP FOR A BOWL OF THIT BO KHO *ON THEIR WAY TO WORK. TRADITIONALLY, IT HAS AN ORANGE HUE FROM THE OIL IN WHICH ANNATTO SEEDS HAVE BEEN FRIED, BUT HERE THE COLOUR COMES FROM TURMERIC.*

SERVES FOUR TO SIX

INGREDIENTS
500g/1¼lb lean beef, cut into
    bitesize cubes
15ml/1 tbsp ground turmeric
30ml/2 tbsp sesame or
    vegetable oil
3 shallots, chopped
3 garlic cloves, chopped
2 red chillies, seeded and chopped
2 lemon grass stalks, cut into several
    pieces and bruised
15ml/1 tbsp curry powder
4 star anise, roasted and ground to
    a powder
700ml/scant 1¼ pints hot beef or
    chicken stock, or boiling water
45ml/3 tbsp *nuoc mam*
30ml/2 tbsp soy sauce
15ml/1 tbsp raw cane sugar
1 bunch fresh basil, stalks removed
salt and ground black pepper
1 onion, halved and finely sliced, and
    chopped fresh coriander (cilantro)
    leaves, to garnish
steamed fragrant or sticky rice, or
    chunks of baguette, to serve

2 Add the curry powder, all but 10ml/ 2 tsp of the roasted star anise, and the beef. Brown the beef, then pour in the stock or water, *nuoc mam*, soy sauce and sugar. Stir and bring to the boil. Reduce the heat and cook gently for about 40 minutes, or until the meat is tender and the liquid has reduced.

3 Season to taste with salt and pepper, stir in the reserved roasted star anise, and add the basil. Transfer the stew to a serving dish and garnish with the sliced onion and coriander leaves.

4 Serve with steamed fragrant or sticky rice, or chunks of baguette.

1 Toss the beef in the ground turmeric and set aside. Heat a wok or heavy pan and add the oil. Stir in the shallots, garlic, chillies and lemon grass, and cook until they become fragrant.

COOK'S TIP
If you prefer to use annatto seeds instead of turmeric, they can be found in some Asian supermarkets. Fry 15ml/1 tbsp seeds in a little oil.

Per portion Energy 314Kcal/1312kJ; Protein 33g; Carbohydrate 17g, of which sugars 11g; Fat 14g, of which saturates 4g; Cholesterol 64mg; Calcium 64mg; Fibre 1.7g; Sodium 150mg

BEEF SATÉ

The spicy peanut paste, saté, is a great favourite in South-east Asia. It is thought to have originated in India. In southern Vietnam, it is used for grilling and stir-frying meats and seafood, as well as for dressing egg noodles and spiking marinades.

SERVES FOUR TO SIX

INGREDIENTS
500g/1¼ lb beef sirloin, cut in
    bitesize pieces
15ml/1 tbsp groundnut (peanut) oil
1 bunch rocket (arugula) leaves
For the saté
60ml/4 tbsp groundnut (peanut) or
    vegetable oil
5 garlic cloves, crushed
5 dried Serrano chillies, seeded and
    ground
10ml/2 tsp curry powder
50g/2oz/⅓ cup roasted peanuts,
    finely ground

1 To make the saté, heat the oil in a wok or heavy pan and stir in the garlic until it begins to colour. Add the chillies, curry powder and peanuts and stir over a gentle heat until the mixture forms a paste. Remove from the heat and leave to cool.

2 Put the beef into a large bowl. Beat the groundnut oil into the saté and add the mixture to the pieces of beef. Mix well, so that the beef is evenly coated, and put aside to marinate for 30–40 minutes.

3 Soak four to six wooden skewers in water for 30 minutes. Prepare a barbecue. Thread the meat on to the skewers and cook for 2–3 minutes on each side. Serve the meat with the rocket leaves for wrapping.

Per portion Energy 433Kcal/1798kJ; Protein 34g; Carbohydrate 4g, of which sugars 1g; Fat 31g, of which saturates 7g; Cholesterol 64mg; Calcium 68mg; Fibre 1.5g; Sodium 100mg

VIETNAMESE BEEF FONDUE WITH PINEAPPLE AND ANCHOVY DIPPING SAUCE

INTRODUCED BY MONGOLIAN TRIBESMEN, AND ADOPTED BY THE CHINESE, BO NHUNG DAM IS AN ANCIENT WAY OF COOKING MEAT. TRADITIONALLY, IT WAS MADE AND SERVED IN A CHINESE LAU, A TURBAN-SHAPED PAN WITH A STOVE UNDERNEATH TO KEEP THE LIQUID SIMMERING.

SERVES FOUR TO SIX

INGREDIENTS
  30ml/2 tbsp sesame oil
  1 garlic clove, crushed
  2 shallots, finely chopped
  2.5cm/1in fresh root ginger, peeled
    and finely sliced
  1 lemon grass stalk, cut into
    several pieces and bruised
  30ml/2 tbsp sugar
  225ml/8½fl oz/1 cup white rice
    vinegar
  700g/1lb 10oz beef fillet, thinly
    sliced into rectangular strips
  salt and ground black pepper
  chopped or sliced salad vegetables,
    herbs and rice wrappers,
    to serve
For the beef stock
  450g/1lb meaty beef bones
  15ml/1 tbsp soy sauce
  15ml/1 tbsp *nuoc mam*
  1 onion, peeled and quartered
  2.5cm/1in fresh root ginger, peeled
    and chopped
  3 cloves
  1 star anise
  1 cinnamon stick
For the dipping sauce
  15ml/1 tbsp white rice vinegar
  juice of 1 lime
  5ml/1 tsp sugar
  1 garlic clove, peeled and
    chopped
  2 Thai chillies, seeded and
    chopped
  12 canned anchovy fillets, drained
  2 slices of pineapple, centre removed
    and flesh chopped

COOK'S TIP
Traditionally, various meats are used for this dish – pork, chicken, and even shellfish and eel. The diners use the rice wrappers to roll up bundles of salad and meat to dip into the sauce. Once all the meat has been cooked, the fragrant broth is poured into bowls to drink.

1 To make the stock, put the beef bones into a deep pan with the other ingredients and cover with 900ml/1½ pints/3¾ cups water. Bring to the boil, reduce the heat and simmer, covered, for 1–2 hours. Remove the lid, turn up the heat and gently boil the stock for a further 30–40 minutes, or until it has reduced. Strain and season with salt. Measure out 300ml/½ pint/1¼ cups and set aside.

2 Meanwhile, make the dipping sauce. In a bowl, mix the vinegar and lime juice with the sugar, until the sugar dissolves. Using a mortar and pestle, crush the garlic and chillies together to form a paste. Add the anchovy fillets and pound them to a paste, then add the pineapple and pound it to a pulp. Stir in the vinegar and lime juice mixture, and set aside.

VARIATION
You could use any dipping sauce of your choice, such as sweet and sour peanut sauce.

3 When ready to eat, heat 15ml/1 tbsp of the sesame oil in a heavy pan, wok or fondue pot. Quickly stir-fry the garlic, shallots, ginger and lemon grass until fragrant and golden, then add the sugar, vinegar, beef stock and the remaining sesame oil. Bring to the boil, stirring constantly until the sugar has dissolved. Season to taste with salt and plenty of freshly ground black pepper.

4 Transfer the pan or fondue pot to a lighted burner at the table. Lay the beef strips on a large serving dish, and put the dipping sauce in a serving bowl. Using chopsticks or fondue forks, each person cooks their own meat in the broth and dips it into the sauce. Serve with salad vegetables, chopped herbs and rice wrappers.

Per portion Energy 412Kcal/1712kJ; Protein 41g; Carbohydrate 17g, of which sugars 15g; Fat 19g, of which saturates 6g; Cholesterol 112mg; Calcium 54mg; Fibre 0.8g; Sodium 1000mg

STIR-FRIED BEEF WITH SESAME SAUCE

VARIATIONS OF THIS DISH CAN BE FOUND ALL OVER VIETNAM AND CAMBODIA. SIMILAR TO STIR-FRIED BEEF WITH SATÉ, THE SPICY PEANUT SAUCE, THIS CAMBODIAN RECIPE HAS A DELICIOUSLY RICH, SPICY AND NUTTY FLAVOUR.

SERVES FOUR

INGREDIENTS
    450g/1lb beef sirloin or fillet,
      cut into thin strips
    15ml/1 tbsp groundnut (peanut)
      or sesame oil
    2 garlic cloves, finely chopped
    2 red Thai chillies, seeded and
      finely chopped
    7.5ml/1½ tsp sugar
    30ml/2 tbsp sesame paste
    30–45ml/2–3 tbsp beef stock
      or water
    sea salt and ground black pepper
    red chilli strips, to garnish
    1 lemon, cut into quarters, to serve
For the marinade
    15ml/1 tbsp groundnut (peanut) oil
    30ml/2 tbsp *tuk trey*
    30ml/2 tbsp soy sauce

1 In a bowl, mix together the ingredients for the marinade. Toss in the beef, making sure it is well coated. Leave to marinate for 30 minutes.

2 Heat the groundnut or sesame oil in a wok or heavy pan. Stir in the garlic and chillies and cook until golden and fragrant. Stir in the sugar. Add the beef, tossing it around the wok to sear it.

3 Stir in the sesame paste and enough stock or water to thin it down. Cook for 1–2 minutes, making sure the beef is coated with the sauce. Season with salt and pepper, garnish with chilli strips and and serve with lemon wedges.

VARIATION
Chicken breast fillet or pork fillet can be used instead of beef.

Per portion Energy 269Kcal/1119kJ; Protein 26.2g; Carbohydrate 2/0g, of which sugars 2.0g; Fat 18g, of which saturates 5g; Cholesterol 65mg; Calcium 31mg; Fibre 0.3g; Sodium 73mg

CHARCOAL-GRILLED BEEF WITH SHRIMP SAUCE

In this Vietnamese dish, thin strips of beef are marinated, chargrilled and served with shrimp sauce — a tasty combination. A teaspoon of shrimp paste is sometimes added to the marinade, but you may find the pungency of the accompanying shrimp sauce is sufficient.

SERVES FOUR

INGREDIENTS

    450g/1lb beef rump, sirloin or fillet,
      cut across the grain into thin strips
    24 bamboo or wooden skewers
    lettuce leaves
    1 small bunch fresh coriander
      (cilantro), to garnish
    Vietnamese shrimp sauce, for dipping
For the marinade
    2 lemon grass stalks, trimmed and
      chopped
    2 shallots, chopped
    2 garlic cloves, peeled and chopped
    1 red Thai chilli, seeded and chopped
    10ml/2 tsp sugar
    30ml/2 tbsp *nuoc mam*
    15ml/1 tbsp soy sauce
    15ml/1 tbsp groundnut (peanut) oil

1 For the marinade, pound the lemon grass, shallots, garlic and chilli with the sugar using a mortar and pestle, until it forms a paste. Beat in the *nuoc mam*, soy sauce and groundnut oil. Toss the beef in the marinade, cover, and marinate for 1–2 hours. Soak the bamboo or wooden skewers in water for 20 minutes so they don't burn over the charcoal.

2 Prepare the charcoal grill, or preheat a conventional grill (broiler). Thread the beef on to the skewers and place them over the charcoal. Cook for not much more than a minute on each side.

3 Wrap the beef in the lettuce leaves, garnish with coriander and serve with the pungent Vietnamese shrimp sauce for dipping.

Per portion Energy 229Kcal/952kJ; Protein 26g; Carbohydrate 1.5g, of which sugars 1.1g; Fat 13g, of which saturates 5g; Cholesterol 65mg; Calcium 10mg; Fibre 0.2g; Sodium 340mg

MINCED MEAT WITH CHARRED AUBERGINE

VARIATIONS OF THIS DISH CROP UP IN DIFFERENT PARTS OF SOUTH-EAST ASIA. TO ATTAIN THE UNIQUE, SMOKY FLAVOUR, THE AUBERGINES ARE CHARRED OVER A FLAME, OR CHARCOAL GRILL, THEN SKINNED, CHOPPED TO A PULP AND ADDED TO THE DISH.

SERVES FOUR

INGREDIENTS

    2 aubergines (eggplant)
    15ml/1 tbsp vegetable or groundnut
       (peanut) oil
    2 shallots, finely chopped
    4 garlic cloves, peeled and
       finely chopped
    1 red Thai chilli, finely chopped
    350g/12oz minced (ground) beef
    30ml/2 tbsp *tuk trey* or *nuoc mam*
    sea salt and ground black pepper
    crusty bread or rice and salad,
       to serve

VARIATION

This dish can also be made with beef or pork – either way it is delicious served with chunks of fresh, crusty bread.

1 Place the aubergines directly over an open flame. Turn them over from time to time, until the skin is charred all over. Put the aubergines into a plastic bag to sweat for a few minutes.

2 Hold each aubergine by its stalk under running cold water, while you peel off the skin. Squeeze out the excess water and chop them roughly on a board.

3 Heat the oil in a large, heavy pan. Stir in the shallots, garlic and chilli and fry until golden. Add the minced beef and stir-fry for about 5 minutes.

4 Stir in the *tuk trey* or *nuoc mam* and the aubergine and cook gently for about 20 minutes, until the meat is tender. Season with salt and pepper and serve with crusty bread or rice and a salad.

Per portion Energy 245Kcal/1019kJ; Protein 19g; Carbohydrate 4g, of which sugars 3.4g; Fat 17g, of which saturates 6g; Cholesterol 53mg; Calcium 23mg; Fibre 2.2g; Sodium 607mg

SEARED GARLIC BEEF DIPPED IN LIME JUICE

POPULAR IN BOTH VIETNAM AND CAMBODIA, THIS DISH CAN BE MADE WITH BEEF OR QUAIL. FLAVOURED WITH LOTS OF GARLIC, THE TENDER CHUNKS OF BEEF ARE WRAPPED IN LETTUCE LEAVES AND DIPPED IN A PIQUANT LIME SAUCE. THE BEEF CAN BE SEARED IN A PAN, OR CHARGRILLED.

SERVES FOUR

INGREDIENTS
    350g/12oz beef fillet or sirloin, cut
        into bitesize chunks
    15ml/1 tbsp sugar
    juice of 3 limes
    2 garlic cloves, crushed
    7.5ml/1½ tsp ground black pepper
    30ml/2 tbsp unsalted roasted
        peanuts, finely chopped
    12 lettuce leaves
For the marinade
    15ml/1 tbsp groundnut (peanut) oil
    45ml/3 tbsp mushroom soy sauce
    10ml/2 tsp soy sauce
    15ml/1 tbsp sugar
    2 garlic cloves, crushed
    7.5ml/1½ tsp ground black pepper

1 To make the marinade, beat together the oil, the two soy sauces and the sugar in a bowl, until the sugar has dissolved. Add the garlic and pepper and mix well. Add the beef and coat in the marinade. Leave for 1–2 hours.

2 In a small bowl, stir the sugar into the lime juice, until it has dissolved. Add the garlic and black pepper and beat well. Stir in the peanuts and put aside.

3 Heat a wok or heavy pan and sear the meat on all sides. Serve immediately with lettuce leaves for wrapping and the lime sauce for dipping.

Per portion Energy 237Kcal/986kJ; Protein 22g; Carbohydrate 5.2g, of which sugars 4.7g; Fat 14g, of which saturates 4g; Cholesterol 51mg; Calcium 12mg; Fibre 0.5g; Sodium 324mg

STIR-FRIED PORK WITH PEANUTS, LIME AND BASIL

PORK OR CHICKEN STIR-FRIED WITH NUTS AND HERBS, WITH A SPLASH OF CITRUS FLAVOUR OR FISH SAUCE, IS EVERYDAY HOME COOKING IN VIETNAM. THE COMBINATION OF LIME, BASIL AND MINT IN THIS RECIPE MAKES IT PARTICULARLY REFRESHING AND TASTY.

SERVES FOUR

INGREDIENTS

    45ml/3 tbsp groundnut (peanut) oil
    450g/1lb pork tenderloin, cut into
      fine strips
    4 spring onions (scallions), chopped
    4 garlic cloves, finely chopped
    4cm/1½in fresh root ginger, peeled
      and finely chopped
    2 green or red Thai chillies, seeded
      and finely chopped
    100g/3½oz/generous ½ cup shelled,
      unsalted peanuts
    grated rind and juice of 2 limes
    30ml/2 tbsp *nuoc mam*
    30ml/2 tbsp grated fresh coconut
    25g/1oz/½ cup chopped fresh
      mint leaves
    25g/1oz/½ cup chopped fresh
      basil leaves
    25g/1oz/½ cup chopped fresh
      coriander (cilantro) leaves
    steamed or sticky rice or rice wrappers,
      salad and a dipping sauce, to serve

1 Heat a large wok or heavy pan and pour in 30ml/2 tbsp of the oil. Add the pork tenderloin and sear over a high heat until browned. Transfer the meat and juices to a plate and set aside.

2 Wipe the wok or pan clean and return to the heat. Pour in the remaining oil and add the spring onions, garlic, ginger and chillies. Stir-fry until the aromas rise, then add the peanuts and stir-fry for 1–2 minutes.

3 Return the meat and its juices to the wok or pan, then stir in the lime rind and juice, and the *nuoc mam*. Add the fresh coconut and herbs, and serve with steamed or sticky rice or with rice wrappers, salad and a dipping sauce.

Per portion Energy 401Kcal/1668kJ; Protein 32g; Carbohydrate 7g, of which sugars 3g; Fat 27g, of which saturates 5g; Cholesterol 71mg; Calcium 42mg; Fibre 1.8g; Sodium 400mg

VIETNAMESE STIR-FRIED PORK RIBS

ADAPTED FROM THE CLASSIC CHINESE SWEET-AND-SOUR SPARE RIBS, THE VIETNAMESE VERSION INCLUDES BASIL LEAVES AND THE FISH SAUCE, NUOC MAM. THIS IS FINGER FOOD, REQUIRING FINGER BOWLS, AND IS PERFECT SERVED WITH STICKY RICE AND A SALAD.

SERVES FOUR TO SIX

INGREDIENTS

    45ml/3 tbsp hoisin sauce
    45ml/3 tbsp *nuoc mam*
    10ml/2 tsp five-spice powder
    45ml/3 tbsp vegetable or sesame oil
    900g/2lb pork ribs
    3 garlic cloves, crushed
    4cm/1½in fresh root ginger, peeled
      and grated
    1 bunch fresh basil, stalks removed,
      leaves shredded

1 In a bowl, mix together the hoisin sauce, *nuoc mam* and five-spice powder with 15ml/1 tbsp of the oil.

2 Bring a large wok or pan of water to the boil, then add the pork ribs, bring back to the boil and blanch for 10 minutes. Lift the pork ribs out with a slotted spoon and drain thoroughly, then set aside.

3 Heat the remaining oil in a clean wok. Add the crushed garlic and grated ginger and cook, stirring, until fragrant, then add the blanched pork ribs.

4 Stir-fry for about 5 minutes, or until the ribs are well browned, then add the hoisin sauce mixture, turning the ribs so that each one is thoroughly coated. Continue stir-frying for 10–15 minutes, or until there is almost no liquid in the wok and the ribs are caramelized and slightly blackened. Add the shredded basil leaves and stir. Serve the ribs straight from the pan, offering dinner guests finger bowls and plenty of napkins to wipe sticky fingers.

Per portion Energy 470Kcal/1965kJ; Protein 44g; Carbohydrate 6g, of which sugars 3g; Fat 31g, of which saturates 12g; Cholesterol 149mg; Calcium 98mg; Fibre 0.1g; Sodium 800mg

GRILLED PORK MEATBALLS <u>WITH</u> SWEET-AND-SOUR PEANUT SAUCE

COOKED AT HOME, OR IN STREET STALLS, THESE MEATBALLS ARE USUALLY SERVED WITH NOODLES AND A DIPPING SAUCE. IN VIETNAM A PEANUT DIPPING SAUCE IS TRADITIONAL. THEY ARE ALSO GOOD SERVED WITH CHOPPED CORIANDER AND LIME WEDGES.

SERVES FOUR

INGREDIENTS
10ml/2 tsp groundnut (peanut) or
  sesame oil
4 shallots, chopped
2 garlic cloves, finely chopped
450g/1lb/2 cups minced
  (ground) pork
30ml/2 tbsp *nuoc mam*
10ml/2 tsp five-spice powder
10ml/2 tsp sugar
115g/4oz/2 cups breadcrumbs or
  30ml/2 tbsp potato starch
1 bunch fresh coriander (cilantro),
  stalks removed
salt and ground black pepper
For the sauce
10ml/2 tsp groundnut (peanut) oil
1 garlic clove, finely chopped
1 red Thai chilli, seeded and
  finely chopped
30ml/2 tbsp roasted peanuts,
  finely chopped
15ml/1 tbsp *nuoc mam*
30ml/2 tbsp rice wine vinegar
30ml/2 tbsp hoisin sauce
60ml/4 tbsp coconut milk
100ml/3½fl oz/scant ½ cup water
5ml/1 tsp sugar

VARIATION
A speciality of central Vietnam, these
meatballs, *nem nuong*, are best threaded
on to skewers and grilled on a barbecue,
but they can also be cooked under a grill
(broiler), or fried in a wok or steamed.

COOK'S TIP
Breadcrumbs make the paste easier to
work with and don't interfere with the
meaty texture of the cooked ball.
However, many Vietnamese prefer potato
starch because it gives the meatball a
smooth, springy texture, although this
does make the paste very sticky to
handle. Work with wet hands to make
it easier.

1 To make the sauce, heat the oil in a
small wok or heavy pan, and stir in the
garlic and chilli. When they begin to
colour, add the peanuts. Stir-fry for a
few minutes, or until the natural oil
from the peanuts begins to weep. Add
the remaining ingredients, except the
sugar, and boil the mixture for a minute.
Adjust the sweetness and seasoning to
your taste by adding sugar and salt,
and set aside.

2 To make the meatballs, heat the oil in
a wok or small pan and add the shallots
and garlic. Stir-fry until golden, then
remove from the heat and leave to cool.
Put the minced pork into a bowl, add
the stir-fried shallots and garlic, and
add the *nuoc mam*, five-spice powder
and sugar. Season with a little salt and
plenty of pepper. Using your hand,
knead the mixture until well combined.
Cover the bowl and chill in the
refrigerator for 2–3 hours to allow the
flavours to mingle. You can make this
mixture a day ahead and leave it to
marinate in the refrigerator overnight.

3 Soak eight wooden skewers in water
for 30 minutes. Meanwhile, knead
the mixture again, then add the
breadcrumbs or potato starch. Knead
well to bind. Divide the mixture into
20 pieces and roll into balls. Thread the
balls on to the skewers. Cook either
over the barbecue or under the grill
(broiler), turning the skewers from time
to time, until well browned.

4 Reheat the sauce, stirring constantly,
and pour into a serving bowl. Arrange
the meatballs on a serving dish with
coriander leaves to wrap around them,
or chop the coriander and use as a
garnish. Serve with the sauce.

Per portion Energy 291Kcal/1216kJ; Protein 28g; Carbohydrate 15g, of which sugars 8g; Fat 14g, of which saturates 3g; Cholesterol 71mg; Calcium 69mg; Fibre 1.3g; Sodium 700mg

PORK COOKED IN A CLAY POT WITH COCONUT

THIS RUSTIC VIETNAMESE DISH IS ONE WHERE VERY LITTLE EFFORT PRODUCES A COMFORTING AND FLAVOURSOME MEAL. IF IT WERE BEING PREPARED FOR A LARGE, HUNGRY FAMILY, IT WOULD TYPICALLY BE SERVED WITH A LIGHT SOUP, STIR-FRIED OR STEAMED RICE, AND A VEGETABLE DISH.

SERVES FOUR

INGREDIENTS
  30ml/2 tbsp sugar
  30ml/2 tbsp *nuoc mam*
  90ml/6 tbsp liquid from a coconut
  350g/12oz pork shoulder, boned and
    cut into bitesize strips
  90g/3½oz fresh coconut, grated
  5ml/1 tsp ground black pepper
  salt
  chopped fresh coriander (cilantro),
    to garnish
  steamed rice, to serve

1 Put the sugar in a pan with 10ml/2 tsp water. Heat it gently until it dissolves and turns to a caramel colour. Remove from the heat and leave to cool.

2 In a bowl, combine the caramel with the *nuoc mam* and coconut liquid. Toss the pork strips in the mixture, making sure they are thoroughly coated, then cover and leave to marinate for 1–2 hours. While still in the bowl, add the grated coconut with the pepper, and mix well.

3 Transfer the pork and the marinating juices to a flameproof clay pot or heavy pan, and pour in 100ml/3½fl oz/scant ½ cup water. Bring to the boil, stir well and reduce the heat. Cover and simmer for 5 minutes. Remove the lid and simmer for a further 5 minutes, or until the sauce has thickened. Season to taste, and garnish with the coriander. Serve with steamed rice.

COOK'S TIPS
• To extract the liquid from a coconut, pierce the soft spot at the top of the fruit with a skewer and pour out the juice. You can then crack the shell and skin the flesh before grating it.
• If you don't have a flameproof clay pot a heavy pan with a lid works just as well.

Per portion Energy 234Kcal/980kJ; Protein 19g; Carbohydrate 11g, of which sugars 10g; Fat 13g, of which saturates 9g; Cholesterol 56mg; Calcium 18mg; Fibre 1.8g; Sodium 600mg

CAMBODIAN BRAISED BLACK PEPPER PORK

ADAPTED FROM A RECIPE BY CORINNE TRANG, THIS CAMBODIAN DISH IS QUICK, TASTY AND BEAUTIFULLY WARMING THANKS TO THE GINGER AND BLACK PEPPER. IT IS SURE TO BE A POPULAR CHOICE FOR A FAMILY MEAL.

SERVES FOUR TO SIX

INGREDIENTS

- 1 litre/1¾ pints/4 cups pork stock or water
- 45ml/3 tbsp *tuk trey*
- 30ml/2 tbsp soy sauce
- 15ml/1 tbsp sugar
- 4 garlic cloves, crushed
- 40g/1½oz fresh root ginger, peeled and finely shredded
- 15ml/1 tbsp ground black pepper
- 675g/1½lb pork shoulder or rump, cut into bitesize cubes
- steamed jasmine rice, crunchy salad and pickles or stir-fried greens, such as water spinach or long beans, to serve

1 In a large heavy pan, bring the stock or water, *tuk trey* and soy sauce to the boil. Reduce the heat and stir in the sugar, garlic, ginger, black pepper and pork. Cover the pan and simmer for about 1½ hours, until the pork is very tender and the liquid has reduced.

2 Serve the pork with steamed jasmine rice, drizzling the braised juices over it, and accompany it with a fresh crunchy salad, pickles or stir-fried greens, such as the delicious stir-fried water spinach with *nuoc cham*, or long beans.

Per portion Energy 147Kcal/619kJ; Protein 24g; Carbohydrate 2.7g, of which sugars 2.7g; Fat 4g, of which saturates 2g; Cholesterol 71mg; Calcium 11mg; Fibre 0.1g; Sodium 81mg

CARAMELIZED PORK IN BAMBOO

THIS DISH IS INSPIRED BY THE REFINED IMPERIAL DISHES OF HUE. IN THE PREPARATION OF DISHES FOR THE DEMANDING NINETEENTH-CENTURY EMPEROR TU DOC, CREATIVITY WAS OF THE ESSENCE. IN THE NORTH, EEL IS GIVEN THIS TREATMENT — IT CAN BE SLIPPED WHOLE INTO THE BAMBOO CAVITY.

SERVES FOUR TO SIX

INGREDIENTS
    1 kg/2¼ lb lean pork shoulder, cut
        into thin strips
    2 large banana leaves, torn into
        wide strips
    chopped fresh coriander (cilantro),
        to garnish
    noodles or rice and *nuoc cham*,
        to serve
For the marinade
    45ml/3 tbsp unrefined or muscovado
        (molasses) sugar
    60ml/4 tbsp *nuoc mam*
    3 shallots, finely chopped
    6 spring onions (scallions), trimmed
        and finely chopped
    1cm/½ in fresh root ginger, peeled
        and finely chopped
    1 green or red Thai chilli, seeded
        and finely chopped

1 To make the marinade, gently heat the sugar in a heavy pan with 15ml/1 tbsp water, stirring constantly until it begins to caramelize. Remove from the heat and stir in the remaining ingredients.

2 Place the pork strips in a bowl and add the marinade. Using your fingers, toss the meat in the marinade, then cover and chill for 1–2 hours.

4 Prepare a barbecue. Tie the bamboo parcels with string and cook over the hot barbecue for about 20 minutes. Open up the parcels, check that the pork is cooked, garnish with coriander and serve with noodles or rice and *nuoc cham*.

VARIATIONS
• This method of using a bamboo tube can also be used to cook whole fish on a barbecue.
• If you can't find banana leaves, use thin, flexible cabbage leaves or vine leaves. Alternatively, wrap the tubes in aluminium foil instead.

COOK'S TIPS
Bamboo is traditionally used as a cooking vessel in central and northern Vietnam. For this recipe, you will need two bamboo tubes, about 25cm/10in long, split in half lengthways and cleaned. You can find them in some Asian stores, or try a do-it-yourself store.

3 Line the inside of two of the bamboo halves with strips of banana leaf. Spoon in the pork, folding the edges over the top. Place the remaining bamboo halves on top to form tubes again, and then tightly wrap a wide strip of banana leaf around the outside of each tube.

Per portion Energy 349Kcal/1469kJ; Protein 44g; Carbohydrate 17g, of which sugars 14g; Fat 12g, of which saturates 4g; Cholesterol 142mg; Calcium 71mg; Fibre 1.2g; Sodium 700mg

CAMBODIAN PORK <u>AND</u> BUTTERNUT CURRY

*THIS CURRY CAN BE MADE WITH BUTTERNUT SQUASH, PUMPKIN OR WINTER MELON. FLAVOURED WITH
KROEUNG, GALANGAL AND TURMERIC, IT IS DELICIOUS SERVED WITH RICE AND A FRUIT-BASED SALAD,
OR EVEN JUST WITH CHUNKS OF FRESH CRUSTY BREAD TO MOP UP THE TASTY SAUCE.*

SERVES FOUR TO SIX

INGREDIENTS
30ml/2 tbsp groundnut (peanut) oil
25g/1oz galangal, finely sliced
2 red Thai chillies, peeled, seeded
  and finely sliced
3 shallots, halved and finely sliced
30ml/2 tbsp *kroeung*
10ml/2 tsp ground turmeric
5ml/1 tsp ground fenugreek
10ml/2 tsp palm sugar
450g/1lb pork loin, cut into
  bitesize chunks
30ml/2 tbsp *tuk prahoc*
900ml/1½ pints/3¾ cups
  coconut milk
1 butternut squash, peeled, seeded
  and cut into bitesize chunks
4 kaffir lime leaves
sea salt and ground black pepper
1 small bunch fresh coriander
  (cilantro), coarsely chopped and
  1 small bunch fresh mint, stalks
  removed, to garnish
rice or noodles and salad, to serve

1 Heat the oil in a large wok or heavy
pan. Stir in the galangal, chillies and
shallots and stir-fry until fragrant. Add
the *kroeung* and stir-fry until it begins to
colour. Add the turmeric, fenugreek
and sugar.

VARIATION
For a vegetarian option, omit the pork
and use baby aubergines (eggplants)
instead. The Cambodian flavourings and
creamy coconut milk work well with
many combinations.

2 Stir in the chunks of pork loin and
stir-fry until golden brown on all sides.
Stir in the *tuk prahoc* and pour in the
coconut milk.

COOK'S TIP
Increase the number of chillies if you
want a really hot curry.

3 Bring to the boil, add the squash and
the lime leaves, and reduce the heat.
Cook gently, uncovered, for 15–20
minutes, until the squash and pork are
tender and the sauce has reduced.
Season to taste. Garnish the curry with
the coriander and mint, and serve with
rice or noodles and salad.

Per portion Energy 188Kcal/789kJ; Protein 18g; Carbohydrate 13.2g, of which sugars 12.2g; Fat 7g, of which saturates 2g; Cholesterol 47mg; Calcium 97mg; Fibre 1.7g; Sodium 220mg

STEWED CARAMELIZED PIG'S FEET

THE VIETNAMESE AND CAMBODIANS COOK EVERY PART OF THE PIG — THE FEET, HOCKS AND SHANKS ARE STEWED SLOWLY. BECAUSE THE COOKING JUICES ARE SO RICH AND VELVETY FROM THE GELATINOUS MEAT, THIS DISH IS BEST SERVED WITH CHUNKS OF BREAD TO MOP UP THE SAUCE.

SERVES FOUR

INGREDIENTS
- 30ml/2 tbsp sugar
- 1 litre/1¾ pints/4 cups pork stock or water
- 30ml/2 tbsp *nuoc mam* or *tuk trey*
- 30ml/2 tbsp soy sauce
- 900g/2lb pig's feet, cleaned
- 4 spring onions (scallions), trimmed, halved and bruised
- 2 lemon grass stalks, trimmed, halved and bruised
- 50g/2oz fresh root ginger, peeled and sliced
- 2 garlic cloves, crushed
- 2 dried red chillies
- 4 star anise
- 4 eggs, hard-boiled and shelled
- crusty bread or jasmine rice and stir-fried greens, to serve

2 Add the pig's feet, spring onions, lemon grass, ginger, garlic, chillies and star anise. Bring to the boil, then reduce the heat and cover the pan. Simmer for 3–4 hours, until the meat is very tender.

3 Skim any fat off the top and drop in the boiled eggs. Simmer uncovered for a further 10 minutes, turning the eggs over from time to time, so that they turn golden. Serve hot with fresh bread or jasmine rice and stir-fried greens.

1 In a heavy pan, melt the sugar with 15ml/1 tbsp water. When it turns golden, remove from the heat and stir in the stock, *nuoc mam* or *tuk trey* and the soy sauce. Put the pan back over the heat and stir until the caramel dissolves.

Per portion Energy 126Kcal/531kJ; Protein 16g; Carbohydrate 8.6g, of which sugars 8.5g; Fat 3g, of which saturates 1g; Cholesterol 47mg; Calcium 19mg; Fibre 0.3g; Sodium 328mg

BAKED CINNAMON MEAT LOAF

SIMILAR TO THE VIETNAMESE STEAMED PÂTÉS, THIS TYPE OF MEAT LOAF IS USUALLY SERVED AS A SNACK OR LIGHT LUNCH, WITH A CRUSTY BAGUETTE. ACCOMPANIED WITH EITHER TART PICKLES OR A CRUNCHY SALAD, AND SPLASHED WITH PIQUANT SAUCE, IT IS LIGHT AND TASTY.

SERVES FOUR TO SIX

INGREDIENTS
    30ml/2 tbsp *nuoc mam*
    25ml/1½ tbsp ground cinnamon
    10ml/2 tsp sugar
    5ml/1 tsp ground black pepper
    15ml/1 tbsp potato starch
    450g/1lb lean minced (ground) pork
    25g/1oz pork fat, very finely chopped
    23 shallots, very finely chopped
    oil, for greasing
    chilli oil or *nuoc cham*, for drizzling
    red chilli strips, to garnish
    bread or noodles, to serve

2 Add the minced pork, the chopped pork fat, and the shallots to the bowl and mix thoroughly. Cover and put in the refrigerator for 3–4 hours.

4 Cover with foil and bake in the oven for 35–40 minutes. If you want the top to turn brown and crunchy, remove the foil for the last 10 minutes.

1 In a large bowl, mix together the *nuoc mam*, ground cinnamon, sugar and ground black pepper. Beat in the potato starch.

3 Preheat the oven to 180°C/350°F/ Gas 4. Lightly oil a baking tin (pan) and spread the pork mixture in it – it should feel springy from the potato starch.

5 Turn the meat loaf out on to a board and slice it into strips. Drizzle the strips with chilli oil or *nuoc cham*, and serve them hot with bread or noodles.

COOK'S TIPS
• Serve the meat loaf as a nibble with drinks by cutting it into bitesize squares or fingers.
• Serve with a piquant sauce for dipping.
• Cut the meat loaf into wedges and take on a picnic to eat with bread and pickles or chutney.
• Fry slices of meat loaf until browned and serve with fried eggs.

Per portion Energy 111Kcal/465kJ; Protein 16g; Carbohydrate 4.8g, of which sugars 2.3g; Fat 3g, of which saturates 1g; Cholesterol 47mg; Calcium 9mg; Fibre 0.2g; Sodium 54mg

RICE AND NOODLES

Rice and noodles form the foundations of every meal. Eaten at any time of day, they are served in dishes such as Rice Porridge for breakfast and stir-fried for snacks. Rice may be served as an accompaniment to the main dish and noodles are often presented as a main dish — such as Cambodian Wheat Noodles with Stir-fried Pork.

STEAMED RICE

LONG GRAIN RICE IS THE MOST FREQUENTLY EATEN GRAIN IN VIETNAM — FRESHLY STEAMED AND SERVED AT ALMOST EVERY MEAL. IF THE MAIN DISH DOESN'T INCLUDE NOODLES, THEN A BOWL OF STEAMED RICE — COM — OR RICE WRAPPERS WILL PROVIDE THE STARCH FOR THE MEAL.

SERVES FOUR

INGREDIENTS
225g/8oz/generous 1 cup long grain
  rice, rinsed and drained
a pinch of salt

1 Put the rice into a heavy pan or clay pot. Add 600ml/1 pint/2½ cups water to cover the rice by 2.5cm/1in. Add the salt, and then bring the water to the boil.

VARIATION
Jasmine rice is delicious and readily available from Asian stores.

2 Reduce the heat, cover the pan and cook gently for about 20 minutes, or until all the water has been absorbed. Remove the pan from the heat and leave to steam, still covered, for a further 5–10 minutes.

3 To serve, simply fluff up with a fork.

Per portion Energy 203Kcal/864kJ; Protein 4g; Carbohydrate 49g, of which sugars 0g; Fat 1g, of which saturates 0g; Cholesterol 0mg; Calcium 2mg; Fibre 0.3g; Sodium 0mg

BAMBOO-STEAMED STICKY RICE

VIETNAMESE STICKY RICE, OR GLUTINOUS RICE, CALLED XOI NEP, *REQUIRES A LONG SOAK IN WATER BEFORE BEING COOKED IN A BAMBOO STEAMER. IT IS USED FOR SAVOURY AND SWEET RICE CAKES, SUCH AS* BANH CHUNG *AND* HUE COM SEN.

SERVES FOUR

INGREDIENTS
350g/12oz/1¾ cups sticky rice

1 Put the rice into a large bowl and fill the bowl with cold water. Leave the rice to soak for at least 6 hours, then drain, rinse thoroughly, and drain again.

VARIATION
Sticky rice is enjoyed as a sweet, filling snack with sugar and coconut milk and, as it is fairly bulky, it is also served with dipping sauces, light dishes and vegetarian meals.

2 Fill a wok or heavy pan one-third full with water. Place a bamboo steamer, with the lid on, over the wok or pan and bring the water to the boil. Uncover the steamer and place a dampened piece of muslin (cheesecloth) over the rack. Tip the rice into the middle and spread it out. Fold the muslin over the rice, cover and steam for 25 minutes until the rice is tender but firm. The measured quantity of rice grains doubles when cooked.

Per portion Energy 314Kcal/1314kJ; Protein 7g; Carbohydrate 66g, of which sugars 0g; Fat 1g, of which saturates 0g; Cholesterol 0mg; Calcium 14mg; Fibre 0g; Sodium 0mg

RICE PORRIDGE

IN CAMBODIA, A STEAMING BOWL OF THICK RICE PORRIDGE OR BOBOR IS A NOURISHING AND SATISFYING BREAKFAST. USUALLY MADE WITH LONG GRAIN RICE, IT CAN BE MADE PLAIN, OR WITH THE ADDITION OF CHICKEN, PORK, FISH OR PRAWNS.

SERVES SIX

INGREDIENTS
   15ml/1 tbsp vegetable or groundnut
      (peanut) oil
   25g/1oz fresh root ginger, shredded
   115g/4oz/generous 1 cup long grain
      rice, rinsed and drained
   1.2 litres/2 pints/5 cups chicken
      stock or water
   30–45ml/2–3 tbsp *tuk trey*
   10ml/2 tsp sugar
   450g/1lb fresh fish fillets, boned
      (any fish will do)
   sea salt and ground black pepper
For the garnish
   15ml/1 tbsp vegetable or groundnut
      (peanut) oil
   2 garlic cloves, finely chopped
   1 lemon grass stalk, trimmed and
      finely sliced
   25g/1oz fresh root ginger, shredded
   a few coriander (cilantro) leaves

1 In a heavy pan heat the oil and stir in the ginger and rice for 1 minute. Pour in the stock and bring it to the boil. Reduce the heat and simmer, partially covered, for 20 minutes, until the rice is tender and the soup is thick. Stir the *tuk trey* and sugar into the soupy porridge. Season and keep the porridge hot.

2 Meanwhile, fill a wok a third of the way with water. Fit a covered bamboo steamer on top and bring the water to the boil so that the steam rises. Season the fish fillets, place them on a plate and put them inside the steamer. Cover and steam the fish until cooked.

3 For the garnish, heat the oil in small wok or heavy pan. Add the chopped garlic, lemon grass and ginger and stir-fry until golden and fragrant. Add chillies to the mixture, if you like.

4 Ladle the rice porridge into bowls. Tear off pieces of steamed fish fillet to place on top. Sprinkle with the stir-fried garlic, lemon grass and ginger, and garnish with a few coriander leaves.

Per portion Energy 152Kcal/636kJ; Protein 15g; Carbohydrate 17g, of which sugars 1.7g; Fat 2g, of which saturates 0.3g; Cholesterol 35mg; Calcium 11mg; Fibre 0g; Sodium 45mg

COCONUT RICE

ORIGINALLY FROM INDIA AND THAILAND, COCONUT RICE IS POPULAR IN CAMBODIA AND SOUTHERN VIETNAM. RICH AND NOURISHING, IT IS OFTEN SERVED WITH A TANGY FRUIT AND VEGETABLE SALAD, SUCH AS THE ONES MADE WITH GREEN PAPAYA OR GREEN MANGO.

SERVES FOUR TO SIX

INGREDIENTS
400ml/14fl oz/1⅔ cups unsweetened coconut milk
400ml/14fl oz/1⅔ cups seasoned chicken stock
225g/8oz/generous 1 cup long grain rice, rinsed in several bowls of water and drained
115g/4oz fresh coconut, grated

COOK'S TIP
As the coconut shells are often halved and used as bowls, they make a perfect serving vessel for this rice, garnished with fresh or roasted coconut or crispy-fried ginger. In the street, this rice is often served on a banana leaf.

1 Pour the coconut milk and stock into a heavy pan and stir well to combine. Bring the liquid to the boil and stir in the rice. Stir once, reduce the heat and cover the pan. Simmer gently for about 25 minutes, until the rice has absorbed all the liquid. Remove from the heat and leave the rice to sit for 10 minutes.

2 Meanwhile, heat a small, heavy pan. Stir in the fresh coconut and roast it until it turns golden with a nutty aroma. Tip the roasted coconut into a bowl.

3 Fluff up the rice with a fork and spoon it into bowls. Scatter the roasted coconut over the top and serve.

Per portion Energy 175Kcal/731kJ; Protein 3g; Carbohydrate 33.5g, of which sugars 3.5g; Fat 3g, of which saturates 2g; Cholesterol 0mg; Calcium 28mg; Fibre 0.6g; Sodium 75mg

GARLIC AND GINGER RICE WITH CORIANDER

IN VIETNAM AND CAMBODIA, WHEN RICE IS SERVED ON THE SIDE, IT IS USUALLY STEAMED AND PLAIN, OR FRAGRANT WITH THE FLAVOURS OF GINGER AND HERBS. THE COMBINATION OF GARLIC AND GINGER IS POPULAR IN BOTH COUNTRIES AND COMPLIMENTS ALMOST ANY VEGETABLE, FISH OR MEAT DISH.

SERVES FOUR TO SIX

INGREDIENTS

15ml/1 tbsp vegetable or groundnut
   (peanut) oil
2–3 garlic cloves, finely chopped
25g/1oz fresh root ginger, finely
   chopped
225g/8oz/generous 1 cup long grain
   rice, rinsed in several bowls of
   water and drained
900ml/1½ pints/3¾ cups
   chicken stock
a bunch of fresh coriander (cilantro)
   leaves, finely chopped
a bunch of fresh basil and mint,
   (optional), finely chopped

1 Heat the oil in a clay pot or heavy pan. Stir in the garlic and ginger and fry until golden. Stir in the rice and allow it to absorb the flavours for 1–2 minutes. Pour in the stock and stir to make sure the rice doesn't stick. Bring the stock to the boil, then reduce the heat.

2 Scatter the coriander over the surface of the stock, cover the pan, and leave to cook gently for 20–25 minutes, until the rice has absorbed all the liquid. Turn off the heat and gently fluff up the rice to mix in the coriander. Cover and leave to infuse for 10 minutes before serving.

Per portion Energy 151Kcal/632kJ; Protein 3g; Carbohydrate 30g, of which sugars 0g; Fat 2g, of which saturates 0.3g; Cholesterol 0mg; Calcium 9mg; Fibre 0.1g; Sodium 124mg

SAIGON SOUTHERN-SPICED CHILLI RICE

ALTHOUGH PLAIN STEAMED RICE IS SERVED AT ALMOST EVERY MEAL, MANY SOUTHERN FAMILIES LIKE TO SNEAK IN A LITTLE SPICE TOO. A BURST OF CHILLI FOR FIRE, TURMERIC FOR COLOUR, AND CORIANDER FOR ITS COOLING FLAVOUR, ARE ALL THAT'S NEEDED.

SERVES FOUR

INGREDIENTS

    15ml/1 tbsp vegetable oil
    2–3 green or red Thai chillies,
      seeded and finely chopped
    2 garlic cloves, finely chopped
    2.5cm/1in fresh root ginger, chopped
    5ml/1 tsp sugar
    10–15ml/2–3 tsp ground turmeric
    225g/8oz/generous 1 cup long
      grain rice
    30ml/2 tbsp *nuoc mam*
    600ml/1 pint/2½ cups water or stock
    1 bunch of fresh coriander
      (cilantro), stalks removed, leaves
      finely chopped
    salt and ground black pepper

1 Heat the oil in a heavy pan. Stir in the chillies, garlic and ginger with the sugar. As they begin to colour, stir in the turmeric. Add the rice, coating it well, then pour in the *nuoc mam* and the water or stock – the liquid should sit about 2.5cm/1in above the rice.

2 Tip the rice on to a serving dish. Add some of the coriander and lightly toss together using a fork. Garnish with the remaining coriander.

COOK'S TIP
This rice goes well with grilled and stir-fried fish and shellfish dishes, but you can serve it as an alternative to plain rice. Add extra chillies, if you like.

3 Season with salt and ground black pepper and bring the liquid to the boil. Reduce the heat, cover and simmer for about 25 minutes, or until the water has been absorbed. Remove from the heat and leave the rice to steam for a further 10 minutes.

Per portion Energy 252Kcal/1066kJ; Protein 5g; Carbohydrate 51g, of which sugars 1g; Fat 5g, of which saturates 1g; Cholesterol 0mg; Calcium 24mg; Fibre 0.3g; Sodium 500mg

FRAGRANT RICE <u>WITH</u> CHICKEN, MINT <u>AND</u> NUOC CHAM

FROM THE NORTH OF VIETNAM, THIS REFRESHING DISH CAN BE SERVED SIMPLY, DRIZZLED WITH NUOC CHAM, OR AS PART OF A CELEBRATORY MEAL THAT MIGHT INCLUDE FISH OR CHICKEN, EITHER GRILLED OR ROASTED WHOLE, AND ACCOMPANIED BY PICKLES AND A TABLE SALAD.

2 Put the rice in a heavy pan and stir in the stock. When the rice settles, check that the stock sits roughly 2.5cm/1in above the rice; if not, top it up. Bring the liquid to the boil, cover the pan and cook for about 25 minutes, or until all the water has been absorbed.

3 Remove the pan from the heat and, using a fork, add the shredded chicken, shallots and most of the mint. Cover the pan again and leave the flavours to mingle for 10 minutes. Tip the rice into bowls, or on to a serving dish, garnish with the remaining mint and the spring onions, and serve with *nuoc cham*.

<u>SERVES FOUR</u>

INGREDIENTS
  350g/12oz/1¾ cups long grain rice, rinsed and drained
  2–3 shallots, halved and finely sliced
  1 bunch of fresh mint, stalks removed, leaves finely shredded
  2 spring onions (scallions), finely sliced, to garnish
  nuoc cham, to serve
For the stock
  2 meaty chicken legs
  1 onion, peeled and quartered
  4cm/1½in fresh root ginger, peeled and coarsely chopped
  15ml/1 tbsp *nuoc mam*
  3 black peppercorns
  1 bunch of fresh mint
  sea salt

1 To make the stock, put the chicken legs into a deep pan. Add all the other ingredients, except the salt, and pour in 1 litre/1¾ pints/4 cups water. Bring the water to the boil, skim off any foam, then reduce the heat and simmer gently with the lid on for 1 hour. Remove the lid, increase the heat and simmer for a further 30 minutes to reduce the stock. Skim off any fat, strain the stock and season with salt. Measure 750ml/1¼ pints/3 cups stock. Remove the chicken meat from the bone and shred.

MAKING A MEAL OF IT
To serve this dish as a meal on its own, stir-fry strips of pork, slices of Chinese sausage and a handful of prawns (shrimp) and toss into the rice along with the shredded chicken.

Per portion Energy 370Kcal/1569kJ; Protein 12g; Carbohydrate 79g, of which sugars 1g; Fat 3g, of which saturates 0g; Cholesterol 26mg; Calcium 41mg; Fibre 0.8g; Sodium 200mg

STICKY RICE CAKES FILLED WITH PORK AND LOTUS SEEDS

IN THE OLD IMPERIAL CITY OF HUE, THIS TRADITIONAL DISH, HUE COM SEN, IS PRESENTED LIKE A BEAUTIFUL WOMAN, DRESSED IN A LOTUS LEAF AND GARNISHED WITH A FRESH LOTUS FLOWER. SERVE THE RICE CAKES WITH A SALAD AND DIPPING SAUCE.

MAKES TWO CAKES

INGREDIENTS

15ml/1 tbsp vegetable oil
2 garlic cloves, chopped
225g/8oz lean pork, cut into
  bitesize chunks
30ml/2 tbsp *nuoc mam*
2.5ml/½ tsp sugar
10ml/2 tsp ground black pepper
115g/4oz lotus seeds, soaked for
  6 hours and drained
2 lotus or banana leaves, trimmed
  and cut into 25cm/10in squares
500g/1¼lb/5 cups cooked sticky rice
salt

1 Heat the oil in a heavy pan. Stir in the garlic, until it begins to colour, then add the pork, *nuoc mam*, sugar and pepper. Cover and cook over a low heat for about 45 minutes, or until the pork is tender. Leave to cool.

2 Meanwhile, bring a pan of salted water to the boil. Reduce the heat and add the prepared lotus seeds. Allow them to cook for 10 minutes, or until they are tender, then drain, pat dry and leave to cool.

VARIATIONS
For celebrations over New Year, Tet, there is a similar dish called *banh chung,* which contains mung beans instead of lotus seeds. In southern Vietnam, banana leaves are used to make these parcels, and they make the perfect substitute if you can't find lotus leaves.

3 Using your fingers, shred the cooked pork and place beside the lotus seeds. Lay a lotus leaf or banana leaf on a flat surface and place a quarter of the cooked sticky rice in the middle of the leaf. Flatten the centre of the rice mound slightly and then scatter with half the shredded pork and half the lotus seeds.

4 Drizzle some of the cooking juices from the pork over the top. Place another quarter of the rice on top, moulding and patting it with your fingers to make sure the pork and lotus seeds are enclosed like a cake. Fold the leaf edge nearest to you over the rice, tuck in the sides, and fold the whole packet over to form a tight, square bundle. Tie it with string to secure it and set aside. Repeat with the second leaf and the remaining ingredients.

5 Fill a wok one-third full of water. Place a double-tiered bamboo steamer, with its lid on, on top. Bring the water to the boil, lift the bamboo lid and place a rice cake on the rack in each tier. Cover and steam for about 45 minutes. Carefully open up the parcels and serve.

Per portion Energy 736Kcal/3071kJ; Protein 42g; Carbohydrate 52g, of which sugars 2g; Fat 41g, of which saturates 5g; Cholesterol 1mg; Calcium 107mg; Fibre 3.7g, Sodium 700mg

STIR-FRIED RICE WITH CHINESE SAUSAGE

TRADITIONAL VIETNAMESE STIR-FRIED RICE INCLUDES CHINESE PORK SAUSAGE, OR STRIPS OF PORK COMBINED WITH PRAWNS OR CRAB. PREPARED THIS WAY, THE DISH CAN BE EATEN AS A SNACK, OR AS PART OF THE MEAL WITH GRILLED AND ROASTED MEATS ACCOMPANIED BY A VEGETABLE DISH OR SALAD.

SERVES FOUR

INGREDIENTS

    25g/1oz dried cloud ear (wood ear)
      mushrooms, soaked for 20 minutes
    15ml/1 tbsp vegetable or sesame oil
    1 onion, sliced
    2 green or red Thai chillies, seeded
      and finely chopped
    2 Chinese sausages (15cm/6in long),
      each sliced into 10 pieces
    175g/6oz prawns (shrimp), shelled
      and deveined
    30ml/2 tbsp *nuoc mam*, plus extra
      for drizzling
    10ml/2 tsp five-spice powder
    1 bunch of fresh coriander (cilantro),
      stalks removed, leaves finely
      chopped
    450g/1lb/4 cups cold steamed rice
    ground black pepper

1 Drain the soaked cloud ear mushrooms and cut them into strips. Heat a wok or heavy pan and add the oil. Add the onion and chillies. Fry until they begin to colour, then stir in the mushrooms.

COOK'S TIP
The rice used in these stir-fries is usually made the day before and added cold to the dish.

2 Add the sausage slices, moving them around the wok or pan until they begin to brown. Add the prawns and move them around until they turn opaque. Stir in the *nuoc mam*, the five-spice powder and 30ml/2 tbsp of the coriander.

3 Season well with pepper, then quickly add the rice, making sure it doesn't stick to the pan. As soon as the rice is heated through, sprinkle with the remainder of the coriander and serve with *nuoc mam* to drizzle over it.

Per portion Energy 398Kcal/1673kJ; Protein 19g; Carbohydrate 44g, of which sugars 4g; Fat 18g, of which saturates 5g; Cholesterol 116mg; Calcium 158mg; Fibre 2g; Sodium 800mg

RICE ROLLS STUFFED <u>WITH</u> PORK

THIS TRADITIONAL VIETNAMESE DISH, BANH CUON, IS A CLASSIC. THE STEAMED RICE SHEETS ARE FILLED WITH MINCED PORK, ROLLED UP, DRIZZLED IN SPRING ONION OIL, AND THEN DIPPED IN NUOC CHAM. GENERALLY, THEY ARE EATEN AS A SNACK, OR SERVED AS A STARTER TO A MEAL.

SERVES SIX

INGREDIENTS
  25g/1oz dried cloud ear (wood ear)
    mushrooms, soaked in warm water
    for 30 minutes
  350g/12oz minced (ground) pork
  30ml/2 tbsp *nuoc mam*
  10ml/2 tsp sugar
  15ml/1 tbsp vegetable or groundnut
    (peanut) oil
  2 garlic cloves, finely chopped
  2 shallots, finely chopped
  2 spring onions (scallions), trimmed
    and finely chopped
  24 fresh rice sheets, 7.5cm/3in square
  ground black pepper
  spring onion oil, for drizzling
  nuoc cham, for dipping

COOK'S TIP
To make life easy, prepared, fresh rice
sheets are available in Asian markets.

1 Drain the mushrooms and squeeze out any excess water. Cut off and discard the hard stems. Finely chop the rest of the mushrooms and put them in a bowl. Add the minced pork, *nuoc mam*, and sugar and mix well.

2 Heat the oil in a wok or heavy pan. Add the garlic, shallots and onions. Stir-fry until golden. Add the pork mixture and stir-fry for 5–6 minutes, until the pork is cooked. Season with pepper.

3 Place the rice sheets on a flat surface. Spoon a tablespoon of the pork mixture onto the middle of each sheet. Fold one side over the filling, tuck in the sides, and roll to enclose the filling, so that it resembles a short spring roll.

4 Place the filled rice rolls on a serving plate, drizzle with spring onion oil, and serve with *nuoc cham* or any other chilli or tangy sauce of your choice, for dipping.

Per portion Energy 183Kcal/765kJ; Protein 12g; Carbohydrate 16.2g, of which sugars 2.4g; Fat 8g, of which saturates 2g; Cholesterol 39mg; Calcium 11mg; Fibre 0.2g; Sodium 41mg

FRESH RICE NOODLES

A VARIETY OF DRIED NOODLES IS AVAILABLE IN ASIAN SUPERMARKETS, BUT FRESH ONES ARE QUITE DIFFERENT AND NOT THAT DIFFICULT TO MAKE. THE FRESHLY-MADE NOODLE SHEETS CAN BE SERVED AS A SNACK, DRENCHED IN SUGAR OR HONEY, OR DIPPED INTO A SAVOURY SAUCE OF YOUR CHOICE.

SERVES FOUR

INGREDIENTS
   225g/8oz/2 cups rice flour
   600ml/1 pint/2½ cups water
   a pinch of salt
   15ml/1 tbsp vegetable oil, plus extra
     for brushing
   slivers of red chilli and fresh root
     ginger, and coriander (cilantro)
     leaves, to garnish (optional)

1 Place the flour in a bowl and stir in some of the water to form a paste. Pour in the rest of the water, beating it to make a lump-free batter. Add the salt and oil and leave to stand for 15 minutes.

COOK'S TIP
You may need to top up the water through one of the slits and tighten the cloth.

2 Meanwhile, fill a wide pan with water. Cut a piece of smooth cotton cloth a little larger than the diameter of the pan. Stretch it over the top of the pan, pulling the edges tautly down over the sides, then wind a piece of string around the edge, to secure. Using a sharp knife, make three small slits, about 2.5cm/1in from the edge of the cloth, at regular intervals.

3 Bring the water to the boil. Stir the batter and ladle 30–45ml/2–3 tbsp on to the cloth, swirling it to form a 13–15cm/5–6in wide circle. Cover with a domed lid, such as a wok lid, and steam for 1 minute, or until the noodle sheet is translucent.

4 Carefully insert a spatula or knife under the noodle sheet and prise it off the cloth. (If it doesn't peel off easily, you may need to steam it a little longer.) Transfer the noodle sheet to a lightly oiled baking tray, brush lightly with oil, and cook the remaining batter in the same way.

VARIATION
Fresh noodles are also delicious cut into strips and stir-fried with garlic, ginger, chillies and *nuoc cham* or soy sauce.

Per portion Energy 251Kcal/1046kJ; Protein 4g; Carbohydrate 45g, of which sugars 0g; Fat 5g, of which saturates 1g; Cholesterol 0mg; Calcium 24mg; Fibre 1.1g; Sodium 200mg

NOODLES WITH CRAB AND CLOUD EAR MUSHROOMS

THIS IS A DISH OF CONTRASTING FLAVOURS, TEXTURES AND COLOURS, AND IN VIETNAM IT IS COOKED WITH SKILL AND DEXTERITY. WHILE ONE HAND GENTLY TURNS THE NOODLES IN THE PAN, THE OTHER TAKES CHUNKS OF FRESH CRAB MEAT AND DROPS THEM INTO THE STEAMING WOK TO SEAL.

SERVES FOUR

INGREDIENTS

25g/1oz dried cloud ear (wood ear) mushrooms, soaked in warm water for 20 minutes

115g/4oz dried bean thread (cellophane) noodles, soaked in warm water for 20 minutes

30ml/2 tbsp vegetable or sesame oil

3 shallots, halved and thinly sliced

2 garlic cloves, crushed

2 green or red Thai chillies, seeded and sliced

1 carrot, peeled and cut into thin diagonal rounds

5ml/1 tsp sugar

45ml/3 tbsp oyster sauce

15ml/1 tbsp soy sauce

400ml/14fl oz/1⅔ cups water or chicken stock

225g/8oz fresh, raw crab meat, cut into bitesize chunks

ground black pepper

fresh coriander (cilantro) leaves, to garnish

1 Remove the centres from the soaked cloud ear mushrooms and cut the mushrooms in half. Drain the soaked noodles and cut them into 30cm/12in pieces and put aside.

2 Heat a wok or pan and add 15ml/1 tbsp of the oil. Stir in the shallots, garlic and chillies, and cook until fragrant. Add the carrot rounds and cook for 1 minute, then add the mushrooms. Stir in the sugar with the oyster and soy sauces, followed by the bean thread noodles. Pour in the water or stock, cover the wok or pan and cook for about 5 minutes, or until the noodles are soft and have absorbed most of the sauce.

3 Meanwhile, heat the remaining oil in a heavy pan. Add the crab meat and cook until it is nicely pink and tender. Season well with black pepper. Arrange the noodles and crab meat on a serving dish and garnish with coriander.

Per portion Energy 292Kcal/1224kJ; Protein 16g; Carbohydrate 30g, of which sugars 5g; Fat 13g, of which saturates 2g; Cholesterol 36mg; Calcium 29mg; Fibre 2.5g; Sodium 1000mg

CRISPY EGG NOODLE PANCAKE WITH PRAWNS, SCALLOPS AND SQUID

IN DISHES OF CHINESE ORIGIN, EGG NOODLES ARE USED INSTEAD OF RICE NOODLES. FOR THIS POPULAR DISH, THE VIETNAMESE PREFER TO USE THIN SHANGHAI-STYLE NOODLES, WHICH ARE AVAILABLE ONLY IN CHINESE AND ASIAN MARKETS. SERVE WITH A SALAD OR PICKLED VEGETABLES.

SERVES FOUR

INGREDIENTS
  225g/8oz fresh egg noodles
  60–75ml/4–5 tbsp vegetable oil,
    plus extra for brushing
  4cm/1½in fresh root ginger, peeled
    and cut into matchsticks
  4 spring onions (scallions), trimmed
    and cut into bitesize pieces
  1 carrot, peeled and cut into thin,
    diagonal slices
  8 scallops (halved if large)
  8 baby squid, cut in half
    lengthways
  8 tiger prawns (shrimp), shelled
    and deveined
  30ml/2 tbsp *nuoc mam*
  45ml/3 tbsp soy sauce
  5ml/1 tsp sugar
  ground black pepper
  fresh coriander (cilantro) leaves,
    to garnish
  nuoc cham and/or pickled vegetables,
    to serve

2 Heat 30ml/2 tbsp of the oil in a non-stick, heavy pan. Carefully slide the noodle pancake off the plate into the pan and cook over a medium heat until it is crisp and golden underneath. Add 15ml/1 tbsp oil to the pan, flip the noodle pancake over and crisp the other side too.

3 Meanwhile, heat a wok or heavy pan and add the remaining oil. Stir in the ginger and spring onions, and cook until they become fragrant. Add the carrot slices, tossing them in the wok, for 1–2 minutes.

COOK'S TIP
You can usually ask your fishmonger to prepare the squid, but to prepare squid yourself, get a firm hold of the head and pull it from the body. Reach down inside the body sac and pull out the transparent back bone, as well as any stringy parts. Rinse the body sac inside and out and pat dry. Cut the tentacles off above the eyes and add to the pile of squid you're going to cook. Discard everything else.

4 Add the scallops, squid and prawns, moving them around the wok, so that they sear while cooking. Stir in the *nuoc mam*, soy sauce and sugar and season well with black pepper.

5 Transfer the crispy noodle pancake to a serving dish and tip the seafood on top. Garnish with coriander and serve immediately. To eat, break off pieces of the seafood-covered noodle pancake and drizzle with *nuoc cham*.

1 Bring a large pan of water to the boil. Drop in the noodles, untangling them with chopsticks or a fork. Cook for about 5 minutes, or until tender. Drain thoroughly and spread the noodles out into a wide, thick pancake on a lightly oiled plate. Leave the noodles to dry out a little, so that the pancake holds its shape when it is fried. Noodle nests are a good base for many dishes.

Per portion Energy 807Kcal/3401kJ; Protein 83g; Carbohydrate 53g, of which sugars 48g; Fat 31g, of which saturates 5g; Cholesterol 97.5mg; Calcium 110mg; Fibre 2.3g; Sodium 160mg

FRIED NOODLES WITH SPICY PEANUT SATÉ, BEEF AND FRAGRANT HERBS

IF YOU LIKE CHILLIES AND PEANUTS, THIS DELICIOUS DISH MAKES THE PERFECT CHOICE. THE STRINGY RICE STICKS ARE FIDDLY TO STIR-FRY AS THEY HAVE A TENDENCY TO CLING TO ONE ANOTHER, SO WORK QUICKLY. THIS DISH IS USUALLY SERVED WITH A TABLE SALAD OR PICKLES.

SERVES FOUR

INGREDIENTS
   15–30ml/1–2 tbsp vegetable oil
   300g/11oz beef sirloin, cut against
      the grain into thin slices
   225g/8oz dried rice sticks (vermicelli),
      soaked in warm water for 20 minutes
   225g/8oz/1 cup beansprouts
   5–10ml/1–2 tsp *nuoc mam*
   1 small bunch each of fresh basil
      and mint, stalks removed, leaves
      shredded, to garnish
   pickles, to serve
For the saté
   4 dried Serrano chillies, seeded
   60ml/4 tbsp groundnut (peanut) oil
   4–5 garlic cloves, crushed
   5–10ml/1–2 tsp curry powder
   40g/1½oz/⅓ cup roasted peanuts,
      finely ground

1 To make the saté, grind the Serrano chillies in a mortar with a pestle. Heat the oil in a heavy pan and stir in the garlic until it begins to colour. Add the chillies, curry powder and the peanuts and stir over a low heat, until the mixture forms a paste. Remove the pan from the heat and leave the mixture to cool.

2 Heat a wok or heavy pan, and pour in 15ml/1 tbsp of the oil. Add the sliced beef and cook for 1–2 minutes, and stir in 7.5ml/1½ tsp of the spicy peanut saté. Tip the beef on to a clean plate and set aside. Drain the rice sticks.

VARIATION
Although it is quite similar to *pad Thai*, one of the national noodle dishes of Thailand, the addition of *nuoc mam*, basil and mint give this fragrant dish a distinctly Vietnamese flavour. There are many similar versions throughout South-east Asia, made with prawns (shrimp), pork and chicken.

3 Add 7.5ml/1½ tsp oil to the wok and add the rice sticks and 15ml/1 tbsp saté. Toss the noodles until coated in the sauce and cook for 4–5 minutes, or until tender. Toss in the beef for 1 minute, then add the beansprouts with the *nuoc mam*. Tip the noodles on to a serving dish and sprinkle with the basil and mint. Serve with pickles.

Per portion Energy 603Kcal/2507kJ; Protein 26g; Carbohydrate 52g, of which sugars 2g; Fat 32g, of which saturates 6g; Cholesterol 38mg; Calcium 73mg; Fibre 2.2g; Sodium 200mg

CAMBODIAN WHEAT NOODLES WITH STIR-FRIED PORK

WHEAT NOODLES ARE POPULAR IN CAMBODIA. SOLD DRIED, IN STRAIGHT BUNDLES LIKE STICKS, THEY ARE VERSATILE AND ROBUST. NOODLES DRYING IN THE OPEN AIR, HANGING FROM BAMBOO POLES, ARE COMMON IN THE MARKETS. THIS SIMPLE RECIPE COMES FROM A NOODLE STALL IN PHNOM PENH.

SERVES FOUR

INGREDIENTS
225g/8oz pork loin, cut into thin strips
225g/8oz dried wheat noodles, soaked
   in lukewarm water for 20 minutes
15ml/1 tbsp groundnut (peanut) oil
2 garlic cloves, finely chopped
2–3 spring onions (scallions),
   trimmed and cut into bitesize pieces
45ml/3 tbsp *kroeung*
15ml/1 tbsp *tuk trey*
30ml/2 tbsp unsalted roasted
   peanuts, finely chopped
chilli oil, for drizzling
For the marinade
30ml/2 tbsp *tuk trey*
30ml/2 tbsp soy sauce
15ml/1 tbsp peanut oil
10ml/2 tsp sugar

1 In a bowl, combine the ingredients for the marinade, stirring constantly until the all the sugar dissolves. Toss in the strips of pork, making sure it is well coated in the marinade. Put aside for 30 minutes.

2 Drain the wheat noodles. Bring a large pan of water to the boil. Drop in the noodles, untangling them with chopsticks, if necessary. Cook for 4–5 minutes, until tender. Allow the noodles to drain thoroughly, then divide them among individual serving bowls. Keep the noodles warm until the dish is ready to serve.

3 Meanwhile, heat a wok. Add the oil and stir-fry the garlic and spring onions, until fragrant. Add the pork, tossing it around the wok for 2 minutes. Stir in the *kroeung* and *tuk trey* for 2 minutes – add a splash of water if the wok gets too dry – and tip the pork on top of the noodles. Sprinkle the peanuts over the top and drizzle with chilli oil to serve.

Per portion Energy 357Kcal/1494kJ; Protein 17g; Carbohydrate 51g, of which sugars 4.8g; Fat 9g, of which saturates 2g; Cholesterol 35mg; Calcium 21mg; Fibre 0.7g; Sodium 495mg

VEGETABLE DISHES

Raw, stir-fried, braised, pickled or salted, the Vietnamese

include vegetables in every meal. Side dishes are usually livened

up with exciting spices or herbs, and with many Buddhists

adhering to a vegetarian diet, there are a number of delicious

main dishes too. For a tasty meal at home, try Jungle Curry,

or Cambodian Aubergine Curry, served with rice and

Stir-fried Pineapple with Ginger and Chilli.

LUFFA SQUASH WITH MUSHROOMS, SPRING ONIONS AND CORIANDER

WINTER GOURDS, SUCH AS PUMPKINS, BITTER MELONS, LUFFA SQUASH AND A VARIETY OF OTHER SQUASH THAT COME UNDER THE KABOCHA UMBRELLA, ARE POPULAR INGREDIENTS FOR SOUPS AND BRAISED VEGETABLE DISHES.

SERVES FOUR

INGREDIENTS
    750g/1lb 10oz luffa squash, peeled
    30ml/2 tbsp groundnut (peanut) or
      sesame oil
    2 shallots, halved and sliced
    2 garlic cloves, finely chopped
    115g/4oz/1½ cups button (white)
      mushrooms, quartered
    15ml/1 tbsp mushroom sauce
    10ml/2 tsp soy sauce
    4 spring onions (scallions), cut into
      2cm/¾in pieces
    fresh coriander (cilantro) leaves and
      thin strips of spring onion
      (scallion), to garnish

1 Cut the luffa squash diagonally into 2cm/¾in-thick pieces. Heat the oil in a large wok or heavy pan. Stir in the halved shallots and garlic, stir-fry until they begin to colour and turn golden, then add the mushrooms.

2 Add the mushroom and soy sauces, and the squash. Reduce the heat, cover and cook gently for a few minutes until the squash is tender. Stir in the spring onion pieces, garnish with coriander and spring onion strips, and serve.

Per portion Energy 194Kcal/800kJ; Protein 3g; Carbohydrate 19g, of which sugars 3g; Fat 12g, of which saturates 2g; Cholesterol 0mg; Calcium 31mg; Fibre 5.1g; Sodium 100mg

STIR-FRIED LONG BEANS <u>WITH</u> PRAWNS, GALANGAL <u>AND</u> GARLIC

POPULAR IN BOTH CAMBODIA AND VIETNAM, LONG BEANS — LIKE MANY OTHER VEGETABLES — ARE OFTEN STIR-FRIED WITH GARLIC. THIS CAMBODIAN RECIPE IS LIVENED UP WITH PRAWNS, AS WELL AS OTHER FLAVOURINGS, AND WORKS WELL EITHER AS A SIDE DISH OR ON ITS OWN WITH RICE.

<u>SERVES FOUR</u>

INGREDIENTS
 45ml/3 tbsp vegetable oil
 2 garlic cloves, finely chopped
 25g/1oz galangal, finely shredded
 450g/1lb fresh prawns (shrimp),
  shelled and deveined
 1 onion, halved and finely sliced
 450g/1lb long beans, trimmed and
  cut into 7.5cm/3in lengths
 120ml/4fl oz/½ cup soy sauce
For the marinade
 30ml/2 tbsp *tuk trey*
 juice of 2 limes
 10ml/2 tsp sugar
 2 garlic cloves, crushed
 1 lemon grass stalk, trimmed and
  finely sliced

1 To make the marinade, beat the *tuk trey* and lime juice in a bowl with the sugar, until it has dissolved. Stir in the garlic and lemon grass. Toss in the prawns, cover, and chill for 1–2 hours.

2 Heat 30ml/2 tbsp of the oil in a wok or heavy pan. Stir in the chopped garlic and galangal. Just as they begin to colour, toss in the marinated prawns. Stir-fry for a minute or until the prawns turn pink. Lift the prawns out on to a plate, reserving as much of the oil, garlic and galangal as you can.

3 Add the remaining oil to the wok. Add the onion and stir-fry until slightly caramelized. Stir in the beans, then pour in the soy sauce. Cook for a further 2–3 minutes, until the beans are tender. Add the prawns and stir-fry for a minute until heated through. Serve immediately.

Per portion Energy 215Kcal/897kJ; Protein 23g; Carbohydrate 10g, of which sugars 8.2g; Fat 9g, of which saturates 1g; Cholesterol 219mg; Calcium 140mg; Fibre 2.7g; Sodium 235mg

STIR-FRIED WATER SPINACH WITH NUOC CHAM

IN THE VIETNAMESE COUNTRYSIDE THIS DISH IS A FAVOURITE WITH ROADSIDE VENDORS. ASPARAGUS AND CAULIFLOWER CAN ALSO BE STIR-FRIED IN A SIMILAR MANNER. SERVE ANY OF THESE VERSIONS AS A SIDE DISH TO MEAT OR FISH, OR WITH OTHER VEGETABLE DISHES.

SERVES THREE TO FOUR

INGREDIENTS
   30ml/2 tbsp groundnut (peanut) oil
   2 garlic cloves, finely chopped
   2 red or green Thai chillies, seeded
     and finely chopped
   500g/1¼lb fresh water spinach
   45ml/3 tbsp *nuoc cham*
   salt and ground black pepper

VARIATION
Any type of greens would work,
particularly ordinary spinach, although
tough leaves should be blanched first.

1 Heat a wok or large pan and add the
oil. Stir in the garlic and chillies and
stir-fry for 1 minute, then add the
spinach and toss around the pan.

2 Once the spinach leaves begin to wilt,
add the *nuoc cham*, making sure it
coats the spinach. Season to taste with
salt and pepper and serve immediately.

Per portion Energy 120Kcal/500kJ; Protein 3g; Carbohydrate 5g, of which sugars 3g; Fat 10g, of which saturates 2g; Cholesterol 0mg; Calcium 36mg; Fibre 3.3g; Sodium 200mg

STIR-FRIED PINEAPPLE <u>WITH</u> GINGER <u>AND</u> CHILLI

THROUGHOUT SOUTH-EAST ASIA, FRUIT IS OFTEN TREATED LIKE A VEGETABLE AND TOSSED IN A SALAD, OR STIR-FRIED, TO ACCOMPANY SPICY DISHES. IN THIS CAMBODIAN DISH, THE PINEAPPLE IS COMBINED WITH THE TANGY FLAVOURS OF GINGER AND CHILLI AND SERVED AS A SIDE-DISH.

SERVES FOUR

INGREDIENTS

30ml/2 tbsp groundnut (peanut) oil
2 garlic cloves, finely shredded
40g/1½oz fresh root ginger, peeled
  and finely shredded
2 red Thai chillies, seeded and
  finely shredded
1 pineapple, trimmed, peeled,
  cored and cut into bitesize
  chunks
15ml/1 tbsp *tuk trey*
30ml/2 tbsp soy sauce
15ml–30ml/1–2 tbsp sugar
30ml/2 tbsp roasted unsalted
  peanuts, finely chopped
1 lime, cut into quarters, to serve

1 Heat a large wok or heavy pan and add the oil. Stir in the garlic, ginger and chilli. Stir-fry until they begin to colour, then add the pineapple and stir-fry for a further 1–2 minutes, until the edges turn golden.

2 Add the *tuk trey*, soy sauce and sugar to taste and continue to stir-fry until the pineapple begins to caramelize.

3 Transfer to a serving dish, sprinkle with the roasted peanuts and serve with lime wedges.

Per portion Energy 185Kcal/780kJ; Protein 3g; Carbohydrate 24.1g, of which sugars 23.6g; Fat 9g, of which saturates 1g; Cholesterol 0mg; Calcium 43mg; Fibre 2.9g; Sodium 271mg

CHARRED AUBERGINE WITH A SPRING ONION AND CHILLI DRESSING

ONE OF THE WONDERFUL THINGS ABOUT AUBERGINES IS THAT THEY CAN BE PLACED IN THE FLAMES OF A FIRE, OR OVER HOT CHARCOAL, OR DIRECTLY OVER A GAS FLAME OF A STOVE, AND STILL TASTE GREAT. THIS VIETNAMESE DISH IS SERVED AS A SIDE SALAD TO MEAT AND POULTRY DISHES.

SERVES FOUR

INGREDIENTS

   2 aubergines (eggplants)
   30ml/2 tbsp groundnut (peanut) or
     vegetable oil
   2 spring onions (scallions),
     finely sliced
   2 red Serrano chillies, seeded and
     finely sliced
   15ml/1 tbsp *nuoc mam*
   25g/1oz/½ cup fresh basil leaves
   salt
   15ml/1 tbsp roasted peanuts,
     crushed
   nuoc cham, to serve

1 Place the aubergines over a barbecue or under a hot grill (broiler), or directly over a gas flame, and, turning them, cook until soft when pressed. Put them into a plastic bag to sweat for 1 minute.

2 Holding the aubergines by the stalks, carefully peel off the skin under cold running water. Squeeze the excess water from the peeled flesh, remove the stalk and pull the flesh apart in long strips. Place these strips in a serving dish.

3 Heat the oil in a small pan and quickly stir in the spring onions. Remove the pan from the heat and stir in the chillies, *nuoc mam*, basil leaves and a little salt to taste. Pour this dressing over the aubergines, toss gently and sprinkle the peanuts over the top.

4 Serve at room temperature and, for those who like a little extra fire, splash on some *nuoc cham*.

Per portion Energy 215Kcal/890kJ; Protein 10g; Carbohydrate 6g, of which sugars 4g; Fat 17g, of which saturates 3g; Cholesterol 0mg; Calcium 425mg; Fibre 0.8g; Sodium 700mg

STIR-FRIED ASPARAGUS WITH CHILLI, GALANGAL AND LEMON GRASS

ONE OF THE CULINARY LEGACIES OF FRENCH COLONIZATION IN VIETNAM AND CAMBODIA IS ASPARAGUS. TODAY IT IS GROWN IN VIETNAM AND FINDS ITS WAY INTO STIR-FRIES IN BOTH COUNTRIES. CAMBODIAN IN STYLE, THIS IS A LOVELY WAY TO EAT ASPARAGUS.

SERVES TWO TO FOUR

INGREDIENTS

    30ml/2 tbsp groundnut (peanut) oil
    2 garlic cloves, finely chopped
    2 Thai chillies, seeded and finely
      chopped
    25g/1oz galangal, finely shredded
    1 lemon grass stalk, trimmed and
      finely sliced
    350g/12oz fresh asparagus stalks,
      trimmed
    30ml/2 tbsp *tuk trey*
    30ml/2 tbsp soy sauce
    5ml/1 tsp sugar
    30ml/2 tbsp unsalted roasted
      peanuts, finely chopped
    1 small bunch fresh coriander
      (cilantro), finely chopped

1 Heat a large wok and add the oil. Stir in the garlic, chillies, galangal and lemon grass and stir-fry until they become fragrant and begin to turn golden.

2 Add the asparagus and stir-fry for a further 1–2 minutes, until it is just tender but not too soft.

3 Stir in the *tuk trey*, soy sauce and sugar. Stir in the peanuts and coriander and serve immediately.

VARIATION
This recipe also works well with broccoli, green beans and courgettes (zucchini), cut into strips.

Per portion Energy 117Kcal/482kJ; Protein 5g; Carbohydrate 3.3g, of which sugars 2.7g; Fat 9g, of which saturates 1g; Cholesterol 0mg; Calcium 30mg; Fibre 2g; Sodium 535mg

CRISP-FRIED TOFU IN A TANGY TOMATO SAUCE

THIS IS A LIGHT, TASTY VIETNAMESE DISH. THE BUDDHIST MONKS WHO ADHERE TO A VEGETARIAN DIET ENJOY IT TOO, SIMPLY BY REPLACING THE FISH SAUCE, NUOC MAM, WITH SOY SAUCE.

2 Reserve 30ml/2 tbsp oil in the wok. Add the shallots, chilli, ginger and garlic and stir-fry until fragrant. Stir in the tomatoes, *nuoc mam* and sugar. Reduce the heat and simmer for 10–15 minutes until it resembles a sauce. Stir in 105ml/ 7 tbsp water and bring to the boil.

3 Season with a little pepper and return the tofu to the pan. Mix well and simmer gently for 2–3 minutes to heat through. Garnish with mint leaves and chilli strips and serve immediately.

<u>SERVES FOUR</u>

INGREDIENTS
   vegetable or groundnut (peanut) oil,
      for deep-frying
   450g/1lb firm tofu, rinsed and cut
      into bitesize cubes
   4 shallots, finely sliced
   1 Thai chilli, seeded and chopped
   25g/1oz fresh root ginger, peeled
      and finely chopped
   4 garlic cloves, finely chopped
   6 large ripe tomatoes, skinned,
      seeded and finely chopped
   30ml/2 tbsp *nuoc mam*
   10ml/2 tsp sugar
   mint leaves and strips of red chilli,
      to garnish
   ground black pepper

1 Heat enough oil for deep-frying in a wok or heavy pan. Fry the tofu, in batches, until crisp and golden. Remove with a slotted spoon and drain on kitchen paper.

COOK'S TIP
This recipe is delicious as a side dish or as a main dish with noodles or rice.

Per portion Energy 234Kcal/974kJ; Protein 11g; Carbohydrate 11g, of which sugars 10.1g; Fat 16g, of which saturates 2g; Cholesterol 0mg; Calcium 619mg; Fibre 2.7g; Sodium 25mg

SPICY TOFU WITH LEMON GRASS, BASIL AND PEANUTS

IN VIETNAM, AROMATIC PEPPER LEAVES ARE OFTEN USED AS THE HERB ELEMENT BUT, BECAUSE THESE ARE QUITE DIFFICULT TO FIND OUTSIDE SOUTH-EAST ASIA, YOU CAN USE BASIL LEAVES INSTEAD.

SERVES THREE TO FOUR

INGREDIENTS
3 lemon grass stalks, finely chopped
45ml/3 tbsp soy sauce
2 red Serrano chillies, seeded and
    finely chopped
2 garlic cloves, crushed
5ml/1 tsp ground turmeric
10ml/2 tsp sugar
300g/11oz tofu, rinsed, drained,
    patted dry and cut into
    bitesize cubes
30ml/2 tbsp groundnut (peanut) oil
45ml/3 tbsp roasted peanuts,
    chopped
1 bunch fresh basil, stalks removed
salt

1 In a bowl, mix together the lemon grass, soy sauce, chillies, garlic, turmeric and sugar until the sugar has dissolved. Add a little salt to taste and add the tofu, making sure it is well coated. Leave to marinate for 1 hour.

VARIATION
Lime, coriander (cilantro) or curry leaves would work well in this simple stir-fry.

2 Heat a wok or heavy pan. Pour in the oil, add the marinated tofu, and cook, stirring frequently, until it is golden brown on all sides. Add the peanuts and most of the basil leaves.

3 Divide the tofu among individual serving dishes, scatter the remaining basil leaves over the top and serve hot or at room temperature.

Per portion Energy 120Kcal/500kJ; Protein 3g; Carbohydrate 5g, of which sugars 3g; Fat 10g, of which saturates 2g; Cholesterol 0mg; Calcium 36mg; Fibre 3.3g; Sodium 200mg

DEEP-FRIED VEGETABLES <u>WITH</u> NUOC CHAM

STIR-FRIED, STEAMED OR DEEP-FRIED VEGETABLES SERVED WITH A DIPPING SAUCE ARE COMMON FARE THROUGHOUT SOUTH-EAST ASIA. IN VIETNAM, THEY ARE USUALLY SERVED WITH THE UBIQUITOUS NUOC CHAM; IN CAMBODIA, THEY ARE OFTEN SERVED WITH A PEANUT OR GINGER DIPPING SAUCE.

SERVES FOUR TO SIX

INGREDIENTS
6 eggs
1 long aubergine (eggplant), peeled, halved lengthways and sliced into half moons
1 long sweet potato, peeled and sliced into rounds
1 small butternut squash, peeled, seeded, halved lengthways and cut into half moons
salt and ground black pepper
vegetable oil, for deep-frying
nuoc cham, for dipping

VARIATIONS
Courgettes (zucchini), angled loofah, taro root or pumpkin could also be used.

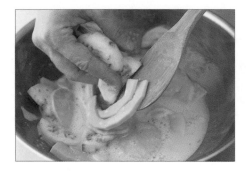

1 Beat the eggs in a wide bowl. Season with salt and pepper. Toss the vegetables in the egg to coat thoroughly.

2 Heat enough oil for deep-frying in a large wok. Cook the vegetables in small batches, making sure there is plenty of egg coating them.

3 When they turn golden, lift them out of the oil with a slotted spoon and drain on kitchen paper.

4 Keep them warm while the remaining vegetables are being fried. Serve warm with *nuoc cham* or a dipping sauce of your choice.

Per portion Energy 280Kcal/1164kJ; Protein 8; Carbohydrate 11.9g, of which sugars 5.7g; Fat 23g, of which saturates 4g; Cholesterol 190mg; Calcium 90mg; Fibre 3.5g; Sodium 84mg

GLAZED PUMPKIN IN COCONUT MILK

PUMPKINS, BUTTERNUT SQUASH AND WINTER MELONS CAN ALL BE COOKED IN THIS WAY.
THROUGHOUT VIETNAM AND CAMBODIA, VARIATIONS OF THIS SWEET, MELLOW DISH ARE OFTEN
SERVED AS AN ACCOMPANIMENT TO RICE OR A SPICY CURRY.

SERVES FOUR

INGREDIENTS
  200ml/7fl oz/scant 1 cup
    coconut milk
  15ml/1 tbsp *nuoc mam* or
    tuk trey
  30ml/2 tbsp palm sugar
  30ml/2 tbsp groundnut (peanut) oil
  4 garlic cloves, finely chopped
  25g/1oz fresh root ginger, peeled and
    finely shredded
  675g/1½lb pumpkin flesh, cubed
  ground black pepper
  a handful of curry or basil leaves,
    to garnish
  chilli oil, for drizzling
  fried onion rings, to garnish
  plain or coconut rice, to serve

1 In a bowl, beat the coconut milk and the *nuoc mam* or *tuk trey* with the sugar, until it has dissolved. Set aside.

2 Heat the oil in a wok or heavy pan and stir in the garlic and ginger. Stir-fry until they begin to colour, then stir in the pumpkin cubes, mixing well.

3 Pour in the coconut milk and mix well. Reduce the heat, cover and simmer for about 20 minutes, until the pumpkin is tender and the sauce has reduced. Season with pepper and garnish with curry or basil leaves and fried onion rings. Serve hot with plain or coconut rice, drizzled with a little chilli oil.

Per portion Energy 114Kcal/477kJ; Protein 1.5g; Carbohydrate 14g, of which sugars 13.4g; Fat 6g, of which saturates 1g; Cholesterol 0mg; Calcium 68mg; Fibre 1.7g; Sodium 323mg

CAMBODIAN AUBERGINE CURRY

AUBERGINE CURRIES ARE POPULAR THROUGHOUT SOUTH-EAST ASIA, THE THAI VERSION BEING THE MOST FAMOUS. ALL ARE HOT AND AROMATIC, ENRICHED WITH COCONUT MILK. THIS KHMER RECIPE USES THE TRADEMARK HERBAL PASTE, KROEUNG.

2 Stir in the coconut milk and stock, and add the aubergines and lime leaves.

3 Partially cover the pan and simmer over a gentle heat for about 25 minutes until the aubergines are tender. Stir in the basil and check the seasoning. Serve with jasmine rice and lime wedges.

SERVES FOUR TO SIX

INGREDIENTS
    15ml/1 tbsp vegetable oil
    4 garlic cloves, crushed
    2 shallots, sliced
    2 dried chillies
    45ml/3 tbsp *kroeung*
    15ml/1 tbsp shrimp paste or *mam tom*
    15ml/1 tbsp palm sugar
    600ml/1 pint/2½ cups coconut milk
    250ml/8fl oz/1 cup chicken stock
    4 aubergines (eggplants), trimmed
        and cut into bitesize pieces
    6 kaffir lime leaves
    1 bunch fresh basil, stalks removed
    jasmine rice and 2 limes, cut into
        quarters, to serve
    salt and ground black pepper

1 Heat the oil in a wok or heavy pan. Stir in the garlic, shallots and whole chillies and stir-fry until they begin to colour. Stir in the *kroeung*, shrimp paste or *mam tom* and palm sugar and stir-fry until the mixture begins to darken.

Per portion Energy 72Kcal/305kJ; Protein 1.6g; Carbohydrate 11.2g, of which sugars 10.7g; Fat 3g, of which saturates 1g; Cholesterol 0mg; Calcium 46mg; Fibre 2.8g; Sodium 113mg

JUNGLE CURRY

VARIATIONS OF THIS FIERY, FLAVOURSOME VEGETARIAN CURRY CAN BE FOUND ALL OVER SOUTHERN VIETNAM. A FAVOURITE WITH THE BUDDHIST MONKS AND OFTEN SOLD FROM COUNTRYSIDE STALLS, IT CAN BE SERVED WITH PLAIN RICE OR NOODLES, OR CHUNKS OF CRUSTY BREAD.

SERVES FOUR

INGREDIENTS

  30ml/2 tbsp vegetable oil
  2 onions, roughly chopped
  2 lemon grass stalks, roughly
    chopped and bruised
  4 green Thai chillies, seeded and
    finely sliced
  4cm/1½ in galangal or fresh root
    ginger, peeled and chopped
  3 carrots, peeled, halved lengthways
    and sliced
  115g/4oz long beans
  grated rind of 1 lime
  10ml/2 tsp soy sauce
  15ml/1 tbsp rice vinegar
  10ml/2 tsp *nuoc mam*
  5ml/1 tsp black peppercorns,
    crushed
  15ml/1 tbsp sugar
  10ml/2 tsp ground turmeric
  115g/4oz canned bamboo shoots
  75g/3oz spinach, steamed and
    roughly chopped
  150ml/¼ pint/⅔ cup coconut milk
  salt
  chopped fresh coriander (cilantro)
    and mint leaves, to garnish

COOK'S TIPS

• Also known as long beans or asparagus beans, snake beans are eaten all over South-east Asia. They may grow up to 40cm/16in long and can be found in Asian stores. There are two common varieties, pale green and darker green, the latter have the better flavour. When buying, choose young, narrow specimens with under-developed seeds, as these will be the most tender. They do not have strings, and preparation is simply trimming and chopping them into short lengths. As they mature, snake beans can become quite tough. They should be used before they turn yellow.
• Jungle curry should be fiery, almost dominated by the chilli. In Vietnam it is often eaten for breakfast or a great pick-me-up at any time of day.

1 Heat a wok or heavy pan and add the oil. Once hot, stir in the onions, lemon grass, chillies and galangal or ginger. Add the carrots and beans with the lime rind and stir-fry for 1–2 minutes.

2 Stir in the soy sauce, rice vinegar and *nuoc mam*. Add the crushed peppercorns, sugar and turmeric, then stir in the bamboo shoots and the chopped spinach.

3 Stir in the coconut milk and simmer for about 10 minutes, until the vegetables are tender. Season with salt. and serve hot, garnished with fresh coriander and mint.

Per portion Energy 159Kcal/660kJ; Protein 3g; Carbohydrate 19g, of which sugars 16g; Fat 8g, of which saturates 1g; Cholesterol 0mg; Calcium 68mg; Fibre 3.7g; Sodium 200mg

VEGETARIAN STIR-FRY <u>WITH</u> PEANUT SAUCE

STIR-FRIED VEGETABLES ARE POPULAR THROUGHOUT SOUTH-EAST ASIA. WHEREVER YOU GO, THERE WILL BE SOME VARIATION ON THE THEME. IN CAMBODIA, THE VEGETABLES ARE SOMETIMES DRIZZLED IN A PEANUT SAUCE LIKE THIS ONE, PARTICULARLY AMONG THE BUDDHIST COMMUNITIES.

SERVES FOUR TO SIX

INGREDIENTS
> 6 Chinese black mushrooms (dried shiitake), soaked in lukewarm water for 20 minutes
> 20 tiger lily buds, soaked in lukewarm water for 20 minutes
> 225g/8oz tofu
> 60ml/4 tbsp sesame or groundnut (peanut) oil
> 1 large onion, halved and finely sliced
> 1 large carrot, finely sliced
> 300g/11oz pak choi (bok choy), the leaves separated from the stems
> 225g/8oz can bamboo shoots, drained and rinsed
> 50ml/2fl oz/¼ cup soy sauce
> 10ml/2 tsp sugar

For the peanut sauce
> 15ml/1 tbsp groundnut (peanut) or sesame oil
> 2 garlic cloves, finely chopped
> 2 red chillies, seeded and finely chopped
> 90g/3½oz/generous ½ cup unsalted roasted peanuts, finely chopped
> 150ml/5fl oz/⅔ cup coconut milk
> 30ml/2 tbsp hoisin sauce
> 15ml/1 tbsp soy sauce
> 15ml/1 tbsp sugar

1 To make the sauce, heat the oil in a small wok or heavy pan. Stir in the garlic and chillies, stir-fry until they begin to colour, then add all the peanuts except 15ml/1 tbsp. Stir-fry for a few minutes until the natural oil from the peanuts begins to weep.

VARIATION
The popular piquant peanut sauce is delicious served hot with stir-fried, deep-fried or steamed vegetables. Alternatively, leave it to cool, garnish with a little chopped mint and coriander (cilantro) and serve it as a dip for raw vegetables, such as strips of carrot, cucumber and celery.

2 Add the remaining ingredients and bring to the boil. Reduce the heat and cook gently until the sauce thickens a little and specks of oil appear on the surface. Put aside.

3 Drain the mushrooms and lily buds and squeeze out any excess water. Cut the mushroom caps into strips and discard the stalks. Trim off the hard ends of the lily buds and tie a knot in the centre of each one. Put the mushrooms and lily buds aside.

4 Cut the tofu into slices. Heat 30ml/2 tbsp of the oil in a wok or heavy pan and brown the tofu on both sides. Drain on kitchen paper and cut it into strips.

5 Heat a wok or heavy pan and add the remaining oil. Stir in the onion and carrot and stir-fry for a minute. Add the pak choi stems and stir-fry for 2 minutes. Add the mushrooms, lily buds, tofu and bamboo shoots and stir-fry for a minute more. Toss in the pak choi leaves, followed by the soy sauce and sugar. Stir-fry until heated through.

6 Heat up the peanut sauce and drizzle over the vegetables in the wok, or spoon the vegetables into individual bowls and top with a little sauce. Garnish with the remaining peanuts and serve.

Per portion Energy 252Kcal/1045kJ; Protein 10g; Carbohydrate 12g, of which sugars 8.5g; Fat 18g, of which saturates 3g; Cholesterol 0mg; Calcium 319mg; Fibre 3.6g; Sodium 1055mg

SALAD ROLLS WITH PUMPKIN, TOFU, PEANUTS AND BASIL

THIS IS ONE OF THE BEST VIETNAMESE "DO-IT-YOURSELF" DISHES. YOU PLACE ALL THE INGREDIENTS ON THE TABLE WITH THE RICE WRAPPERS FOR EVERYONE TO ASSEMBLE THEIR OWN ROLLS. IN TOWNS ALL OVER SOUTHERN VIETNAM, BO BIA (SALAD ROLL) CARTS COME OUT IN THE WARM WEATHER.

SERVES FOUR TO FIVE

INGREDIENTS
    30ml/2 tbsp groundnut (peanut) or
        sesame oil
    175g/6oz tofu, rinsed and
        patted dry
    4 shallots, halved and sliced
    2 garlic cloves, finely chopped
    350g/12oz pumpkin flesh,
        cut into thin slices
    1 carrot, cut into thin slices
    15ml/1 tbsp soy sauce
    4 green Thai chillies, seeded
        and finely sliced
    1 small, crisp lettuce,
        leaves separated
    1 bunch fresh basil, stalks removed
    115g/4oz/⅔ cup roasted peanuts,
        chopped
    100ml/3½fl oz/scant ½ cup
        hoisin sauce
    20 dried rice wrappers
    salt
    nuoc cham, to serve (optional)

1 In a heavy frying pan, heat half of the oil. Place the block of tofu in the pan and sear on both sides. Transfer to a plate and cut into thin strips.

2 Heat the remaining oil in the pan and stir in the shallots and garlic. Add the pumpkin and carrot, then pour in the soy sauce and 120ml/4fl oz/½ cup water. Add salt to taste and cook gently until the vegetables have softened.

3 Meanwhile, arrange the tofu, chillies, lettuce, basil, roasted peanuts and hoisin sauce in separate dishes and put them on the table.

4 Fill a bowl with hot water and place it in the middle of the table, or fill a small bowl for each person. Place the stack of rice wrappers beside it. Spoon the vegetable mixture into a dish and add to the bowls of ingredients on the table.

5 To eat, take a rice wrapper and dip it in the water for a few seconds to soften. Lay the wrapper flat on the table or on a plate and, just off-centre, spread a few strips of lettuce, followed by the pumpkin mixture, some tofu, a sprinkling of chillies, a drizzle of hoisin sauce, some basil leaves and peanuts, layering the ingredients in a neat stack.

6 Pull the shorter edge of the wrapper (the side with filling on it) up over the stack, tuck in the sides and roll into a tight cylinder. Dip the roll into *nuoc cham*.

VARIATIONS
Squash, courgette (zucchini) or aubergine (eggplant) could be used in the filling, and cured Chinese sausage is often used instead of tofu.

Per portion Energy 402Kcal/1669kJ; Protein 14g; Carbohydrate 29g, of which sugars 13g; Fat 26g, of which saturates 5g; Cholesterol 0mg; Calcium 321mg; Fibre 4.1g; Sodium 400mg

SALADS
AND PICKLES

Raw vegetables are enjoyed pickled or in salads. Often the

salads incorporate raw or lightly seared fish or shellfish, such

as in Cambodian Raw Fish Salad. Fresh herbs and chillies are

added in liberal quantities, as in Sweet-and-Sour Cucumber

with Chillies, Coriander and Mint. Many dishes are served

with a table salad which includes lettuce leaves to wrap around

the food and strips of cucumber, carrot and beansprouts.

SWEET-AND-SOUR CUCUMBER WITH CHILLIES, CORIANDER AND MINT

SHORT, FAT CUCUMBERS ARE A COMMON SIGHT IN THE MARKETS OF VIETNAM. THIS SALAD IS A GREAT ADDITION TO A SUMMER BARBECUE OR THE SALAD TABLE, AND IS A DELIGHTFUL ACCOMPANIMENT TO ANY MEAT, POULTRY AND SEAFOOD DISHES.

SERVES FOUR TO SIX

INGREDIENTS
  2 cucumbers
  30ml/2 tbsp sugar
  100ml/3½fl oz/½ cup rice vinegar
  juice of half a lime
  2 green Thai chillies, seeded and
    finely sliced
  2 shallots, halved and finely sliced
  1 small bunch each fresh coriander
    (cilantro) and mint, stalks removed,
    leaves finely chopped
  salt
  fresh coriander leaves, to garnish

COOK'S TIP
Decorate the dish with edible flowers, such as nasturtiums, to add colour.

1 Use a vegetable peeler to remove strips of the cucumber peel. Halve the cucumbers lengthways and cut into slices. Place the slices on a plate and sprinkle with a little salt. Leave them to stand for 15 minutes. Rinse well, drain the slices and pat them dry with kitchen paper.

2 In a bowl, mix the sugar with the vinegar until it has dissolved, then stir in the lime juice and a little salt to taste.

3 Add the chillies, shallots, herbs and cucumber to the dressing and leave to stand for 15–20 minutes. Garnish with coriander leaves and a flower, if you like.

Per portion Energy 59Kcal/248kJ; Protein 2g; Carbohydrate 12g, of which sugars 11g; Fat 0g, of which saturates 0g; Cholesterol 0mg; Calcium 63mg; Fibre 0.8g; Sodium 200mg

VIETNAMESE TABLE SALAD

WHEN THIS VIETNAMESE TABLE SALAD SA LACH DIA IS SERVED ON ITS OWN, THE VEGETABLES AND FRUIT ARE USUALLY FOLDED INTO LITTLE PACKETS USING LETTUCE LEAVES OR RICE WRAPPERS, AND THEN DIPPED IN A SAUCE, OR ADDED BIT BY BIT TO BOWLS OF RICE OR NOODLES.

SERVES FOUR TO SIX

INGREDIENTS
1 crunchy lettuce, leaves separated
half a cucumber, peeled and
  thinly sliced
2 carrots, peeled and finely sliced
200g/7oz/scant 1 cup beansprouts
2 unripe star fruit, finely sliced
2 green bananas, finely sliced
1 firm papaya, cut in half, seeds
  removed, peeled and finely sliced
1 bunch each fresh mint and basil,
  stalks removed
juice of 1 lime
dipping sauce, to serve

1 Arrange the salad ingredients attractively on a large plate, with the lettuce leaves placed on one side so that they can be used as wrappers.

2 Squeeze the lime juice over the sliced fruits, particularly the bananas to help them retain their colour, and place the salad in the middle of the table. Serve with a dippping sauce.

Per portion Energy 108Kcal/455kJ; Protein 4g; Carbohydrate 21g, of which sugars 12g; Fat 1g, of which saturates 0g; Cholesterol 0mg; Calcium 110mg; Fibre 42g; Sodium 20mg

GREEN MANGO SALAD

ALTHOUGH THE ORANGE AND YELLOW MANGOES AND PAPAYAS ARE DEVOURED IN VAST QUANTITIES WHEN RIPE AND JUICY, THEY ARE ALSO POPULAR WHEN GREEN. THEIR TART FLAVOUR AND CRUNCHY TEXTURE MAKE THEM IDEAL FOR SALADS AND STEWS.

SERVES FOUR

INGREDIENTS
   450g/1lb green mangoes
   grated rind and juice of 2 limes
   30ml/2 tbsp sugar
   30ml/2 tbsp *nuoc mam*
   2 green Thai chillies, seeded and
     finely sliced
   1 small bunch fresh coriander
     (cilantro), stalks removed,
     finely chopped
   salt

1 Peel, halve and stone (pit) the green mangoes, and slice them into thin strips.

2 In a bowl, mix together the lime rind and juice, sugar and *nuoc mam*. Add the mango strips with the chillies and coriander. Add salt to taste and leave to stand for 20 minutes to allow the flavours to mingle before serving.

Per portion Energy 92Kcal/391kJ; Protein 1g; Carbohydrate 22g, of which sugars 15g; Fat 0g; Cholesterol 0mg; Calcium 32mg; Fibre 33g; Sodium 0.5g

LOTUS STEM SALAD ^{WITH} SHALLOTS AND SHREDDED FRESH BASIL

YOU MAY BE LUCKY ENOUGH TO FIND FRESH LOTUS STEMS IN AN ASIAN MARKET, OR, AS HERE, YOU CAN USE THE ONES PRESERVED IN BRINE. ALTERNATIVELY, TRY THIS RECIPE WITH FRESHLY STEAMED, CRUNCHY ASPARAGUS TIPS.

SERVES FOUR

INGREDIENTS
    half a cucumber
    225g/8oz jar preserved lotus stems,
       drained and cut into 5cm/2in strips
    2 shallots, finely sliced
    25g/1oz/½ cup fresh basil
       leaves, shredded
    salt
    fresh coriander (cilantro) leaves,
       to garnish
For the dressing
    juice of 1 lime
    30ml/2 tbsp *nuoc mam*
    1 red Thai chilli, seeded and chopped
    1 garlic clove, crushed
    15ml/1 tbsp sugar

1 To make the dressing, mix together the dressing ingredients in a bowl and set aside.

COOK'S TIPS
The Vietnamese love the lotus plant because it symbolizes purity and perfection. Every part of the plant is used: the flowers are laid at shrines and temples; the stamens are steeped to make a soothing tea; the seeds are dried for desserts and cakes; and the stems and roots are sliced up for soups and salads, where they absorb the flavours of the dressing while retaining a crunchy texture.

  If you cannot find the stems, lotus roots make a good substitute and are readily available in Asian markets. They grow in sausage-like links, each one about 18–23cm/7–9in long. Once the mud that coats them has been washed off, a pale beige-pink skin is revealed. When buying fresh lotus roots, choose ones that feel heavy for their size, as this is an indication that they are full of liquid. They should be peeled and soaked in water with a little lemon juice before being added to the salad, to retain their pale colour.

2 Peel the cucumber and cut it into 5cm/2in batons. Soak the batons in cold salted water for 20 minutes. Put the lotus stems into a bowl of water. Using a pair of chopsticks, stir the water so that the loose fibres of the stems wrap around the sticks.

3 Drain the stems and put them in a bowl. Drain the cucumber batons and add to the bowl, then add the shallots, shredded basil leaves and the prepared dressing. Leave the salad to marinate for 20 minutes before serving. Garnish with fresh coriander leaves.

Per portion Energy 43Kcal/181kJ; Protein 1g; Carbohydrate 9g, of which sugars 6g; Fat 0g, of which saturates 0g; Cholesterol 0mg; Calcium 40mg; Fibre 0.5g; Sodium 300mg

PICKLED VEGETABLES

EVERYDAY VIETNAMESE AND CAMBODIAN PICKLES GENERALLY CONSIST OF CUCUMBER, DAIKON AND CARROT — GREEN, WHITE AND ORANGE IN COLOUR — AND ARE SERVED FOR NIBBLING ON, AS PART OF THE TABLE SALAD, OR AS AN ACCOMPANIMENT TO GRILLED MEATS AND SHELLFISH.

SERVES FOUR TO SIX

INGREDIENTS
  300ml/½ pint/1¼ cups white
    rice vinegar
  90g/3½oz/½ cup sugar
  450g/1lb carrots, cut into 5cm/2in
    matchsticks
  450g/1lb daikon, halved lengthways,
    and cut into thin crescents
  600g/1lb 6oz cucumber, partially
    peeled in strips and cut into
    5cm/2in matchsticks
  15ml/1 tbsp salt

1 In a large bowl, whisk the vinegar with the sugar, until it dissolves.

2 Add the carrots and daikon to the vinegar mixture and toss well to coat. Cover them and place in the refrigerator for 24 hours, turning them occasionally.

3 Put the cucumber on a plate and sprinkle with the salt. Leave for 30 minutes, then rinse under cold water and drain well. Add to the carrot and daikon and toss well in the pickling liquid. Cover and refrigerate as before.

4 Lift the vegetables out of the pickling liquid to serve, or spoon them into a jar and store in the refrigerator.

Per portion Energy 104Kcal/438kJ; Protein 2g; Carbohydrate 24g, of which sugars 24g; Fat 0.5g, of which saturates 0.2g; Cholesterol 0mg; Calcium 59mg; Fibre 3.1g; Sodium 1013mg

CAMBODIAN PICKLED GINGER

THE CAMBODIANS LOVE COOKING WITH GINGER. WARMING, GOOD FOR THE HEART, AND BELIEVED TO AID DIGESTION, IT FINDS ITS WAY INTO SALADS, SOUPS, STIR-FRIES AND PUDDINGS. CHINESE IN ORIGIN, PICKLED GINGER IS OFTEN SERVED AS A CONDIMENT WITH BROTHS, NOODLES AND RICE.

SERVES FOUR TO SIX

INGREDIENTS
    225g/8oz fresh young ginger, peeled
    10ml/2 tsp salt
    200ml/7fl oz/1 cup white rice vinegar
    50g/2oz/¼ cup sugar

1 Place the ginger in a bowl and sprinkle with salt. Cover and place in the refrigerator for 24 hours.

COOK'S TIP
Juicy and tender with a pinkish-yellow skin, young ginger is less fibrous than the mature rhizome. When pickled in vinegar, the flesh turns pale pink.

2 Drain off any liquid and pat the ginger dry with a clean dishtowel. Slice each knob of ginger very finely along the grain, like thin rose petals, and place them in a clean bowl or a sterilized jar suitable for storing.

3 In a small bowl beat the vinegar and 50ml/2fl oz/¼ cup water with the sugar, until it has dissolved. Pour the pickling liquid over the ginger and cover or seal. Store in the refrigerator or a cool place for about a week.

Per portion Energy 36Kcal/151kJ; Protein 0.2g; Carbohydrate 9.1g, of which sugars 9.1g; Fat 0.1g, of which saturates 0g; Cholesterol 0mg; Calcium 20mg; Fibre 0.4g; Sodium 678mg

CAMBODIAN SOYA BEANSPROUT SALAD

HIGH IN PROTEIN AND FAT, SOYA BEANSPROUTS ARE PARTICULARLY FAVOURED IN CAMBODIA. UNLIKE MUNG BEANSPROUTS, THEY ARE SLIGHTLY POISONOUS WHEN RAW AND NEED TO BE PARBOILED BEFORE USING. TOSSED IN A SALAD, THEY ARE OFTEN EATEN WITH NOODLES AND RICE.

2 Bring a pan of salted water to the boil. Drop in the beansprouts and blanch for a minute only. Drain and refresh under cold water until cool. Drain again and put them into a clean dishtowel. Shake out the excess water.

3 Put the beansprouts into a bowl with the spring onions. Pour over the dressing and toss well. Garnish with coriander leaves and serve.

SERVES FOUR

INGREDIENTS
   450g/1lb fresh soya beansprouts
   2 spring onions (scallions), finely
   sliced
   1 small bunch fresh coriander
   (cilantro), stalks removed
For the dressing
   15ml/1 tbsp sesame oil
   30ml/2 tbsp *tuk trey*
   15ml/1 tbsp white rice vinegar
   10ml/2 tsp palm sugar
   1 red chilli, seeded and finely sliced
   15g/½oz fresh young root ginger,
   finely shredded

1 First make the dressing. In a bowl, beat the oil, *tuk trey* and rice vinegar with the sugar, until it dissolves. Stir in the chilli and ginger and leave to stand for 30 minutes to allow the flavours to develop.

Per portion Energy 76Kcal/317kJ; Protein 3.4g; Carbohydrate 8.6g, of which sugars 6.5g; Fat 3.3g, of which saturates 0.5g; Cholesterol 0mg; Calcium 27mg; Fibre 1.8g; Sodium 6mg

BANANA BLOSSOM SALAD WITH PRAWNS

BANANA BLOSSOM IS VERY POPULAR — THE PURPLISH-PINK SHEATHS ARE USED FOR PRESENTATION, THE PETALS AS A GARNISH, AND THE POINTED, CREAMY YELLOW HEART IS TOSSED IN SALADS, WHERE IT IS COMBINED WITH LEFTOVER GRILLED CHICKEN OR PORK, STEAMED OR GRILLED PRAWNS, OR TOFU.

SERVES FOUR

INGREDIENTS
- 2 banana blossom hearts
- juice of 1 lemon
- 225g/8oz prawns (shrimp), cooked and shelled
- 30ml/2 tbsp roasted peanuts, finely chopped, fresh basil leaves and lime slices, to garnish

For the dressing
- juice of 1 lime
- 30ml/2 tbsp white rice vinegar
- 60ml/4 tbsp *nuoc mam* or *tuk trey*
- 45ml/3 tbsp palm sugar
- 3 red Thai chillies, seeded and finely sliced
- 2 garlic cloves, peeled and finely chopped

2 To make the dressing, beat the lime juice, vinegar, and *nuoc mam* or *tuk trey* with the sugar in a small bowl, until it has dissolved. Stir in the chillies and garlic and set aside.

3 Drain the sliced banana blossom and put it in a bowl. Add the prawns and pour over the dressing. Toss well and garnish with the roasted peanuts, basil leaves and lime slices.

1 Cut the banana blossom hearts into quarters lengthways and then slice them very finely crosswise. To prevent them discolouring, tip the slices into a bowl of cold water mixed with the lemon juice and leave to soak for about 30 minutes.

COOK'S TIP
Banana blossom doesn't actually taste of banana. Instead, it is mildly tannic, similar to an unripe persimmon – a taste and texture that complements chillies, lime and the local fish sauce.

VARIATION
If you cannot find banana blossom hearts in Asian supermarkets, you can try this recipe with raw, or lightly steamed or roasted, fresh artichoke hearts.

Per portion Energy 103Kcal/438kJ; Protein 11g; Carbohydrate 15g, of which sugars 13g; Fat 0.5g, of which saturates 0.1g; Cholesterol 110mg; Calcium 54mg; Fibre 0.7g; Sodium 109mg

GRILLED PRAWN SALAD WITH PEANUTS AND POMELO

THIS REFRESHING SALAD IS TYPICAL OF THE SALADS OF CENTRAL AND SOUTHERN VIETNAM, WHERE FRUIT, VEGETABLES, MEAT, FISH AND SHELLFISH ARE ALL TOSSED TOGETHER IN ONE DISH. IT MAKES A GREAT ADDITION TO A BARBECUE: COOK THEM ON A PIECE OF FOIL LAID ON TOP OF THE GRIDDLE.

SERVES FOUR

INGREDIENTS
    16 raw tiger prawns (jumbo shrimp),
        peeled and deveined
    1 small cucumber, peeled and cut
        into matchsticks
    1 pomelo, separated into segments
        and cut into bitesize pieces
    1 carrot, peeled and cut into
        matchsticks
    1 green Serrano chilli, seeded and
        finely sliced
    30ml/2 tbsp roasted peanuts,
        roughly chopped
    juice of half a lime
    60ml/4 tbsp *nuoc cham*
    vegetable oil, for griddling
    1 small bunch fresh basil,
        stalks removed
    1 small bunch coriander (cilantro),
        stalks removed
    salt
For the marinade
    30ml/2 tbsp *nuoc mam*
    30ml/2 tbsp soy sauce
    15ml/1 tbsp groundnut (peanut) or
        sesame oil
    1 shallot, finely chopped
    1 garlic clove, crushed
    10ml/2 tsp raw cane sugar

1 In a wide bowl, combine all the marinade ingredients. Add the prawns, making sure they are coated, and set aside for 30 minutes.

2 Sprinkle the cucumber matchsticks with salt and leave for 15 minutes. Rinse and drain the cucumber and mix in a large bowl with the pomelo, carrot, chilli and peanuts. Add the lime juice and *nuoc cham* and toss well.

3 If using a barbecue, prepare the barbecue and lay a piece of foil on top. Put the marinated prawns on the foil and cook on both sides until opaque. Alternatively, to griddle the prawns, wipe a hot griddle with a little oil, and cook the prawns on both sides until they turn opaque.

4 Once cooked, toss the prawns into the salad with the herbs and serve.

COOK'S TIP
Larger and sweeter than grapefruits, yellow pomelos are piled high on stalls in the coastal regions, where people often peel them on a hot day to make an impromptu salad with a little salt and a few herbs. They are available in many Asian markets and stores but, if you can't find them, use a sweet, pink grapefruit instead. Or select juicy oranges – peel them, cut them into fine slices, remove the pips, and quarter each slice. The zesty, refreshing flavour of the citrus fruits makes this a lovely summer salad.

Per portion Energy 219Kcal/912kJ; Protein 14g; Carbohydrate 14g, of which sugars 9g; Fat 12g, of which saturates 2g; Cholesterol 98mg; Calcium 121mg; Fibre 1.4g; Sodium 500mg

CAMBODIAN RAW FISH SALAD

SWEET-FLESHED FRESHWATER FISH AND SHELLFISH ARE OFTEN EATEN RAW IN CAMBODIA, PLUCKED STRAIGHT FROM THE WATER, OR TOSSED IN A MARINADE. WRAPPED IN A LETTUCE LEAF WITH EXTRA LEAFY HERBS, OR SERVED WITH NOODLES, THIS CAMBODIAN SALAD, KOY PA, IS LIGHT AND DELICIOUS.

SERVES FOUR TO SIX

INGREDIENTS

450g/1lb white fish fillets, boned
  and finely sliced
juice of 4 limes
30ml/2 tbsp *tuk trey*
4 spring onions (scallions),
  finely sliced
2 garlic cloves, finely sliced
1 fresh red chilli, seeded and
  finely sliced
1 small bunch fresh coriander
  (cilantro), stalks removed
lettuce leaves, to serve

1 Place the sliced fish in a large bowl. Pour over the juice of 3 limes and toss well, making sure all the fish is coated Cover and chill in the refrigerator for 24 hours.

2 Drain the fish and place in a clean bowl with the juice of the remaining lime, the *tuk trey*, spring onions, garlic, chilli and coriander. Toss well and serve with lettuce leaves.

Per portion Energy 66Kcal/280kJ; Protein 14g; Carbohydrate 1.2g, of which sugars 1.1g; Fat 0.6g, of which saturates 0.1g; Cholesterol 35mg; Calcium 11mg; Fibre 0.2g; Sodium 402mg

CHICKEN AND SHREDDED CABBAGE SALAD

IN SOME VIETNAMESE AND CAMBODIAN HOUSEHOLDS, A WHOLE CHICKEN IS COOKED IN WATER WITH HERBS AND FLAVOURINGS TO MAKE A BROTH. THE CHICKEN IS THEN SHREDDED. SOME OF THE MEAT GOES BACK INTO THE BROTH, THE REST IS TOSSED IN A SALAD.

SERVES FOUR TO SIX

INGREDIENTS
450g/1lb chicken, cooked and torn into thin strips
1 white Chinese cabbage, trimmed and finely shredded
2 carrots, finely shredded or grated
a small bunch fresh mint, stalks removed, finely shredded
1 small bunch fresh coriander (cilantro) leaves, to garnish
For the dressing
30ml/2 tbsp vegetable or groundnut (peanut) oil
30ml/2 tbsp white rice vinegar

45ml/3 tbsp *nuoc mam* or *tuk trey*
juice of 2 limes
30ml/2 tbsp palm sugar
2 red Thai chillies, seeded and finely chopped
25g/1oz fresh young root ginger, sliced
3 garlic cloves, crushed
2 shallots, finely chopped

1 First make the dressing. In a bowl, beat the oil, vinegar, *nuoc mam* or *tuk trey*, and lime juice with the sugar, until it has dissolved. Stir in the other ingredients and leave to stand for about 30 minutes to let the flavours mingle.

2 Put the cooked chicken strips, cabbage, carrots and mint in a large bowl. Pour over the dressing and toss well. Garnish with coriander leaves and serve.

Per portion Energy 142Kcal/597kJ; Protein 19; Carbohydrate 5.7g, of which sugars 5.1g; Fat 4.8g, of which saturates 0.7g; Cholesterol 53mg; Calcium 53mg; Fibre 1.9g; Sodium 57mg

CAMBODIAN RAW BEEF SALAD <u>WITH</u> PEANUTS

THERE ARE MANY RECIPES FOR BEEF SALADS THROUGHOUT SOUTH-EAST ASIA, SUCH AS THE VIETNAMESE GOI BO, BUT THIS CAMBODIAN RECIPE, PLEAH SAIKO, IS QUITE DISTINCTIVE AS IT USES THE FLAVOURSOME FISH EXTRACT, TUK PRAHOC, AND ROASTED PEANUTS.

2 Meanwhile, in a small bowl, beat the remaining *tuk prahoc* with the juice of the third lime. Stir in the remaining sugar, until it dissolves, and put aside.

3 Put the beef slices, drained of any remaining liquid, in a clean bowl. Add the chilli, peanuts and coriander. Toss with the dressing, garnish with coriander leaves and serve immediately.

SERVES FOUR

INGREDIENTS
    45ml/3 tbsp *tuk prahoc*
    juice of 3 limes
    45ml/3 tbsp palm sugar
    2 lemon grass stalks, trimmed and
        finely sliced
    2 shallots, peeled and finely sliced
    2 garlic cloves, finely chopped
    450g/1lb beef fillet, very
        finely sliced
    1 red chilli, seeded and finely sliced
    50g/2oz roasted, unsalted peanuts,
        finely chopped or crushed
    1 small bunch fresh coriander
        (cilantro), finely chopped, plus extra
        leaves, to garnish

1 In a bowl, beat 30ml/2 tbsp *tuk prahoc* with the juice of 2 limes and 30ml/2 tbsp of the sugar, until the sugar has dissolved. Add the lemon grass, shallots and garlic and mix well. Toss in the slices of beef, cover and place in the refrigerator for 1–2 hours.

Per portion Energy 321Kcal/1343kJ; Protein 29g; Carbohydrate 15g, of which sugars 14g; Fat 16g, of which saturates 5g; Cholesterol 65mg; Calcium 48mg; Fibre 1.6g; Sodium 78mg

SEARED BEEF SALAD ᴵᴺ ᴬ LIME DRESSING

*THIS DISH, GOI BO, IS AN INDO-CHINESE FAVOURITE AND VERSIONS OF IT ARE ENJOYED IN VIETNAM,
THAILAND, CAMBODIA AND LAOS. IT IS ALSO ONE OF THE TRADITIONAL DISHES THAT APPEAR IN THE
BO BAY MON — BEEF SEVEN WAYS FEAST — IN WHICH SEVEN DIFFERENT BEEF DISHES ARE SERVED.*

SERVES FOUR

INGREDIENTS
   about 7.5ml/1½ tsp vegetable oil
   450g/1lb beef fillet, cut into steaks
    2.5cm/1in thick
   115g/4oz/½ cup beansprouts
   1 bunch each fresh basil and mint,
    stalks removed, leaves shredded
   1 lime, cut into slices, to serve
For the dressing
   grated and juice (about 80ml/3fl oz)
    of 2 limes
   30ml/2 tbsp *nuoc mam*
   30ml/2 tbsp raw cane sugar
   2 garlic cloves, crushed
   2 lemon grass stalks, finely sliced
   2 red Serrano chillies, seeded and
    finely sliced

3 Drain the meat of any excess juice
and transfer it to a wide serving bowl.
Add the beansprouts and herbs and
toss it all together. Serve with lime slices
to squeeze over.

1 To make the dressing, beat the lime
rind, juice and *nuoc mam* in a bowl
with the sugar, until the sugar dissolves.
Stir in the garlic, lemon grass and
chillies and set aside.

2 Pour a little oil into a heavy pan and
rub it over the base with a piece of
kitchen paper. Heat the pan and sear
the steaks for 1–2 minutes each side.
Transfer them to a board and leave to
cool a little. Using a sharp knife, cut the
meat into thin slices. Toss the slices in
the dressing, cover and leave to
marinate for 1–2 hours.

COOK'S TIP
It is worth buying an excellent-quality
piece of tender fillet steak for this recipe
as the meat is only just seared.

Per portion Energy 233Kcal/979kJ; Protein 26g; Carbohydrate 12g, of which sugars 9g; Fat 9g, of which saturates 3g; Cholesterol 69mg; Calcium 74mg; Fibre 0.5g; Sodium 400mg

DIPS, SAUCES AND CONDIMENTS

Dips, sauces and condiments are present at every meal. Ranging from the local fermented fish sauce to a tangy condiment flavoured with lemon grass or ginger, the Vietnamese and Cambodians love to dip their food in a sauce. To spike noodles and grilled meats, there is always hot chilli sauce, Nuoc Cham, *and vegetables are delicious with a spicy peanut sauce,* Nuoc Leo. *And for an authentic dish Cambodian Herbal Paste,* kroeung, *is essential.*

NUOC CHAM

THERE ARE MANY VERSIONS OF THIS POPULAR CHILLI DIPPING SAUCE, VARYING IN DEGREES OF SWEETNESS, SOURNESS AND HEAT. SOME PEOPLE ADD RICE VINEGAR TO THE MIX.

MAKES ABOUT 200ML/7FL OZ/SCANT 1 CUP

INGREDIENTS
    4 garlic cloves, roughly chopped
    2 red Thai chillies, seeded and
        roughly chopped
    15ml/1 tbsp sugar
    juice of 1 lime
    60ml/4 tbsp *nuoc mam*

1 Using a mortar and pestle, pound the garlic with the chillies and sugar and grind to make a paste.

2 Squeeze in the lime juice, add the *nuoc mam* and then stir in 60–75ml/4–5 tbsp water to taste. Blend well.

Per portion Energy 140Kcal/593kJ; Protein 5.; Carbohydrate 30g, of which sugars 24g; Fat 0.4g, of which saturates 0.1g; Cholesterol 0mg; Calcium 30mg; Fibre 2.4g; Sodium 4277mg

NUOC LEO

THIS HOT PEANUT DIPPING SAUCE IS POPULAR THROUGHOUT VIETNAM. ADJUST THE PROPORTIONS OF CHILLI, SUGAR OR LIQUID, ADDING MORE OR LESS ACCORDING TO TASTE. THIS IS ESPECIALLY GOOD SERVED WITH STEAMED, STIR-FRIED OR DEEP-FRIED VEGETABLES.

MAKES ABOUT 300ML/10FL OZ/2¼ CUPS

INGREDIENTS
    15ml/1 tbsp vegetable oil
    2 garlic cloves, finely chopped
    2 red Thai chillies, seeded
        and chopped
    115g/4oz/⅔ cup unsalted roasted
        peanuts, finely chopped
    150ml/¼ pint/⅔ cup chicken stock
    60ml/4 tbsp coconut milk
    15ml/1 tbsp hoisin sauce
    15ml/1 tbsp *nuoc mam*
    15ml/1 tbsp sugar

2 Simmer until the sauce thickens and oil appears on the surface.

1 Heat the oil in a small wok and stir in the garlic and chillies. Stir-fry until they begin to colour, then add all but 15ml/1 tbsp of the peanuts. Stir-fry for a few minutes until the oil from the peanuts begins to weep. Add the remaining ingredients and bring to the boil.

COOK'S TIP
If you don't use it in one sitting, this sauce will keep in the refrigerator for about one week.

3 Transfer the sauce to a serving dish and garnish with the reserved peanuts.

Per portion Energy 848Kcal/3525kJ; Protein 31g; Carbohydrate 39g, of which sugars 31g; Fat 64g, of which saturates 11g; Cholesterol 0mg; Calcium 104mg; Fibre 8g; Sodium 2498mg

NUOC XA OT

THIS LEMON GRASS, CHILLI AND SOY DIPPING SAUCE OFTEN ACCOMPANIES FISH DISHES OR FRIED
TOFU. IT IS ALSO POPULAR WITH ROASTED MEATS.

MAKES 100ML/3½FL OZ/SCANT ½ CUP

INGREDIENTS
30ml/2 tbsp vegetable oil
1 lemon grass stalk, outer leaves
removed, finely chopped
1 garlic clove, crushed
2 spring onions (scallions),
finely sliced
2 red Thai chillies, seeded and
finely sliced
75ml/5 tbsp soy sauce

1 Heat the oil in a small wok or heavy
pan and stir in the lemon grass, garlic,
spring onions and chillies.

2 Stir-fry until the lemon grass turns
golden, then quickly stir in the soy
sauce. Remove from the heat and pour
the *nuoc xa ot* into a serving bowl.

VARIATION
If you have already made up a quantity
of the Cambodian paste, *kroeung*, mix
several tablespoons of it with the *nuoc
xa ot* to make a Cambodian version.

Per portion Energy 279Kcal/1156kJ; Protein 6g; Carbohydrate 14g, of which sugars 8g; Fat 22g, of which saturates 3g; Cholesterol 0mg; Calcium 33mg; Fibre 2.3g; Sodium 5345mg

NUOC MAM GUNG

THIS INTENSELY FLAVOURED GINGER SAUCE IS SERVED AS AN ACCOMPANIMENT TO GRILLED OR ROASTED
POULTRY AND FISH DISHES. IT IS ALSO DRIZZLED OVER PLAIN NOODLES OR RICE TO GIVE THEM A
LITTLE EXTRA SPIKE, AND IS A GOOD SAUCE TO SERVE WITH VIETNAMESE BEEF FONDUE.

MAKES ABOUT 150ML/¼ PINT/⅔ CUP

INGREDIENTS
15ml/1 tbsp *nuoc mam*
juice of 1 lime
5ml/1 tsp honey
75g/3oz fresh root ginger, peeled
and grated
2 red Thai chillies, seeded and
finely chopped
100ml/3½fl oz/scant ½ cup sesame
or groundnut (peanut) oil

1 In a bowl, mix the *nuoc mam* with the
lime juice, honey, ginger and chillies.

2 Add the oil, mix well and leave to
stand for at least 30 minutes.

Per portion Energy 763Kcal/3147kJ; Protein 1g; Carbohydrate 17g, of which sugars 16.3g; Fat 77g, of which saturates 9g; Cholesterol 0mg; Calcium 38mg; Fibre 1.6g; Sodium 1117mg

CAMBODIAN HERBAL PASTE

THIS PASTE, KNOWN AS KROEUNG, COULD BE DESCRIBED AS THE ESSENCE OF CAMBODIA. LEMON GRASS, GALANGAL AND TURMERIC ARE THREE OF THE KEY FLAVOURS IN KHMER COOKING. THIS VERSATILE PASTE IS USED TO FLAVOUR MANY MARINADES, SOUPS AND STIR-FRIES.

MAKES ABOUT 150ML/¼ PINT/⅔ CUP

INGREDIENTS
    3 lemon grass stalks, trimmed, with
      outer leaves removed,
      and chopped
    25g/1oz galangal, peeled and chopped
    25g/1oz fresh turmeric, peeled
      and chopped
    8 garlic cloves, crushed
    1 small onion or 2 shallots,
      finely chopped
    4 kaffir lime leaves, ribs removed
    2.5ml/½ tsp sea salt

1 Using a mortar and pestle, grind the ingredients to a paste, adding a little water to bind. Or simply put all the ingredients in a food processor with 15–30ml/1–2 tbsp water and process until they form a paste.

2 Spoon the paste into a jar or small bowl and cover. Keep the *kroeung* in the refrigerator for up to a week.

Per portion Energy 25Kcal/105kJ; Protein 1g; Carbohydrate 5.2g, of which sugars 3.8g; Fat 0.2g, of which saturates 0g; Cholesterol 0mg; Calcium 36mg; Fibre 1.4g; Sodium 1014mg

CAMBODIAN TAMARIND DIPPING SAUCE

VARIATIONS OF THIS FRUITY DIPPING SAUCE ARE POPULAR WITH STEAMED OR GRILLED FISH AND SHELLFISH. THE COOKED FISH IS BROKEN INTO CHUNKS AND DIPPED INTO THE SAUCE.

MAKES ABOUT 175ML/6FL OZ/¾ CUP

INGREDIENTS
    30ml/2 tbsp tamarind concentrate
    2.5ml/½ tsp sugar
    15ml/1 tbsp *tuk trey*
    1 fresh red chilli, seeded and
      finely chopped

COOK'S TIP
If you find that the tamarind concentrate is too thick, thin it down with the juice of half a lemon rather than with water so that you don't lose the trademark sour flavour of the tamarind.

1 In a small bowl blend the tamarind concentrate with 50ml/2fl oz/¼ cup water and the sugar. Stir in the *tuk trey* and most of the chilli. Garnish with the reserved chilli and serve.

Per portion Energy 61Kcal/257kJ; Protein 2g; Carbohydrate 13g, of which sugars 12g; Fat 0.6g, of which saturates 0.1g; Cholesterol 0mg; Calcium 15mg; Fibre 2.2g; Sodium 1074mg

VIETNAMESE SHRIMP SAUCE

POPULAR AS A CONDIMENT FOR ROASTED AND GRILLED MEATS, THIS SAUCE IS ALSO ADDED TO SOUPS, BROTHS AND NOODLES. AS IT INCLUDES THE FIERCELY PUNGENT FERMENTED SHRIMP PASTE MAM TOM, *THIS SAUCE IS POWERFUL AND SHOULD BE USED IN MODERATION.*

MAKES ABOUT 200ML/7FL OZ/SCANT 1 CUP

INGREDIENTS
- 3 garlic cloves, chopped
- 1 fresh red chilli, seeded and chopped
- 1 small bunch fresh coriander (cilantro), stalks removed
- 30ml/2 tbsp sugar
- juice of 3 limes
- 30ml/2 tbsp *mam tom*
- 30ml/2 tbsp *nuoc mam*

1 Using a mortar and pestle, pound the garlic, chilli, coriander and sugar to a paste. Add the lime juice, *mam tom* and *nuoc mam*. Mix well and serve.

Per portion Energy 362Kcal/1521kJ; Protein 13g; Carbohydrate 47g, of which sugars 39g; Fat 15g, of which saturates 2.7g; Cholesterol 0mg; Calcium 149mg; Fibre 6.8g; Sodium 23mg

FRIED BLACK CHILLI SAUCE

THAI IN ORIGIN, THIS SPICY, SALTY SAUCE ADDS A UNIQUE FLAVOUR TO MANY SOUPS, SUCH AS THE SOUR FISH SOUP ENJOYED THROUGHOUT VIETNAM AND CAMBODIA. IT IS ALSO SERVED AS A DIPPING SAUCE FOR GRILLED AND ROASTED MEATS IN CAMBODIA.

MAKES ABOUT 200ML/7FL OZ/SCANT 1 CUP

INGREDIENTS
- 50g/2oz dried shrimp, soaked in water for 20 minutes
- 12 dried red chillies, soaked in water for 20 minutes
- 120ml/4fl oz/½ cup vegetable oil
- 8 garlic cloves, finely chopped
- 4 shallots or 1 onion, chopped
- 30ml/2 tbsp Thai shrimp paste
- 30ml/2 tbsp palm sugar

1 Drain the shrimp and, using a mortar and pestle, pound them to a paste. Drain the chillies, remove the stalks and seeds and chop them finely.

2 Heat the oil in a wok and stir-fry the garlic and shallots or onion until fragrant. Add the pounded shrimp, chillies, Thai shrimp paste and palm sugar. Stir-fry until the chillies are dark in colour. Remove from the heat and pour into a bowl. Serve hot or cold.

Per portion Energy 1059Kcal/4389kJ; Protein 30g; Carbohydrate 43g, of which sugars 40g; Fat 86g, of which saturates 10g; Cholesterol 253mg; Calcium 653mg; Fibre 2g; Sodium 2171mg

SPRING ONION OIL

MANY DISHES CALL FOR A FLAVOURED OIL TO BE DRIZZLED OVER NOODLES, OR BRUSHED ON GRILLED MEAT. IN VIETNAM, SPRING ONION OIL IS ALMOST ALWAYS AT HAND, READY TO BE SPLASHED INTO SOUPS, AND OVER MANY NOODLE AND STIR-FRIED DISHES.

MAKES ABOUT 250ML/8FL OZ/1 CUP

INGREDIENTS
   250ml/8fl oz/1 cup vegetable or
      groundnut (peanut) oil
   15 spring onions (scallions), trimmed
      and finely sliced

COOK'S TIP
It is important not to fry the spring onions for too long: they should be golden and sweet. If they become dark brown, they will have a bitter taste. Many South-east Asian cooks prepare batches of this garnish to keep at hand for the week's cooking. Refrigerate after making up a batch. They will keep for 2 weeks.

1 Heat the oil, stir in the spring onions and fry until golden. Pour the oil into a heatproof jug (pitcher) and leave to cool.

2 Pour the oil into a glass bottle or jar, seal tightly, and store in a cool place.

Per portion Energy 1698Kcal/6985kJ; Protein 3g; Carbohydrate 4g, of which sugars 4g; Fat 186g, of which saturates 22g; Cholesterol 0mg; Calcium 59mg; Fibre 2.3g; Sodium 11mg

FRIED SHALLOTS

SHALLOTS FRIED WITH A COMBINATION OF GINGER, SPRING ONIONS AND GARLIC, OR JUST ONE OR TWO OF THESE FLAVOURINGS, LEND A CRUNCH AND A SWEETNESS TO FINISHED DISHES. SERVED AS GARNISHES OR CONDIMENTS, THEY ARE FOUND THROUGHOUT SOUTH-EAST ASIA.

TO GARNISH THREE TO FOUR DISHES

INGREDIENTS
150ml/¼ pint/⅔ cup vegetable or
   groundnut (peanut) oil
6 shallots, halved lengthways and
   sliced along the grain
50g/2oz fresh root ginger, peeled and
   cut into fine strips
6 spring onions (scallions), trimmed,
   cut into 2.5cm/1in pieces and
   halved lengthways
3 garlic cloves, halved lengthways
   and cut into thin strips

1 Heat the oil in a wok or small pan. Stir in the shallots, ginger, spring onions and garlic. Stir-fry until golden, but not brown. Remove with a slotted spoon and drain on kitchen paper.

2 Leave to cool and store in a jar in the refrigerator for up to 1 week. Use as a garnish or put it on the table as a condiment. The leftover, flavoured oil can be used for stir-fries.

Per portion Energy 471Kcal/1942kJ; Protein 4g; Carbohydrate 14g, of which sugars 9g; Fat 44.7g, of which saturates 5.2g; Cholesterol 0mg; Calcium 77mg; Fibre 3.7g; Sodium 38mg

SWEET SNACKS

Juicy fruit and sweet snacks are enjoyed by all Vietnamese and Cambodians. Rather than being served at the end of a meal, sweet snacks are devoured on a whim. Ripe fruit is peeled and eaten or crushed into juice; ice cream is made with the flesh of pungent durian and exotic flavours such as star anise. Hot, sweet soups such as Sweet Mung Bean Soup, and Vietnamese Fried Bananas and other fried delicacies disappear rapidly.

VIETNAMESE FRIED BANANAS

WHEREVER YOU GO IN VIETNAM, YOU WILL FIND FRIED BANANAS. THEY ARE EATEN HOT, STRAIGHT FROM THE PAN, AS A QUICK AND TASTY SNACK. FOR A MORE INDULGENT TREAT, THEY MIGHT BE COMBINED WITH ONE OF THE LOVELY FRENCH-STYLE ICE CREAMS.

SERVES FOUR

INGREDIENTS
4 ripe but firm bananas
vegetable oil, for deep-frying
caster (superfine) sugar, for sprinkling
For the batter
115g/4oz/1 cup rice flour or plain
(all-purpose) flour
2.5ml/½ tsp baking powder
45ml/3 tbsp caster (superfine) sugar
150ml/¼ pint/⅔ cup water
150ml/¼ pint/⅔ cup beer

1 To make the batter, sift the flour with the baking powder into a bowl. Add the sugar and beat in a little of the water and beer to make a smooth paste. Gradually beat in the rest of the water and beer to form a thick batter. Leave to stand for 20 minutes.

2 Peel the bananas and cut them in half crossways, then in half again lengthways. Heat enough vegetable oil for deep-frying in a wok or a large, heavy pan.

3 Cook the bananas in batches, so they don't stick together in the pan. Dip each one into the beer batter, making sure it is well coated, and carefully slip it into the hot oil. Use tongs or chopsticks for turning and make sure each piece is crisp and golden all over.

4 Drain the fried bananas on kitchen paper and sprinkle them with sugar. Serve immediately and eat hot.

Per portion Energy 290Kcal/1211kJ; Protein 3g; Carbohydrate 48g, of which sugars 22g; Fat 9g, of which saturates 1g; Cholesterol 0mg; Calcium 22mg; Fibre 1.7g; Sodium 600mg

DEEP-FRIED MUNG BEAN DUMPLINGS

SWEET AND SAVOURY RICE DUMPLINGS ARE POPULAR SNACKS IN VIETNAM. IN THIS DISH, DAU XANH VUNG, THE POTATO AND RICE-FLOUR DUMPLINGS ARE STUFFED WITH THE CLASSIC VIETNAMESE FILLING OF SWEETENED MUNG BEAN PASTE AND THEN ROLLED IN SESAME SEEDS.

SERVES SIX

INGREDIENTS
    100g/3½oz/scant ½ cup split
      mung beans, soaked for 6 hours
      and drained
    115g/4oz/generous ½ cup caster
      (superfine) sugar
    300g/10½oz/scant 3 cups glutinous
      rice flour
    50g/2oz/½ cup rice flour
    1 medium potato, boiled in its skin,
      peeled and mashed
    75g/3oz/6 tbsp sesame seeds
    vegetable oil, for deep-frying

1 Put the mung beans in a large pan with half the caster sugar and pour in 450ml/¾ pint/scant 2 cups water. Bring to the boil, stirring constantly until all the sugar has dissolved. Reduce the heat and simmer gently for 15–20 minutes until the mung beans are soft. You may need to add more water if the beans are becoming dry, otherwise they will burn on the bottom of the pan.

2 Once the mung beans are soft and all the water has been absorbed, reduce the beans to a smooth paste in a mortar and pestle or food processor and leave to cool.

3 In a large bowl, beat the flours and remaining sugar into the mashed potato. Add about 200ml/7fl oz/scant 1 cup water to bind the mixture into a moist dough. Divide the dough into 24 pieces, roll each one into a small ball, then flatten with the heel of your hand to make a disc and lay out on a lightly floured board.

VARIATION
These little fried dumplings may also be filled with a sweetened red bean paste, sweetened taro root or, as in China, a lotus paste. Alternatively, the dumplings can be steamed and then soaked in syrup. Both versions are very popular throughout Vietnam.

4 Divide the mung bean paste into 24 small portions. Place one portion of mung bean paste in the centre of a dough disc. Fold over the edges of the dough and then shape into a ball. Repeat for the remaining dumplings.

5 Spread the sesame seeds on a plate and roll the dumplings in them until evenly coated. Heat enough oil for deep-frying in a wok or heavy pan. Fry the balls in batches until golden. Drain on kitchen paper and serve warm.

Per portion Energy 321Kcal/1346kJ; Protein 7g; Carbohydrate 40g, of which sugars 21g; Fat 16g, of which saturates 2g; Cholesterol 0mg; Calcium 104mg; Fibre 3.1g; Sodium 0mg

Sweet Mung Bean Soup

In Hue, sweet soups are a great favourite. In the restaurants and parks along the Perfume River, people pause for a while to enjoy a bowl of soup made with different sorts of beans, rice, tapioca, bananas or even lotus seeds and root vegetables sucii as taro.

SERVES FOUR TO SIX

INGREDIENTS
  225g/8oz/1 cup skinned split mung
    beans, soaked in water for 3 hours
    and drained
  500ml/17fl oz/2¼ cups
    coconut milk
  50g/2oz/¼ cup caster (superfine)
    sugar
  toasted coconut shavings (optional),
    to serve

COOK'S TIP
Be sure to buy the bright yellow, peeled, split mung beans for this soup rather than the whole green ones. Split mung beans are available in Asian stores.

1 Put the mung beans in a pan and pour in 500ml/17fl oz/2¼ cups water. Bring the water to the boil, stirring constantly, then reduce the heat and simmer gently for 15–20 minutes until all the water has been absorbed and the mung beans are soft enough to purée. Press the beans through a sieve (strainer), or purée them in a blender.

2 In a large heavy pan, heat the coconut milk with the caster sugar, stirring until the sugar has dissolved. Gently stir in the puréed mung beans, making sure the soup is thoroughly mixed and heated through. Serve hot in individually warmed bowls sprinkled with toasted coconut shavings, if you like.

Per portion Energy 240Kcal/1025kJ; Protein 15g; Carbohydrate 45g, of which sugars 20g; Fat 1g, of which saturates 0g; Cholesterol 0mg; Calcium 57mg; Fibre 0g; Sodium 100mg

TAPIOCA WITH BANANA AND COCONUT

POPULAR IN BOTH VIETNAM AND CAMBODIA, THIS IS THE TYPE OF DESSERT THAT EVERYBODY'S MOTHER OR GRANDMOTHER MAKES. SWEET AND NOURISHING, IT IS MADE WITH TAPIOCA PEARLS COOKED IN COCONUT MILK AND SWEETENED WITH BANANAS AND SUGAR.

SERVES FOUR

INGREDIENTS
   550ml/18fl oz/2½ cups water
   40g/1½oz tapioca pearls
   550ml/18fl oz/2½ cups coconut milk
   90g/3½oz/½ cup sugar
   3 ripe bananas, diced
   salt

COOK'S TIP
A pinch of salt added to this recipe enhances the flavour of the coconut milk and counterbalances the sweetness. You can try the recipe with sweet potato, taro root, yellow corn or rice.

1 Pour the water into a pan and bring it to the boil. Stir in the tapioca pearls, reduce the heat and simmer for about 20 minutes, until translucent. Add the coconut milk, sugar and a pinch of salt. Cook gently for 30 minutes.

2 Stir in the diced bananas and cook them for 5–10 minutes until soft. Spoon into individual warmed bowls and serve immediately.

Per portion Energy 226Kcal/964kJ; Protein 1.5g; Carbohydrate 57.2g, of which sugars 45.9g; Fat 0.7g, of which saturates 0.4g; Cholesterol 0mg; Calcium 57mg; Fibre 0.9g; Sodium 154mg.

STICKY RICE <u>WITH</u> DURIAN SAUCE

THROUGHOUT SOUTH-EAST ASIA, PEOPLE ENJOY A SNACK OF SWEET STICKY RICE. EVERY CULTURE HAS THEIR OWN FAVOURITE VERSION OF THIS SNACK — SOME LIKE IT SERVED WITH SWEETENED RED BEANS, OTHERS WITH MANGO, AND THE CAMBODIANS EAT IT WITH A DOLLOP OF DURIAN SAUCE.

SERVES FOUR TO SIX

INGREDIENTS
115g/4oz/generous ½ cup sticky
  glutinous rice, rinsed, and soaked in
  plenty of water for at least 6 hours
550ml/18fl oz/2½ cups coconut milk
30ml/2 tbsp palm sugar
115g/4oz fresh durian flesh, puréed
salt

1 Drain the sticky rice. Fill a wok a third of the way up with water. Fit a bamboo steamer into the wok and put the lid on. Bring the water to the boil, place a piece of dampened muslin (cheesecloth) over the bamboo rack and spoon the rice into it, leaving space all around for the steam to come through.

2 Carefully fold the muslin over the rice, cover the steamer, and steam for about 20 minutes, until the rice is translucent and tender but still has a bite to it.

3 In a heavy pan, heat the coconut milk with a pinch of salt and the sugar, until it has dissolved.

4 Beat in the puréed durian. Pour a little less than half of the mixture into a small pan and set aside. Add the cooked rice to the remaining mixture and mix well. Put the lid on the pan and simmer for a further 15 minutes. Divide the sweetened rice among individual bowls. Heat the reserved sauce in the small pan and pour it over the rice.

Per portion Energy 111Kcal/470kJ; Protein 2g; Carbohydrate 25.4g, of which sugars 10g; Fat 0.4g, of which saturates 0.2g; Cholesterol 0mg; Calcium 39mg; Fibre 0.2g; Sodium 101mg

COCONUT RICE PUDDING WITH PINEAPPLE

THIS RICE PUDDING IS A FRENCH-INSPIRED DESSERT. WHEN SERVED IN THE VIETNAMESE HOME, IT MIGHT BE ACCOMPANIED BY FRUITS IN SYRUP, OR SAUTÉED BANANAS OR PINEAPPLE, AS HERE. IT NEEDS LONG, SLOW COOKING IN A LOW OVEN. IT IS WELL WORTH THE WAIT.

SERVES FOUR TO SIX

INGREDIENTS

  90g/3½oz/½ cup pudding rice
  600ml/1 pint/2½ cups
    coconut milk
  300ml/½ pint/1¼ cups full-fat
    (whole) milk
  75g/2¾oz/scant ½ cup caster
    (superfine) sugar
  25g/1oz/2 tbsp butter, plus extra
    for greasing
  45ml/3 tbsp grated fresh or
    desiccated (dry unsweetened
    shredded) coconut, toasted
  1 small, ripe pineapple
  30ml/2 tbsp sesame oil
  5cm/2in piece of fresh root ginger,
    peeled and grated
shavings of toasted coconut,
  to garnish

2 After 30 minutes, take the dish out and gently stir in the toasted coconut. Return it to the oven for a further 1½ hours, or until almost all the milk is absorbed and a golden skin has formed on top of the pudding.

3 Using a sharp knife, peel the pineapple and remove the core, then cut the flesh into bitesize cubes.

4 Towards the end of the cooking time, heat the oil in a large wok or heavy pan. Stir in the ginger, stir-fry until the aroma is released, then add the pineapple cubes, turning them over to sear on both sides. Sprinkle with the remaining sugar and continue to cook until the pineapple is slightly caramelized.

5 Serve the pudding spooned into bowls and topped with the hot, caramelized pineapple and toasted coconut.

1 Preheat the oven to 150°C/300°F/ Gas 2. Grease an ovenproof dish. In a bowl, mix the rice with the coconut milk, milk and 50g/2oz/¼ cup of the sugar and pour it into the ovenproof dish. Dot pieces of butter over the top and place the dish in the oven.

VARIATIONS
The Vietnamese love sticky rice and mung bean puddings and always sprinkle a little extra sugar over the top to serve. You can also heat up a little sweetened coconut cream and pour it over the top. For a slightly different flavour, you could also serve the rice pudding with slices of seared mango or banana instead of the sauteed pineapple.

Per portion Energy 414Kcal/1735kJ; Protein 6g; Carbohydrate 56g, of which sugars 39g; Fat 19g, of which saturates 9g; Cholesterol 24mg; Calcium 156mg; Fibre 1.6g; Sodium 200mg

PUMPKIN PUDDING IN BANANA LEAVES

NATIVE TO CAMBODIA, NOM L'POH IS A TRADITIONAL PUDDING THAT CAN BE MADE WITH SMALL, SWEET PUMPKINS, OR BUTTERNUT SQUASH. THIS IS A VERY MOREISH DESSERT, OR SNACK, WHICH CAN BE EATEN HOT, AT ROOM TEMPERATURE, OR COLD.

2 In a pan, heat the coconut milk with the sugar and a pinch of salt. Blend the tapioca starch with 15ml/1 tbsp water and 15ml/1 tbsp of the hot coconut milk. Add it to the coconut milk and beat well. Beat the mashed pumpkin into the coconut milk or, if using a blender, add the coconut milk to the pumpkin and purée together.

3 Spoon equal amounts of the pumpkin purée into the centre of each banana leaf square. Fold in the sides and thread a cocktail stick (toothpick) through the open ends to enclose the purée.

4 Fill the bottom third of a wok with water. Place a bamboo steamer on top. Place as many stuffed banana leaves as you can into the steamer, folded side up – you may have to cook them in batches. Cover the steamer and steam parcels for 15 minutes. Unwrap them and serve hot or cold.

SERVES SIX

INGREDIENTS
  1 small pumpkin, about 1.3kg/3lb, peeled, seeded and cubed
  250ml/8fl oz/1 cup coconut milk
  45ml/3 tbsp palm sugar
  15ml/1 tbsp tapioca starch
  12 banana leaves, cut into 15cm/6in squares
  salt

VARIATION
You can also try sweet potatoes, cassava or taro root in this recipe.

1 Bring a pan of salted water to the boil. Add the pumpkin flesh and cook for 15 minutes, or until tender. Drain and mash with a fork or purée in a blender.

Per portion Energy 60Kcal/257kJ; Protein 1g; Carbohydrate 13.6g, of which sugars 12.7g; Fat 0.5g, of which saturates 0.3g; Cholesterol 0mg; Calcium 64mg; Fibre 1.7g; Sodium 46mg

BAKED PUMPKIN WITH COCONUT CUSTARD

THIS IS A TRADITIONAL DESSERT FROM CAMBODIA AND THAILAND. ONCE THE CUSTARD-FILLED PUMPKIN IS BAKED, THE FLESH IS SCOOPED OUT WITH THE CUSTARD AND A HOT COCONUT SAUCE IS DRIZZLED OVER THE TOP. SWEET AND FRAGRANT, THIS IS SHEER INDULGENCE.

SERVES FOUR TO EIGHT

INGREDIENTS
   1 small pumpkin, about 1.3kg/3lb,
     halved, seeded and fibres removed
   400ml/14fl oz/1⅔ cups
     coconut milk
   3 large (US extra large) eggs
   45ml/3 tbsp palm sugar, plus a
     little extra for sprinkling
   salt
For the sauce
   250ml/8fl oz/1 cup coconut cream
   30ml/2 tbsp palm sugar

1 Preheat the oven to 180°C/350°F/ Gas 4. Place the pumpkin halves, skin side down, in a baking dish.

3 Bake in the oven for 35–40 minutes. The pumpkin should feel tender when a skewer is inserted in it, and the custard should feel firm when lightly touched. If you like, you can brown the top further under the grill (broiler).

4 Just before serving, heat the coconut cream in a pan with a pinch of salt and the sugar. Scoop out servings of pumpkin flesh with the custard and place it in bowls. Pour a little sweetened coconut cream over the top to serve.

2 In a large bowl, whisk the coconut milk with a pinch of salt, the eggs and sugar, until the mixture is thick and smooth. Pour the custard into each pumpkin half and sprinkle a little extra sugar over the top of the custard and the rim of the pumpkin.

COOK'S TIP
Choose a small pumpkin as it will be more fragrant and less fibrous than a larger one.

VARIATION
This recipe can also be made with butternut or acorn squash and, interestingly, with halved avocados, mangoes and papayas, although the quantity of custard and cooking times may have to be adjusted.

Per portion Energy 217Kcal/906kJ; Protein 4.5g; Carbohydrate 16g, of which sugars 16g; Fat 15g, of which saturates 12g; Cholesterol 71mg; Calcium 71mg; Fibre 1.3g; Sodium 88mg

COCONUT CRÈME CARAMEL

BASED ON THE CLASSIC FRENCH DESSERT, THIS VIETNAMESE VERSION IS MADE WITH COCONUT MILK.
POPULAR THROUGHOUT VIETNAM, IT IS SERVED BOTH AS A SNACK AND AS A DESSERT IN RESTAURANTS,
WHERE IT IS SOMETIMES GARNISHED WITH MINT LEAVES.

SERVES FOUR TO SIX

INGREDIENTS
   4 large (US extra large) eggs
   4 egg yolks
   50g/2oz/¼ cup caster (superfine)
     sugar
   600ml/1 pint/2½ cups coconut
     milk
   toasted slivers of coconut,
     to decorate
For the caramel
   150g/5oz/¾ cup caster (superfine)
     sugar

1 Preheat the oven to 160°C/325°F/
Gas 3. To make the caramel, heat the
sugar and 75ml/5 tbsp water in a heavy
pan, stirring constantly until the sugar
dissolves. Bring to the boil and, without
stirring, let the mixture bubble until it is
dark golden and almost like treacle.

2 Pour the caramel into an ovenproof
dish, tilting the dish to swirl it around
so that it covers the bottom and sides –
you will need to do this quickly.
Put the dish aside and leave the
caramel to set.

3 In a bowl, beat the eggs and egg
yolks with the caster sugar. Heat the
coconut milk in a small pan, but don't
allow it to boil. Then gradually pour it
on to the egg mixture, while beating
constantly. Pour the mixture through a
sieve (strainer) over the caramel in the
dish or individual ramekins.

4 Set the dish or ramekins in a bain-
marie. You can use a roasting pan or
wide oven dish half-filled with water.
Place it in the oven for about 50
minutes, or until the custard has just
set, but still feels soft when touched
with the fingertips. Leave the dish to
cool, then chill in the refrigerator for at
least 6 hours, or overnight.

COOK'S TIP
• You can use this recipe to make six
small individual desserts using ramekin
dishes instead of a large dish.

VARIATION
• If you are not keen on coconut, you
can use full-fat fresh milk instead of
coconut milk and infuse it with a vanilla
pod, orange peel or aniseed.

5 To serve, loosen the custard around
the sides using a thin, sharp knife.
Place a flat serving plate over the top
and invert the custard, holding on to the
dish and plate at the same time. Shake
it a little before removing the inverted
dish, then carefully lift it off as the
caramel drizzles down the sides and
forms a puddle around the pudding.

6 Decorate the custard with fresh grated
coconut and mint leaves, and serve.

VARIATION
For an alternative garnish, try toasted
coconut or make a small batch of sugar
syrup with finely shredded ginger or
orange peel.

Per portion Energy 256Kcal/1078kJ; Protein 9g; Carbohydrate 31g, of which sugars 31g; Fat 11g, of which saturates 4g; Cholesterol 338mg; Calcium 79mg; Fibre 0.4g; Sodium 200mg

JUNGLE FRUITS ᴵᴺ LEMON GRASS SYRUP

THIS EXOTIC AND REFRESHING FRUIT SALAD CAN BE MADE WITH ANY COMBINATION OF TROPICAL FRUITS — JUST GO FOR A GOOD BALANCE OF COLOUR, FLAVOUR AND TEXTURE. YOU CAN ALSO FLAVOUR THE SYRUP WITH GINGER RATHER THAN LEMON GRASS, IF YOU PREFER.

SERVES SIX

INGREDIENTS
   1 firm papaya
   1 small pineapple
   2 small star fruit, sliced into stars
   12 fresh lychees, peeled and stoned
     (pitted) or 14oz/400g can lychees
   2 firm yellow or green bananas, peeled
     and cut diagonally into slices
mint leaves, to decorate
For the syrup
   115g/4oz/generous ½ cup caster
     (superfine) sugar
   2 lemon grass stalks, bruised and
     halved lengthways

2 Peel and halve the papaya, remove the seeds and slice the flesh crossways. Peel the pineapple and slice it into rounds. Remove the core and cut each round in half. (Keep the core and slice it for a stir-fry.)

3 Put all the fruit into a bowl. Pour the syrup, including the lemon grass stalks, over the top and toss to combine. Cover and chill for 6 hours, or overnight. Before serving, remove the lemon grass stalks and decorate with mint leaves.

1 To make the syrup, put 225ml/ 7½ fl oz/1 cup water into a heavy pan with the sugar and lemon grass stalks. Bring to the boil, stirring constantly until the sugar has dissolved, then reduce the heat and simmer for 15 minutes. Leave to cool.

Per portion Energy 160Kcal/683kJ; Protein 1g; Carbohydrate 41g, of which sugars 40g; Fat 0g, of which saturates 0g; Cholesterol 0mg; Calcium 22mg; Fibre 1.8g; Sodium 0mg

CASSAVA SWEET

THIS TYPE OF SWEET AND STICKY SNACK IS USUALLY SERVED WITH A CUP OF LIGHT JASMINE TEA.
MORE LIKE AN INDIAN HELVA THAN A CAKE, THIS RECIPE CAN ALSO BE MADE USING SWEET POTATOES
OR YAMS IN PLACE OF THE CASSAVA.

SERVES SIX TO EIGHT

INGREDIENTS
  butter, for greasing
  350ml/12fl oz/1½ cups coconut milk
  115g/4oz/generous ½ cup palm sugar
  2.5ml/½ tsp ground aniseed
  salt
  675g/1½lb cassava root, peeled
  and coarsely grated

COOK'S TIP
To prepare the cassava for grating, use a
sharp knife to split the whole length of
the root and then carefully peel off the
skin. Simply grate the peeled root using
a coarse grater.

1 Preheat the oven to 190°C/375°F/
Gas 5 and grease a baking dish with
butter. In a bowl, whisk the coconut
milk with the palm sugar, ground
aniseed and a pinch of salt, until the
sugar has dissolved.

2 Beat the grated cassava root into the
coconut mixture and pour into the
greased baking dish. Place it in the
oven and bake for about 1 hour, or until
it is golden on top. Leave the sweet to
cool a little in the dish before serving
warm or at room temperature.

Per portion Energy 254Kcal/1086kJ; Protein 1g; Carbohydrate 64g, of which sugars 25g; Fat 1g, of which saturates 1g; Cholesterol 2mg; Calcium 39mg; Fibre 1.8g; Sodium 0.2g

SWEET RICE DUMPLINGS IN GINGER SYRUP

OFTEN COOKED FOR TET AND OTHER VIETNAMESE CELEBRATIONS, THESE RICE DUMPLINGS ARE FILLED WITH THE TRADITIONAL MUNG BEAN PASTE AND THEN SIMMERED IN A GINGER-INFUSED SYRUP. THE DOUGH IS MADE WITH GLUTINOUS RICE FLOUR TO ATTAIN THE DESIRED SPRINGY, CHEWY TEXTURE.

SERVES FOUR TO SIX

INGREDIENTS

For the syrup
   25g/1oz fresh root ginger, peeled and
     finely shredded
   115g/4oz/generous ½ cup sugar
   400ml/14fl oz/1⅔ cups water

For the filling
   40g/1½oz dried split mung beans,
     soaked for 6 hours and drained
   25g/1oz/2 tbsp sugar

For the dough
   225g/8oz/2 cups sticky glutinous
     rice flour
   175ml/6fl oz/¾ cup boiling water

1 To make the syrup, stir the ginger and sugar in a heavy pan over a low heat, until the sugar begins to brown. Take the pan off the heat to stir in the water – it will bubble and spit. Return the pan to the heat and bring to the boil, stirring all the time. Reduce the heat and simmer for 5 minutes.

2 To make the filling, put the soaked mung beans in a pan with the sugar and pour in enough water to cover. Bring to the boil, stirring all the time until the sugar has dissolved. Reduce the heat and simmer for 15–20 minutes until the mung beans are soft – you may need to add more water if the beans are getting dry.

COOK'S TIP
These dumplings are popular at Vietnamese weddings. Coloured red with food dye, they represent good fortune.

3 Once soft enough and when all the water has been absorbed, pound to a smooth paste and leave to cool.

4 Using your fingers, pick up teaspoon-sized portions of the filling and roll them into small balls – there should be roughly 16–20.

5 To make the dough, put the flour in a bowl. Make a well in the centre and gradually pour in the water, drawing in the flour from the sides. Mix to form a dough, then cover and leave to stand until cool enough to handle. Dust a surface with flour and knead the dough for a few minutes, until soft, smooth and springy.

6 Divide the dough in half and roll each half into a sausage, about 25cm/10in long. Divide each sausage into 8–10 pieces, and roll each piece into a ball. Take a ball of dough and flatten it in the palm of your hand. Place a ball of the mung bean filling in the centre of the dough and seal it by pinching and rolling the dough. Repeat with the remaining balls.

7 Bring a deep pan of water to the boil. Drop in the filled dumplings and cook for a few minutes, until they rise to the surface. Once cooked, drain the dumplings in a colander. Heat the syrup in a heavy pan, drop in the cooked dumplings, and simmer for 2–3 minutes. Leave to cool and serve at room temperature, or chilled.

VARIATIONS
• For a spicy version, the syrup can be flavoured with a mixture of ginger, cloves, aniseed and cinnamon sticks.
• The dumplings can be filled with a sweetened purée of cooked sweet potato, mashed banana or even a mixture of chopped dried fruits.

Per portion Energy 231Kcal/975kJ; Protein 2.7g; Carbohydrate 54.7g, of which sugars 24.5g; Fat 0.3g, of which saturates 0g; Cholesterol 0mg; Calcium 23mg; Fibre 0.9g; Sodium 4mg.

GOLDEN THREADS

OFTEN SOLD AS A SNACK IN THE STREET MARKETS OF CAMBODIA, THESE DELICATE GOLDEN THREADS, OR VAWEE, ARE ALSO FREQUENTLY USED IN RESTAURANTS AS A DECORATIVE GARNISH FOR SOME OF THE CUSTARDS AND RICE PUDDINGS.

SERVES TWO TO FOUR AS A SNACK

INGREDIENTS

450ml/¾ pint/scant 2 cups water
225g/8oz/generous 1 cup caster
 (superfine) sugar
30ml/2 tbsp rose water
12 egg yolks, lightly beaten together,
 and strained through a sieve

1 In a heavy pan, stir the water and sugar over a high heat, until the sugar dissolves. Bring to the boil, then reduce the heat and continue to stir for 5–10 minutes, until it begins to thicken. Add the rose water and continue to boil gently for 2–3 minutes. Pour the egg yolk into a piping (icing) bag with a single-hole nozzle, or use a jug (pitcher) with a narrow spout.

2 Carefully drip some of the egg yolk into the simmering syrup, moving backwards and forwards to form long threads or in a circular motion to form round ones. Cook the threads for about 30 seconds then, using a slotted spoon or chopsticks, lift them out of the syrup and on to a dish. Continue with the rest of the egg yolk, cooking in batches.

3 Serve the golden threads as a snack, or use them to garnish sweet rice dishes and fruit salads.

COOK'S TIPS
• Although considered a Thai speciality in Cambodia, these threads probably originated in India, or the Middle East, where traditional sweet threads and pastries are often poached, or soaked, in rose-scented syrup.
• It is important to keep the consistency of the syrup loose and flowing, not too thick, by adding more water if necessary while cooking the threads, which should be smooth. They may not be perfect on the first few occasions, as it takes a little practice to control the flow of the egg into the syrup, as well as lifting them out quickly while still golden.

Per portion Energy 1619Kcal/6811kJ; Protein 36g; Carbohydrate 235g, of which sugars 235g; Fat 66g, of which saturates 19g; Cholesterol 2419mg; Calcium 400mg; Fibre 0g; Sodium 122mg

COCONUT SORBET

DELICIOUSLY REFRESHING AND COOLING, THIS TROPICAL SORBET CAN BE FOUND IN DIFFERENT VERSIONS ALL OVER SOUTH-EAST ASIA. OTHER CLASSIC VIETNAMESE SORBETS ARE MADE WITH LYCHEES, PINEAPPLE, WATERMELON AND LEMON GRASS.

SERVES SIX

INGREDIENTS
  175g/6oz/scant 1 cup caster
    (superfine) sugar
  120ml/4fl oz/½ cup coconut milk
  50g/2oz/⅔ cup grated or desiccated
    (dry unsweetened shredded)
    coconut
  a squeeze of lime juice

1 Place the sugar in a heavy pan and add 200ml/7fl oz/scant 1 cup water. Bring to the boil, stirring constantly, until the sugar has dissolved completely. Reduce the heat and simmer for 5 minutes to make a light syrup.

2 Stir the coconut milk into the sugar syrup, along with most of the coconut and the lime juice. Pour the mixture into a bowl or freezer container and freeze for 1 hour.

3 Take the sorbet out of the freezer and beat it with a fork, or blend it in a food processor, until it is smooth and creamy, then return it to the freezer and leave until frozen.

4 Before serving, allow the sorbet to stand at room temperature for 10–15 minutes to soften slightly.

5 Serve in small bowls and decorate with the remaining grated coconut.

COOK'S TIP
Light and refreshing, this sorbet is very welcome on a hot day, or as a palate refresher during a spicy meal. You could serve it in coconut shells, garnished with sprigs of fresh mint.

Per portion Energy 170Kcal/718kJ; Protein 1g; Carbohydrate 32g, of which sugars 32g; Fat 5g, of which saturates 5g; Cholesterol 4mg; Calcium 11mg; Fibre 1.1g; Sodium 0mg

DURIAN ICE CREAM

FOLLOWING THE FRENCH INFLUENCE, THE VIETNAMESE HAVE COME UP WITH SOME EXCITING ICE CREAM RECIPES USING LOCAL FRUITS AND FLAVOURINGS. BECAUSE THE NOTORIOUSLY PUNGENT DURIAN IS ONE OF THEIR FAVOURITE FRUITS, IT IS NO SURPRISE THAT IT IS USED TO MAKE ICE CREAM.

2 Strain the milk and egg mixture into a heavy pan and place it over the heat, stirring constantly, until it thickens and forms a creamy custard. Leave to cool.

3 Purée the durian flesh. Strain the custard into a bowl, then whisk in the cream. Fold in the durian flesh, making sure it is thoroughly combined.

4 Pour the mixture into an ice cream maker and churn until frozen. Alternatively, pour into a freezerproof container and freeze for 4 hours, beating twice with a fork or whisking with an electric mixer to break up the ice crystals.

COOK'S TIP
The Vietnamese name for the strong-smelling fruit durian is *saw rieg* (one's sorrow), but the sweet, creamy, yellow flesh of the fruit is delicious. The problem is getting to this nectar. With its tough, brownish skin covered in thorns, and the overwhelming smell as you cut into it, you might wonder if it's worth the effort. Be assured though – it definitely is. Just hold your nose and persevere.

SERVES EIGHT

INGREDIENTS
 6 egg yolks
 115g/4oz/generous ½ cup caster
  (superfine) sugar
 500ml/17fl oz/2¼ cups full-fat
  (whole) milk
 350g/12oz durian flesh
 300ml/½ pint/1¼ cups double
  (heavy) cream

VARIATION
Other tropical fruits used to make ice cream include banana, mango and papaya, often spiked with lime zest.

1 In a bowl, whisk the egg yolks and sugar together until light and frothy. In a heavy pan, heat the milk to just below boiling point, then pour it slowly into the egg mixture, whisking constantly.

Per portion Energy 392Kcal/1692kJ; Protein 32g; Carbohydrate 69g, of which sugars 32g; Fat 27g, of which saturates 15g; Cholesterol 211mg; Calcium 117mg; Fibre 0g; Sodium 40mg

STAR ANISE ICE CREAM

THIS SYRUP-BASED ICE CREAM IS FLAVOURED WITH THE CLEAN, WARMING TASTE OF STAR ANISE AND WILL PUNCTUATE THE END OF A SPICY VIETNAMESE OR CAMBODIAN MEAL PERFECTLY, LEAVING YOU WITH A REALLY EXOTIC TASTE IN YOUR MOUTH.

SERVES SIX TO EIGHT

INGREDIENTS
  500ml/17fl oz/2¼ cups double (heavy) cream
  8 whole star anise
  90g/3½oz/½ cup caster (superfine) sugar
  4 large (US extra large) egg yolks
  ground star anise, to decorate

1 In a heavy pan, heat the cream with the star anise to just below boiling point, then remove from the heat and leave to infuse until cool.

COOK'S TIP
Spices play an important role in the ice creams from the south of Vietnam, with their lively tastes of cinnamon, clove, star anise and pandanus leaf. This ice cream is often served as a palate cleanser.

2 In another pan, dissolve the sugar in 150ml/¼ pint/⅔ cup water, stirring constantly. Bring to the boil for a few minutes to form a light syrup, then leave to cool for 1 minute.

3 Whisk the egg yolks in a bowl. Trickle in the hot syrup, whisking constantly, until the mixture becomes mousse-like. Pour in the infused cream through a sieve (strainer), and continue to whisk.

4 Pour the mixture into an ice cream maker and churn until frozen. Alternatively, pour the mixture into a freezerproof container and freeze for 4 hours, beating twice with a fork or whisking with an electric mixer to break up the ice crystals. To serve, dust with a little ground star anise.

Per portion Energy 393Kcal/1623kJ; Protein 3g; Carbohydrate 14g, of which sugars 14g; Fat 37g, of which saturates 22g; Cholesterol 198mg; Calcium 45mg; Fibre 0g; Sodium 10mg

SWEET SOYA MILK <u>WITH</u> PANDANUS

IN THE STREETS AND MARKETS OF VIETNAM AND CAMBODIA, FRESHLY MADE SOYA MILK IS SOLD DAILY. OFTEN INFUSED WITH PANDANUS LEAVES, OR GINGER, AND SERVED HOT OR CHILLED, IT IS A SWEET AND NOURISHING DRINK, ENJOYED BY CHILDREN AND ADULTS.

MAKES 1.2 LITRES/2 PINTS/5 CUPS

INGREDIENTS

    225g/8oz/1¼ cups soya beans,
      soaked overnight and drained
    1.5 litres/2½ pints/6¼ cups water
    2 pandanus leaves, slightly bruised
    15ml/2 tbsp sugar

VARIATION

To make ginger-flavoured soya milk, stir in 25g/1oz grated ginger with the sugar. Bring the liquid to the boil and simmer for 10 minutes, then turn off the heat and leave to infuse for 20 minutes more.

1 Put a third of the soya beans into a blender with a third of the water. Blend until thick and smooth. Pour the purée into a bowl and repeat with the rest of the beans. Strain the purée through a fine sieve (strainer) to extract the milk. Discard the solids. Line the sieve with a piece of muslin (cheesecloth), then strain the milk again.

2 Pour the milk into a pan and bring it to the boil. Stir in the pandanus leaves with the sugar, until it has dissolved. Return the milk to the boil, reduce the heat and simmer for 10 minutes.

3 Remove the pandanus leaves, then ladle the hot milk into cups and serve, You can also leave it to cool, then chill in the refrigerator.

Per portion Energy 384Kcal/1584kJ; Protein 35g; Carbohydrate 9.g, of which sugars 9g; Fat 19g, of which saturates 4g; Cholesterol 0mg; Calcium 156mg; Fibre 0g; Sodium 384mg

RAINBOW DRINK

THIRST-QUENCHING AND APPETIZING AT THE SAME TIME, RAINBOW DRINKS ARE A DELIGHTFUL SOUTH-EAST ASIAN TREAT. TWO KINDS OF SWEETENED BEANS ARE COLOURFULLY LAYERED WITH CRUSHED ICE, DRENCHED IN COCONUT MILK AND TOPPED WITH JELLIED AGAR AGAR.

SERVES FOUR

INGREDIENTS
   50g/2oz dried split mung beans,
      soaked for 4 hours and drained
   50g/2oz red azuki beans, soaked for
      4 hours and drained
   25g/1oz/2 tbsp sugar
For the syrup
   300ml/½ pint/1¼ cups coconut
      milk
   50g/2oz/¼ cup sugar
   25g/1oz tapioca pearls
   crushed ice, to serve
   15g/½oz jellied agar agar, soaked
      in warm water for 30 minutes
      and shredded into long strands,
      to decorate

2 In a heavy pan, bring the coconut milk to the boil. Reduce the heat and stir in the sugar, until it dissolves. Add the tapioca pearls and simmer for about 10 minutes, until they become transparent. Leave to cool and chill in the refrigerator.

3 Divide the beans among four tall glasses, add a layer of crushed ice, then the azuki beans and more ice. Pour the coconut syrup over the top and decorate with strands of agar agar. Serve immediately with straws and long spoons.

1 Put the mung beans and azuki beans into two separate pans with 15gl/½oz/ 1 tbsp sugar each. Pour in enough water to cover and, stirring all the time, bring it to the boil. Reduce the heat and leave both pans to simmer for about 15 minutes, stirring from time to time, until the beans are tender but not mushy – you may have to add more water. Drain the beans, leave to cool and chill separately in the refrigerator.

COOK'S TIP
Many variations of rainbow drinks are served throughout South-east Asia, some combining ingredients such as lotus seeds, taro, sweet potato, and tapioca pearls with exotic fruits. Served in tall, clear glasses in the markets, restaurants and bars they are popular in both Vietnam and Cambodia.

Per portion Energy 188Kcal/800kJ; Protein 6g; Carbohydrate 42g, of which sugars 25g; Fat 0.5g, of which saturates 0.2g; Cholesterol 0mg; Calcium 55mg; Fibre 2.5g; Sodium 87mg

SHOPPING INFORMATION

AUSTRALIA

Asian Supermarkets Pty Ltd
116 Charters Iowers Road
Townsville QLD 4810
Tel: (07) 4772 3997
Fax: (07) 4771 3919

Kongs Trading Pty Ltd
8 Kingscote Street
Kewdale WA 6105
Tel: (08) 9353 3380
Fax: (08) 9353 3390

Duc Hung Long Asian
 Foodstore
95 The Crescent
Fairfield NSW 2165
Tel: (02) 9728 1092

Exotic Asian Groceries Q
 Supercentre
Cnr Market and Bermuda
 Streets
Mermaid Waters QLD 4218
Tel: (07) 5572 8188

Saigon Asian Food Retail and
 Wholesale
6 Cape Street
Dickson ACT 2602
Tel: (02) 6247 4251

The Spice and Herb Asian Shop
200 Old Cleveland Road
Capalaba QLD 4157
Tel: (07) 3245 5300

Sydney Fish Market Pty Ltd
Cnr Pyrmont Bridge Road and
 Bank Street
Pyrmont NSW 2009
Tel: (02) 9660 1611

Harris Farm Markets
Sydney Markets
Flemongton NSW 2140
Tel: (02) 9746 2055

Burlington Supermarkets
Chinatown Mall
Fortitude Valley QLD 4006
Tel: (07) 3216 1828

CANADA

Dahl's Oriental Food
822 Broadview
Toronto
Ontario M4K 2P7
Tel: (416) 463-8109

Hong Kong Emporium
364 Young Street,
Toronto
Ontario M5B 1S5
Tel: (416) 977-3386

SOUTH AFRICA

Akhalwaya and Sons
Gillies Street
Burgersdorp
Johannesburg
Tel: (11) 838-1008

Kashmiri Spice Centre
95 Church Street
Mayfair, Johannesburg
Tel: (11)839-3883

Haribak and Sons Ltd
31 Pine Street
Durban
Tel: (31) 32-662

UNITED KINGDOM

Good Harvest Fish Market
14 Newport Place
London WC2H 7PR
Tel: 020 7437 0712

Golden Gate Supermarket
16 Newport Place
London WC2H 7JS
Tel: 020 7437 6266

Hopewell Emporium
2f Dyne Road
London NW6 7XB
Tel: 020 7624 5473

Loon Fung Supermarket
42–44 Gerrard Street
London W1V 7LP
Tel: 020 7437 7332

Manila Supermarket
11–12 Hogarth Place
London SW5 0QT
Tel: 020 7373 8305

Miah, A. and Co
20 Magdalen Street
Norwich NR3 1HE
Tel: 01603 615395

New Peking Supermarket
59 Westbourne Grove
London W2 4UA
Tel: 020 7928 8770

Newport Supermarket
28–29 Newport Court
London WC2H 7PQ
Tel: 020 7437 2386

Rum Wong Supermarket
London Road
Guildford GU1 2AF
Tel: 01483 451568

S. W. Trading Ltd
Horn Lane
London SE10 0RT
Tel: 020 8293 9393

Tawana
18–20 Chepstow Road
London W2 5BD
Tel: 020 7221 6316

Wing Tai
11a Aylesham Centre
Rye Lane
London SE15 5EW
Tel: 020 7635 0714

Wing Yip
395 Edgware Road
London NW2 6LN
Tel: 020 7450 0422
also at
Oldham Road
Ancoats
Manchester M4 5HU
Tel: 0161 832 3215
and
375 Nechells Park Road
Nechells
Birmingham B7 5NT
Tel: 0121 327 3838

Mail Order Companies
Fiddes Payne Herbs and
 Spices Ltd
Unit 3B, Thorpe Way, Banbury
Oxfordshire OX16 8XL
Tel: 01295 253 888

Fox's Spices
Mason's Road
Stratford-upon-Avon
Warwickshire CV37 9XN
Tel: 01789 266 420

UNITED STATES

Ai Hoa
860 North Hill Street
Los Angeles, CA 90026
Tel (213) 482-48

Asian Food Market
6450 Market Street
Upper Darby, PA 19082
Tel: (610) 352-4433

Asian Foods, Etc.
1375 Prince Avenue
Atlanta, GA 30341
Tel: (404) 543-8624

Asian Foods Ltd.
260–280 West Lehigh
   Avenue
Philadelphia, PA 19133
Tel: (215) 291-9500

Asian Market
2513 Stewart Avenue
Las Vegas, NV 89101
Tel: (702) 387-3373

Asian Market
18815 Eureka Road
South Gate, MI 48195
Fax: (734) 246-4795

Augusta Market Oriental Foods
2117 Martin Luther King Jr.
   Boulevard
Atlanta, GA 30901
Tel: (706) 722-4988

Bachri's Chili & Spice Gourmet
5617 Villa Haven
Pittsburgh, PA 15236
Tel: (412) 831-1131

Bangkok Market
4757 Melrose Avenue
Los Angeles, CA 90029
Tel: (203) 662-7990

Bharati Food & Spice Center
6163 Reynolds Road Suite G
Morrow, GA 30340
Tel: (770) 961-9007

First Asian Food Center
3420 East Ponce De Leon Ave
Scottsdale, GA 30079
Tel: (404) 292-6508

The House of Rice Store
3221 North Hayden Road
Scottsdale, AZ 85251
Tel: (480) 947-6698

Han Me Oriental Food & Gifts
2 E. Derenne Avenue
Savannah, GA 31405
Tel: (912) 355-6411

Hong Tan Oriental Food
2802 Capitol Street
Savannah, GA 31404
Tel: (404) 233-9184

Huy Fong Foods Inc.
5001 Earle Avenue
Rosemead, CA 91770
Tel: (626) 286-8328

Khanh Tam Oriental Market
4051 Buford Highway NE
Atlanta, GA 30345
Tel: (404) 728-0393

Norcross Oriental Market
6062 Norcross-Tucker Road
Chamblee, GA 30341
Tel: (770) 496-1656

Oriental Grocery
11827 Del Amo Boulevard
Cerritos, CA 90701
Tel: (310) 924-1029

Oriental Market
670 Central Park Avenue
Yonkers, NY 10013
(212) 349-1979

The Oriental Pantry
423 Great Road
Acton, MA 01720
Tel: (978) 264-4576

Saigon Asian Market
10090 Central Avenue
Biloxi, MS 39532
Tel: (228) 392-8044

Unimart American and Asian
   Groceries
1201 Howard Street
San Francisco, CA94103
Tel: (415) 431-0362

AUTHOR'S ACKNOWLEDGEMENTS

In a book of this nature, there is always a great deal of research involved. For this I must mention the *Essentials of Asian Cuisine* by Corinne Trang, the most informative book on culinary cultures of South-east Asia; *South East Asian Food* by Rosemary Brissenden; *Authentic Vietnamese Cooking* by Corinne Trang, *A Vietnamese Feast* by Andy Lee; and the excellent *Rough Guide to Vietnam*, and *Lonely Planet Guide to Cambodia*. On the ground, I would like to say a big thank you to Douglas Toidy and Le Huong at their Vung Tau fish farm, and to Peter Grant at Frank's, Singapore. And, I would like to thank the team at Anness Publishing Ltd.

   For spices and pastes from Southeast Asia and other parts of the world, I rely on the best global mail order company there is: Seasoned Pioneers Ltd, 101 Summers Road, Brunswick Business Park, Liverpool, L3 4BJ. Tel: +44 (0) 151 709 9330. Or look up: www.seasonedpioneers.com – they can deliver to any location in the world.

PUBLISHER'S ACKNOWLEDGEMENTS

The publisher would like to thank Martin Brigdale for his stunning photography throughout the book, apart from the following images:
t = top; b = bottom; r = right; l = left
Alamy pages 6t (J Marshall/Tribaleye Images). 11br (E J Baumeister Jr), 14b (Robert Harding Picture Library), 15b (World Religions Photo Library), 18t (J Marshall/Tribaleye Images), 18b (Robert Harding Picture Library); Robert Harding Picture Library pages 8tr, 8bl, 10t, 12b, 15t, 16bl, 17br; Superstock Ltd pages 11tr, 13b, 14t, 16tr, 16bl, 19tr, 24bl, 28tr, 28bl, 52tr; Travel-ink pages 6b, 7t, 7b, 12t, 17bl, 19 bl, 60bl.

INDEX